How To Become A
MENTAL HEALTH LEADER
Within The Workplace

James Fairview

First Edition Published 2020
© James Fairview

A catalogue record for this book
is available from The British Library

ISBN: 978-1-78324-159-0

CONTENTS

LIST OF FIGURES

LIST OF TABLES

ABBREVIATIONS

ACAS	The Advisory, Conciliation and Arbitration Service
ADD	Attention deficit disorder
ADHD	Attention deficit hyperactivity disorder
AIR	All-injury rate
APA	American Psychiatric Association
BME/BAME	Black and minority ethnic/black, Asian and minority ethnic
COPFS	Crown Office and Procurator Fiscal Service
CP	Competent person
C-PTSD	Complex post-traumatic stress disorder
CSR	Corporate social responsibility
D&I	Diversity and inclusion
D-PTSD	Delayed-onset post-traumatic stress disorder
EMS	Environmental management system
ICO	Information Commissioner's Office
IOSH	Institution of Occupational Safety and Health
ISO	International Standards Organisation
HASAWA	The Health and Safety at Work etc. Act 1974
H&S	Health and safety
HR	Human resources
HSA	Health and Safety Authority of Ireland
HSE	Health and Safety Executive
LTIR	Lost-time injury rate
MHA	Mental Health America
MHSWR	The Management of Health and Safety at Work Regulations 1999
NAMI	National Alliance on Mental Illness
NEBOSH	National Examination Board for Occupational Safety and Health

OH	Occupational health
OSHA	Occupational Safety and Health Administration
PTSD	Post-traumatic stress disorder
QMS	Quality management system
ROI	Return on investment
RoSPA	Royal Society for the Prevention of Accidents
RP	Responsible person
SR	Social responsibility
TTC	Time To Change
UN	United Nations
US/USA	United States/United States of America
WHO	World Health Organization

FOREWORD

To nurses, doctors, first responders, childcare workers, military service personnel and others whose occupation is intrinsically more dangerous to mental health, you have my utmost admiration, appreciation and respect. Because trauma is an intrinsic and inescapable part of the nursing occupation and can lead to post-traumatic stress disorder, 30% of any profits from the sale of this book will be donated to Cavell Nurses' Trust.

CAVELL NURSES' TRUST

When nurses suffer hardship, Cavell Nurses' Trust gives help.
We're here for nurses and midwives.

We transform their lives. The nurses, midwives and healthcare assistants we help say they're often happier, healthier and able to stay in or return to work.

Cavell Nurses' Trust is the charity supporting UK nurses, midwives and healthcare assistants, both working and retired, when they're suffering personal or financial hardship often due to illness, disability, older age and domestic abuse.

From simple, essential support like money to repair a broken cooker or boiler, to vital life-changing aid like helping a family flee their home due to domestic abuse, Cavell Nurses' Trust is here to help. The numbers seeking our help increase year on year so it's clear there's a need for nursing professionals to access our support.

If you'd like to speak with someone,
please give us a call on:
01527 595 999

Our address:
Cavell Nurses' Trust, Grosvenor House,
Prospect Hill, Redditch, Worcestershire B97 4DL

Web site:
https://www.cavellnursestrust.org/

ACKNOWLEDGEMENTS

As with most publications, this book is the result of a team effort. Grace Fairley of the Big Wide Word provided editorial services, making the book a far better product than I could have achieved alone, so she has my thanks. Proofreading was provided by Suzanne Williams of Quick Brown Fox Transcription Services and Ralph Percival of Ralph Design provided the designs for all figures. They both have my thanks. David Whincup of law firm Squire Patton Boggs (UK) LLP played a valuable role in helping clarify many of the legal aspects addressed in this book. David has my thanks. Special thanks too, to Jessica Piper LLB; LLM (Cantab) & Emily Dixon LLB; MA (both solicitors admitted in England & Wales) for their advice and input on the employment law references. Jessica and Emily are both employed by Ashtons Legal, one of East Anglia's leading law firms. My thanks also go to Lyn Nesbitt-Smith of LNS Indexing for producing such a comprehensive index. Finally, I would like to thank the many people and organisations who have given their permission to use the material referred to in this book. The people and organisations referred to above have helped bring a degree of clarity to the area of workplace mental health, which is in desperate need of fresh thinking. Hopefully, this book makes good use of their contributions.

All references in this book from UK Government sources contain public sector information licensed under the Open Government Licence v3.0, available at: *http://www.nationalarchives. gov.uk/doc/open-government-licence/version/3/.*

INTRODUCTION

If you are a leader or manager, you may find yourself wondering how to design and implement your organisation's mental health management system. *How to Become a Mental Health Leader Within the Workplace* will guide you through this process and provide you with a strategic management system, along with ideas and initiatives that are practical, easy to understand and easy to implement. The book will also go a long way to helping you meet your legal obligations under health and safety legislation as it relates to mental health, and will help you prepare for the forthcoming ISO 45003, which relates to psychological health and safety. It also sets out a 10-point plan to bring about national policy-level change to workplace mental health.

The language of mental health can be imprecise. In this book, I refer to mental health issues, mental disability, mental illness, mental ill-health and mental health disorders. I use these broad terms when I talk about people with mental health issues, whether the issues are short or long term, diagnosed or undiagnosed. This book is applicable to leaders and managers of employees who might have any kind of mental health issue, from anxiety to agoraphobia, from depression to dementia and from stress to schizophrenia.

Our World in Data (Ritchie and Roser, 2018) estimates there are about 792 million people in the world who live with a mental health disorder – about 10.7% of the world's population. This figure is misleading, however, because many people live with poor mental health without a diagnosis. When we take undiagnosed conditions into account, it is possible that more than a billion people worldwide are living with a mental health issue. Long-term conditions, such as depression, can blight lives. Short-term conditions, such as stress, can overwhelm people. There are many reasons people might develop such conditions and nobody is immune; anyone can be affected at any time of their life, although some people are more at risk than others.

Naturally, many people with mental health issues are in employment and many employers will want to develop an effective support system for them. This book has been written with the aim of helping employers do just that. It sets out a strategic management system to aid leaders and managers in managing and supporting employees struggling with their mental health.

The approach to mental health management in this book is based on methods that will feel familiar to many organisational leaders and managers, because it takes its lead from established physical health and safety management methods. The methods presented here are practical, simple to understand and easy to implement.

How to Become a Mental Health Leader Within the Workplace is a management book. It focuses on providing readers with a mental health management system, along with related models and frameworks, as well as suggestions about procedures and processes (see Figure 0.1).

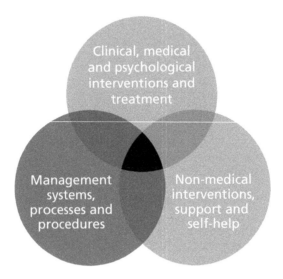

Figure 0.1 *Where* How to Become a Mental Health Leader Within the Workplace *is positioned in existing literature*

There are some things that are outside the remit of this book, of course. It does not offer guidance on medical diagnosis and treatment, and it does not provide information on non-medical interventions, such as therapies, mindfulness and resilience training. These are available elsewhere, through the healthcare system or from myriad workplace mental health practitioners. Neither does this book provide legal advice, although chapter 5 explores some aspects of the law that employers might wish to consider when developing a workplace mental health management system.

For leaders and managers, the management of mental health at work may feel like a daunting challenge. There are so many types of mental health condition, such diverse causes and contributory factors, and such a bewildering array of available medical and non-medical treatments, that the sheer complexity of mental health might seem overwhelming. But it need not be.

When organisations address physical health and safety, they are not expected to become experts in how to diagnose high blood pressure, set a bone fracture or treat a blood infection. Physical health conditions may initially be treated with first aid if they occur at work but the injured employee will then be transferred to the healthcare system for appropriate medical treatment and recovery support. The same applies to mental health.

Employers have the same two health and safety responsibilities for mental health as they do for physical health: first, to prevent injury and illness; and second, to provide first aid. This book sets out a management approach that addresses the employer's first responsibility – to prevent and minimise harm to employees' mental health at work.

This book does not provide information about the employer's second responsibility – to provide mental health first aid. Advice and training on this are widely available these days, for example, from St John's Ambulance (www.sja.org.uk). Mental health first aid is not part of the mental health management system offered in this book; it is assumed that organisations will explore mental health first aid elsewhere and include it in the many arrangements that should be implemented through a mental health policy.

Part I of this book focuses exclusively on the 'backstory' of workplace mental health management. The methods presented in Part II can be applied equally to mental health and to wellbeing. Wellbeing has an increasingly high profile and is a popular focus for many employers today. Although it does touch on the subject, this book does not cover wellbeing as such, taking a focused approach to mental health rather than the broad approach taken by wellbeing. However, many of the management methods set out in Part II can be applied to wellbeing approaches.

Part I explores the scale of the mental health issue, encourages the reader to develop empathy with employees with poor mental health and presents methods by which physical health and safety is managed. It goes on to consider the differences between the management of physical health and safety and the management of mental health, before exploring aspects of the law that employers might contemplate when developing a mental health management system. The chapter closes by considering the positive case for employing people with mental health issues, as well as some of the challenges involved in determining how best to manage them.

Chapter 1 explores the 'problem' of mental health. It begins by offering definitions of mental health and mental ill-health. The methods presented in this book can be applied equally to all employees with mental ill-health, no matter what their mental health issue. The chapter goes on to explore the scale of the mental health crisis and reveals the rates of mental illness in the UK and the United States. The four phases that people with poor mental health might experience are explained, along with the main causes of poor mental health and the prevalence of key conditions. Significant attention is given to PTSD and the rate at which it occurs in some occupations, such as nursing. After setting out the uncertain nature of the challenge faced by employers when tackling mental health, along with some of the reasons for this uncertainty, the chapter goes on to consider some of the contemporary responses being taken by employers to address mental health in the workplace.

Chapter 2 aims to build the reader's empathy with those employees with poor mental health. It considers the journey of discovery people with mental health issues may travel, based on their lived experience, and sets out some of the decisions they are likely to be confronted with along the way. It continues by presenting the dilemma many employees with mental health issues face when they are considering whether to divulge their mental health condition to their employer, along with the range of reactions that can arise should they do so, including stigma and bullying. The chapter concludes by exploring the knock-on effects of mental health conditions and how these can create a 'cycle of suffering'.

Chapter 3 introduces the reader to core aspects of physical health and safety management. The chapter provides foundation knowledge, setting out the well-known methods for managing physical health and safety upon which this book's approach to managing mental health at work is built. Here, leaders and managers may find some familiar themes, whilst this chapter will assist readers with less health and safety management experience to quickly grasp the mental health management system proposed in the book.

Chapter 4 considers the key differences between the management of physical health and safety, and the management of mental health. It explores how the two types of health management have developed over time and why mental health lags behind workplace physical health and safety management. The tangibility of physical and mental health is considered, with the reader's attention being especially drawn to visible and invisible causes, effects and control methods. The chapter continues by introducing the notion of technical ambiguity at the macro (national) and micro (employer) levels, which acts as a barrier that governments and employers should be aware of and that might affect how workplace mental health strategies and plans are developed and implemented. The chapter goes on to consider further differences between physical and mental health management as those differences relate to leadership commitment and to employee engagement. It concludes by considering how physical and mental health and safety laws are enforced, including the use of sanctions to control market practice.

Chapter 5 provides readers with an understanding of the law as it relates to workplace mental health. Whilst not providing advice or even definitive guidance, it seeks to give a detailed explanation of the law, so as to comprehensively inform leaders and managers about the various legal issues they should be aware of when contemplating the development of a workplace mental health management system. Central to this chapter are the tort of negligence, the Equality Act 2010, the Data Protection Act 2010 and the Health and Safety at Work etc Act 1974 (HASAWA). A definition of the term 'mental disability' is provided, along with a discussion about the definition's shortcomings. Laws as they relate to confidentiality are briefly considered. Existing health and safety legislation is examined to determine how it applies to mental health. Finally, the tort of negligence is examined. Throughout the chapter, questions are posed that test the effectiveness of laws in protecting people with mental health issues.

The main negligence defences available to employers are presented, partly to help employers develop mental health management practices that minimise the risk of litigation and partly to help support employers should they find themselves facing related claims.

Chapter 6 considers the legal, moral, technical and commercial arguments for hiring and supporting employees with mental health issues. The legal argument relates to the rights of people with a mental disability. The moral argument assumes that employers wish to 'do the right thing', so encourages them to employ people with mental health issues, in line with corporate social responsibility (CSR) and social wellbeing policies. The technical argument raises the possibility that some employees with mental health issues may possess 'super-powers' that can be of benefit to organisations. Finally, the commercial argument shows that when companies make a financial investment in employees' wellbeing there is a clear return on investment. These arguments aim to address some of the fears around employing and supporting people with poor mental health. They justify why, based on one or more of four arguments, employing people with mental health issues should be approached positively.

Chapter 7 brings Part I to a close by considering some of the challenges an employer may face during their quest to become mental-health-friendly. It begins by exploring how, if the employer fails to be proactive, an employee's perception of the employer's mental health culture may develop. The chapter goes on to explore how the employer might proactively shape the employee's perception of the organisation's culture, along with methods the employer might use to do so. The chapter also discusses some of the perceived concerns surrounding the employment of people with mental health issues, and attempts to put these concerns into perspective.

Part II of *How to Become a Mental Health Leader Within the Workplace* explores the concerns and benefits of using a management systems approach to manage workplace mental health. It presents a '7 Principles' framework for managing workplace mental health, which comprises: 1) the management system; 2) commitment; 3) policy; 4) risk assessments; 5) the hierarchy of controls; 6) consultation; and 7) reporting. Part II concludes with recommendations that are set out in a 10-point plan. These recommendations aim at national policy-level to bring about seismic change to workplace mental health.

Chapter 8 explores aspects of managing workplace mental health through the use of a management system. It considers arguments against doing this; there is a school of thought that believes that mental health is not best managed through an impersonal and bureaucratic process, given that it is a personal, intimate issue, requiring care and compassion. This is countered with arguments in favour of a management system approach, with reference to other settings in which a high degree of care and compassion is also necessary, with the case for utilising a management systems approach to workplace mental health being made.

Chapter 9 introduces the first of the '7 Principles', *the management system* itself, through which workplace mental health can be managed. This system uses the core principles of safety management advocated by the UK's safety enforcer, the Health and Safety Executive (HSE), and by the Occupational Safety and Health Administration (OSHA) in the United States. The chapter also sets out the world-renowned 'Plan-Do-Check-Act' model, linking this approach to workplace mental health management. Having drawn from these two well-established management approaches, an overarching management system for managing workplace mental health is presented. This system effectively allows leaders and managers to manage mental health in a similar way to physical health. The chapter goes on to set out the aims of the management system's other six 'principles', referring back to the physical health and safety management methods in chapter 3 on which the '7 Principles' workplace mental health management system is based.

The second principle, *commitment*, is explored in chapter 10. The chapter offers a definition of commitment, drawing on the term's use in physical health and safety management. It discusses ways to achieve management and workforce 'buy-in' to mental health plans, with the aim of ensuring that the commitment to mental health runs throughout the entire organisation. The chapter explores 'the commitment cycle', a six-step approach that leaders and managers can use to establish organisational and individual commitment to mental health through: 1) leadership; 2) managing practice; 3) influencing perceptions; 4) building trust; 5) establishing commitment; and 6) recognising good behaviours. It discusses how the cycle of commitment establishes and reinforces commitment, along with the perils that can arise from breaking the cycle.

The third principle, *policy*, is the subject of chapter 11, which first explores policies as they are used in physical health and safety management. The chapter then suggests a similar structure for the design of a workplace mental health policy, which should be based upon: a statement of intent, which sets out the organisation's commitment to mental health; the organisation and management structure as it relates to mental health; and the arrangements to be put in place to implement the mental health policy. Ten such arrangements are presented as examples, providing practical guidance for leaders and managers.

Chapter 12 examines the fourth principle, *risk assessments*. The HSE provides a useful five-step approach to risk assessments: 1) identify the hazards; 2) identify who can be harmed and how; 3) assess the risks and determine control measures; 4) write up the risk assessment and implement it; 5) and review the risk assessment. The chapter comprehensively addresses the first step – identify mental health hazards. It reveals the '12 *general* mental health risk factors' and the '12 *workplace* mental health risk factors', providing employers with the '12 x 12' mental health risk factors that identify work and non-work hazards, and providing leaders and managers with a crucial starting point when considering which mental health hazards to 'risk assess'. The remaining four steps of the risk assessment process are explored, providing readers with a comprehensive understanding of how to identify and control workplace and other mental health risks.

Most current approaches to mental health management start with control measures – that is to say, reducing symptoms using methods such as resilience and mindfulness training. Chapter 13 takes a more preventative approach, as is required by the physical health and safety management doctrine. The chapter sets out the fifth principle, the *hierarchy of controls*. This internationally recognised, strategic approach to risk control provides leaders and managers with a proven approach to controlling workplace mental health risks. The hierarchy of controls offers an approach that focuses on the six control methods of: i) elimination; ii) substitution; iii) isolation; iv) engineering controls; v) administrative controls; vi) and personal protective equipment (PPE), with the most effective methods being used first; these being elimination and substitution. Each of these 'controls' as it relates to mental health is explored and examples relevant to mental health are presented, providing leaders and managers with useful insights into the technique.

The sixth principle, *consultation*, is the subject of chapter 14. The chapter reflects upon this well-known practice in the context of workplace mental health. It presents the justification for mental health consultation, along with some typical aims of consultation. Various methods of engaging employees in consultation are explored, along with some thoughts about the governance of consultations; these are necessary as, in some countries including the UK, workforce consultation in respect of health and safety is a legal requirement. The consultation process itself is explored, including how events and employee surveys can be organised to encourage engagement. Potential solutions to the question 'should I use engagement surveys to ask employees about their mental health?' are explored. The chapter ends with a discussion of how consultations can be held at organisational and individual levels.

Chapter 15 looks at the seventh and final principle, *reporting*. It considers the aims of mental health reporting, along with the type of mental health reports leaders and managers might wish to utilise and implement. The chapter explores numerous measures of mental health performance, and provides leaders and managers with ideas about how to monitor the effectiveness of their mental health management system at strategic and tactical levels. *Direct* and *indirect* measures, along with *input* and *output* measures are contemplated, with all found to have a place in the mental health reporting model. In addition, the four strategic measures of workplace mental health performance are also introduced, these being: attendance; engagement; productivity and loyalty. The chapter continues by considering the purpose of mental health performance reporting, including the aims of creating action plans and driving continual improvement. It closes with an examination of how errors and bias in reporting can occur; these being common problems when measuring and reporting on workplace mental health.

In Chapter 16, conclusions are drawn and recommendations made in the form of a 10-point plan of action that aims to bring about a seismic change at UK national policy level. These 10 actions focus especially on the perceived weaknesses in leadership, related laws and in law enforcement that were identified in chapters 4 and 5. In this chapter, it is argued that legal principles that protect people under the Equality Act 2010 should be reviewed and revised. The chapter also calls for greater clarity about the applicability of health and safety law to workplace mental health, before continuing by setting out recommendations that address conflicts between employment law and health and safety law. The chapter continues by proposing specific actions to introduce new employer reporting obligations that, like actions proposed earlier, lay the foundations for more stringent law enforcement. The chapter concludes by calling upon prominent figures in society to take up the challenge of helping to bring about these policy-level changes, so improving the effectiveness with which workplace mental health is managed, to the benefit of society as a whole.

The book concludes with a summary in chapter 17, which recaps on the main take-outs from each chapter and summarises the proposed 10-point plan of national policy-level actions.

How to Become a Mental Health Leader Within the Workplace is intended to share knowledge and ideas rather than serve as a definitive guide. It has been written for employers, providing them with a strategic and structured management system approach through which they can effectively support their employees. Although it has been written for employers, the book recognises that the workplace mental health relationship between employers and employees is inequitable. It examines this inequity and presents the case for change. In many instances, employers are unsure what to do about mental health, and many employees feel unsupported by their employer. This book aims to address these points by improving employers' understanding of mental health and the certainty with which they address it, which in turn should help them to provide improved support to employees. The 10-point plan set out here also aims to make the workplace mental health relationship between employers and employees more equitable. Today, some of the legal principles examined in chapter 5 seem out of date; they are causing confusion and are in desperate need of review. Changes to these laws, along with changes to the workplace mental health regulatory system, are therefore proposed with the aim of bringing about a seismic change in workplace mental health.

This book is perhaps naïve, but also ambitious, misguided but innovative, limited but expertly informed. It is a cornucopia; a mental health melange, based on lived experience, extensive research, leadership and management skills, academic understanding and legal expertise. It seeks to provide an insightful, challenging and sometimes opinionated view of workplace mental health management. Most of all, this book aims to be thought-provoking. It is a foundation upon which you can build.

Workplace mental health management is a rapidly emerging discipline. It is rising up the organisational agenda but, even so, progress is slow. This book describes how people are ten times more likely to experience mental harm than physical injury. Despite this, despite the management of mental health being a legal requirement and despite far greater awareness, key mental health output indicators have deteriorated or remained disappointing. Many employers are still not sure how to approach mental health. It seems that a lack of under-standing, along with uncertainty about how to act, is leading to reticence on the subject. However, for employers, the need to address mental health is becoming ever more pressing.

Having reached a twenty-year low in 2007, the UK suicide rate trend over the past decade or so is concerning. The 2019 figure, expected in September 2020, is set to determine if 2017 was an aberration that masked a continuing and concerning long-term trend of deterioration, or whether 2018 was the aberration, with 2019 data representing a return to a desperately sought lower rate, for which so many strive (Figure 0.2).

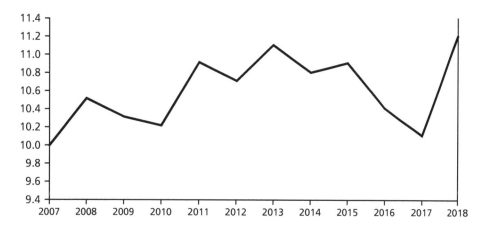

Figure 0.2 *UK suicide rate – all persons: deaths per 100,000 population*

Looking beyond the suicide rate to the numbers of people living with poor mental health, over the past thirty years, according to some reports, stress, depression and anxiety have doubled (Figure 0.3).

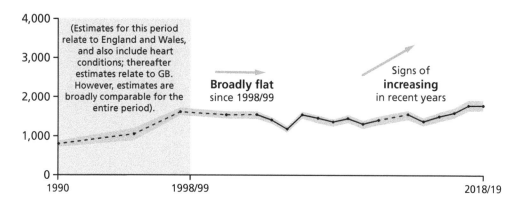

Figure 0.3 *Rate of self-reported stress, depression or anxiety*

Source: HSE online

Notably, there has been a particularly rapid increase in reported mental health conditions in the last five years, despite mental health awareness being at its height.

These two trends of an increasing suicide rate and an increased number of people reporting stress, depression and anxiety suggest mental health has now become a far more pressing issue for employers, warranting you give the issue of workplace mental health more urgent attention.

The workplace mental health management methods set out in this book will directly support you and your organisation's efforts to manage and improve the mental health of employees. Doing so effectively may help your organisation improve productivity and performance. You can become a mental health leader where you work, bringing about great benefits for your organisation, by applying the many easy-to-understand and easy-to-implement methods set out in *How to Become a Mental Health Leader Within the Workplace*.

References

Health and Safety Executive (online) Historical Picture Statistics in Great Britain, 2019 – Trends in work-related ill health and workplace injury. Available at: *https://www.hse.gov.uk/ statistics/history/index.htm#* (accessed 18 April 2020).

Office for National Statistics (online). *Suicides in the UK Statistical bulletins*. Available at: *https:// www.ons.gov.uk/peoplepopulationandcommunity/birthsdeathsandmarriages/deaths/ bulletins/suicidesintheunitedkingdom/previousReleases* (accessed on 20 Feb 2020).

Ritchie, H. & Roser, M. (2018) Mental health. *Our World in Data*. Available at: *https:// ourworldindata.org/mental-health* (accessed 5 December 2019).

PART I

THE MENTAL HEALTH PROBLEM

Mental health has reached a crisis point in the twenty-first century, and we can probably say this is true throughout the world. Yet in many ways our approach to tackling workplace mental health issues is still in its infancy. Even today, many employers do not consider their employees' mental health at all, let alone explore the strategies they might put in place to aid them. Only four in ten organisations (39%) have policies or systems in place to support employees with common mental health issues (Stevenson and Farmer, 2017).

In the UK, reports suggest that one in four people will experience mental ill-health each year (Mind, 2017a). In the United States, the figure is one in five (National Alliance on Mental Illness, 2019). With a combined population of 400 million people, this equates to 80 million people in the UK and the United States experiencing mental health issues every year. The scale of the issue is immense. Taking a worst-case scenario, mental health issues outweighing workplace physical injuries by a factor of ten (Figure 1.1).

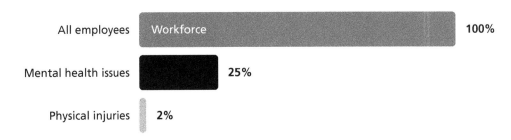

Figure 1.1 *The scale of the mental health crisis*
Source: Mind, 2017a (mental health issues); based on HSE, online, a (physical injuries)

Official figures vary. In the UK, the Health and Safety Executive (HSE) – the UK Government's health and safety enforcer – reported 1.4 million cases in 2018/19, of which 0.6 million (43%) related to work-related stress, depression or anxiety (HSE, online, b).

Of course, not all people experiencing mental health issues have a severe or chronic condition. Many suffer with short-term stress, for example, which passes as their circumstances change. However, the population is ageing (UN, online) and, as the population ages, the risk of people suffering from repeated past trauma also increases. Increasing distress can result from the cumulative impact of exposure to traumatic events throughout life, which contributes significantly to post-traumatic stress in older adulthood (Ogle et al., 2013). In other words, population ageing may be contributing towards an overall deterioration in mental health. Not only is the population ageing, but the workforce is also ageing. In the UK, this is partly because of age equality and age-related legislation (AgeUK, 2019). Given that older people are likely to have experienced a higher number of past traumatic events than younger people, and given that the workforce is ageing, the mental health issue as it affects employers is a growing problem. Further concern arises from the fact that systematic reviews consistently show that people with mental disorders have an increased risk of premature death (Plana-Ripoll et al., 2019). This effect on life expectancy should be of concern to our wider society as well as employers. Maintaining good mental health and improving poor mental health may positively contribute towards extending life expectancy.

Before dwelling further on the mental health problem as it affects employers, I want to take a look at what we mean by mental health.

Mental Health and Wellbeing

The aim of mental health management is perhaps obvious. The World Health Organization (WHO) describes mental health as 'a state of well-being in which every individual realizes his or her own potential, can cope with the normal stresses of life, can work productively and fruitfully, and is able to make a contribution to her or his community' (WHO, 2019a). This definition is comprehensive, if a little theoretical.

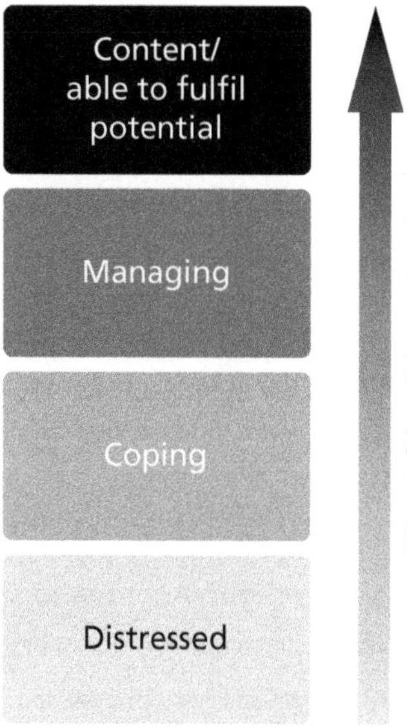

Figure 1.2 illustrates the four phases of mental health. Some people with mental health issues are unable to function in a way that might be considered normal. They might find usual daily activities – organising themselves, engaging other people and concentrating on tasks – virtually impossible. People in this category may not be able to cope mentally with the day-to-day stresses of life. These people can be considered *distressed*.

Figure 1.2 *The four phases of mental health*

People who have mental health issues, but are able to get by day-to-day, can be said to be *coping*. They may have unfulfilling lives, however, and each day may be a struggle. They are not in distress but may not be able to think or plan ahead and are far from realising their potential.

People with mental health issues can be said to be *managing* when they can do more than cope, enjoying relationships and activities on a day-to-day basis, and looking and planning ahead to some degree. These people may be unable to take the next step of becoming deeply fulfilled, however, perhaps because of anxiety, depression or another chronic condition, which holds them back.

A person may be considered *content* or fulfilled if they gain pleasure from several aspects of life. They might be regarded as living a full life and able to fulfil their potential. Here, the emphasis must be placed on the person's *ability* to fulfil their potential and not on the *attainment* of their potential. Many people have the ability to progress further in whatever they pursue but some may lack the desire or commitment to do so, whether inside or outside work. This might be because of an underlying *contentment* that is not related to mental ill-health. Many people in the workplace are content in their role, harbouring no ambition to be promoted, and are happy to continue in the same role for many years to come. Perhaps it is to be envied when people find contentment at work despite not fulfilling their potential. These employees are often the backbone of an organisation, providing stability when so many other things may be changing. It could be that contentment should be the aim of mental health and wellbeing programmes, rather than the WHO's aspiration for *every* person to *realise* their potential, which some might regard as unrealistic. The proportion of people experiencing contentment appears low, however, with only a minority of people (13%) reporting that they live with high levels of good mental health (Mental Health Foundation, 2017).

Given the ambiguity that can arise in any definition of mental health and wellbeing, employers might start by considering the state of mind they would like their employees to achieve, then employ methods such as those described in this book to bring that desired mental health state about.

Causes of Mental Ill-Health

I now turn my attention to the factors that can undermine good mental health, starting with a couple of definitions of mental ill-health.

According to the American Psychiatric Association, mental ill-health can be described as: 'health conditions involving changes in emotion, thinking or behaviour (or a combination of these). Mental illnesses are associated with distress and/or problems functioning in social, work or family activities' (APA, 2018).

Other definitions may be a little more specific, such as this one from Everymind: 'A mental illness is a disorder diagnosed by a medical professional that significantly interferes with an individual's cognitive, emotional or social abilities' (Everymind, online).

Everymind's definition places an emphasis on diagnosis by a medical professional. Of course, people may have a mental health condition that is undiagnosed or self-diagnosed, and in fact it is believed the number of people experiencing such conditions may be far higher than this definition provides for. This point illustrates an important issue around mental health: it is far less *quantifiable* than physical health because it is largely *intangible*.

But what exactly causes mental ill-health? As explained by Everymind (online):

> There are different types of mental illness and they occur with varying degrees of severity. Examples include mood disorders (such as depression, anxiety and bipolar disorder), psychotic disorders (such as schizophrenia), eating disorders and personality disorders.

Mental ill-health is broader than mental illness, as is perhaps obvious. In addition to the above conditions, long and short-term conditions may affect people. Stress, low mood, eating disorders, phobias and many more issues can all be linked to poor mental health.

Causes of mental ill-health can be attributed to three basic factors: the person; their circumstances; and their relationships (Figure 1.3).

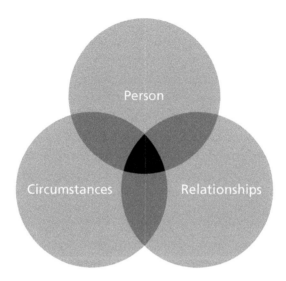

Figure 1.3 *Causes of mental ill-health*

Figure 1.3 shows where the causes of mental ill-health can be found.

The person: This relates to the person as an individual, including their genetics, values and beliefs, along with their preferences and disposition. Examples of mental ill-health located in the person themselves might include genetic or hereditary conditions such as schizophrenia, bipolar disorder, major depressive disorder, autism spectrum disorders and attention deficit hyperactivity disorder (ADHD). Genetic conditions can make sufferers more susceptible to stress, anxiety and other conditions. For example, children with ADHD (a mostly genetic condition) are three times more likely to suffer from anxiety (Rosen, online). About 50% of adults with ADHD are also likely to suffer with anxiety (Anxiety and Depression Association of America, online). This compares with just 5.9% of people without ADHD who suffer with anxiety (Mind, 2017a). Conditions such as vertigo, which have a link with mental health, may be included in the category of mental ill-health located in the person. A person's religious or other personal beliefs might also be said to come into this category, as these factors can affect health, for example, when the person refuses a blood transfusion. The *person* relates to characteristics particular to the individual, whether conscious or subconscious. The *person* also relates to an individual's current state of health, fitness, hygiene and so on. Some of these factors will be directly affected by lifestyle choices, such as diet and exercise. Chronic physical health conditions (eg. chronic back conditions) can also have an adverse effect upon mental health.

Circumstances: These can relate to a person's environment, living conditions and working conditions, along with the tasks, actions and activities they undertake day-to-day. They can relate to a person's past, as well as their present. Conditions relating to their past might include 'a rocky childhood; a violent assault; a car accident' (Harvard Health Publishing, 2019). People who work in child protection, accident and emergency, and war zones may be especially vulnerable if they have witnessed the trauma of others, or they may have suffered trauma themselves. Past suffering and the witnessing of trauma in others are both key causes of poor mental health. Current circumstances such as poverty can also affect a person's mental health, possibly to a chronic extent if no obvious short-term solution can be found. In such cases the person may well carry their worries with them into work, potentially undermining their performance there. People who have suffered significant past trauma (by which I mean severe or multiple incidents) may be more susceptible to stress, anxiety and other conditions in the present because present-day stresses add to and compound past traumatic experiences.

Relationships: This refers to the person's individual family relationships, friendships, professional and work-related relationships, along with relationships formed through social, leisure and recreational activities. Relationships may cause or contribute towards poor mental health. Toxic relationships can take many forms – 'toxic partners, toxic friendships, toxic parent/child relationships, or toxic coworkers', as Carter (2011) points out. Many adults spend more time at work than with loved ones. Toxic workplace relationships (including bullying) may have a significant effect on the state of an employee's mental health. People who have suffered significant relationship problems (such as being beaten as a child) may be susceptible to stress, anxiety and other conditions and may be 'triggered' by toxic workplace relationships.

Factors in a person's past, which can be related to the *person*, their *circumstances* or their *relationships*, can thus make the person far more susceptible to mental health problems in later life.

The UK's Health and Safety Executive (HSE) provides a useful starting point for us to examine the causes of workplace stress. The HSE states that stress at work can be caused by six issues: demands, control, support, relationships, role and change (HSE, online, c). This is not an exhaustive list (indeed, this book identifies a further six workplace stressors as well as non-workplace stressors), so employers should not assume the HSE's guidance is comprehensive. As an employer, your task is to undertake your own risk assessments and identify those risks that are relevant to your own workplace and workforce.

At some time, 70% of employees have suffered from a condition related to mental health (Smith, 2017). Business in the Community (2019) found that 39% of employees experienced poor mental health where work was a contributing factor. They also found this statistic deteriorated, from 36% in the prior year. Breaking this statistic down, it is evident differing factors affect mental health.

A recent study found that 42.2% of all employees have suffered from stress, and that stress accounts for many of the mental health issues that 61% of all employees reportedly experience (Smith, 2017). Smith, of Benenden Health, found that the top three underlying causes of mental ill-health were:

- Increased workload   (38.2% of respondents)
- Financial concerns   (17.9% of respondents)
- Workplace bullying   (9.5% of respondents)

Two of the three causes of mental ill-health provided in Figure 1.3 – *circumstances* and *relationships* – are evident in these findings. Two of the top three causes of mental ill-health – increased workload and workplace bullying – specifically arise at work. Financial concerns may well develop outside of work, say because of debt, but low pay may also be a contributory factor. Thus, all three causes could arise at work or be exacerbated by the employer and the workplace. The results of this study closely match those of other studies.

For example, a study by the Chartered Institute of Personnel and Development (CIPD, 2018a) found that a high proportion of employees reported factors in their top three causes of stress at work as:

- Workload   (60% of respondents)
- Management style   (32% of respondents)
- Non-work factors – relationships/family   (27% of respondents)
- Considerable organisational change   (26% of respondents)
- Pressure to meet targets and deadlines   (24% of respondents)
- Relationships at work   (23% of respondents)
- Non-work factors – personal illness   (22% of respondents)

Additionally, the most recent Labour Force Survey identified causes of workplace stress related to workload (44%) and workplace violence, threats and bulling (13%) (HSE, 2019).

Focusing on the issue of bullying, in the United States the Workplace Bullying Institute (2017) found that 61% of Americans were aware of abusive conduct in the workplace and that 40% of bullied employees were believed to have suffered adverse health effects.

Although it is true that these studies indicate that employee experiences can vary between workplaces, broad themes emerge that allow us to determine the factors most likely to cause mental harm. We can take account of these mental health risk factors when we assess workplace mental health risks, which is the subject of chapter 12.

Factors that may affect the culture of a workplace and drive behaviours such as workplace bullying might include: geographic location; management style; ethnic mix of workforce; age mix; gender mix; and the industry in which the organisation operates. These are just a few examples, so each employer should undertake their own research to identify the issues that affect the mental health of their own workforce.

It is likely that mental health issues are caused by a combination of factors, although some people will be more deeply affected by certain things than others (Mind, 2017b). It is more than possible that some employees experience multiple causes of mental ill-health simultaneously. The CIPD (2018a) study that found the 'top three' workplace stressors demonstrated that employee stress is caused by more than one factor.

The scale of the mental health issue and the number of causes of poor workplace mental health, combined with the wide range of responses open to an employer, demonstrate why employers should take strategic action.

Prevalence of Mental Health Conditions

Mental health is complex. There are many types of condition, each of which can have a wide range of symptoms, with symptoms varying from person to person. Each condition can have different characteristics, making the challenge of managing mental health difficult for the person with the condition, as well as for their employer.

The prevalence of specific mental health conditions has been established (Mind, 2017a), with forms of anxiety and depression or a combination of these, along with PTSD, being the most common (Table 1.1).

Table 1.1   *Prevalence of mental health conditions*

Condition	Prevalence per 100 people
General anxiety disorder	5.9
Depression	3.3
Phobias	2.4
OCD	1.3
Panic disorder	0.6
Post-traumatic stress disorder (PTSD)	4.4
Mixed anxiety and depression	7.8

Source: Mind, 2017a

I established earlier that many people may experience several or even numerous causes of mental ill-health. A combination of factors – say, a genetic mental health condition, a sudden bereavement and a severe car accident leading to a chronic physical condition such as a back or neck problem, plus poor financial circumstances – may have a cumulative or compound effect.

One area of mental health that seems to be overlooked by many employers is that of past trauma. It is common for people to carry these 'burdens' from the past in the form of PTSD (Table 1.1), yet little if anything is done by employers to help employees come to terms with past trauma.

Whether they experienced a stillbirth or miscarriage, or a sudden and unexpected bereavement, or were witness to trauma in an accident and emergency room or war zone, many have experienced events that will haunt them forever. Some people experience numerous such events.

The compound effect of repeated trauma, along with the severity of each traumatic experience, can be devastating, so it is worth exploring this area further.

Complex and Repeated Trauma

Trauma can be considered to be 'the result of extraordinarily stressful events that shatter your sense of security, making you feel helpless' (Robinson et al., 2019). Some people may well experience numerous 'extraordinarily stressful events' in their lives.

Clearly, the older people become, so the compound effect of these stressful events builds: 'The cumulative impact of exposure to traumatic events throughout the life course contributes significantly to post-traumatic stress in older adulthood' (Ogle et al., 2013).

Women may suffer types of emotional distress that men struggle to relate to, for example, as a result of miscarriage, mastectomy and hysterectomy. 'Approximately 9% of women experience postpartum post-traumatic stress disorder (PTSD) following childbirth' (Postpartum Support International, online). 'Women have a two to three times higher risk of developing post-traumatic stress disorder (PTSD) compared to men' (Olff, 2017).

As you can see from Table 1.1, PTSD is prevalent in 4.4% of the population (Mind, 2017a). The Advisory Board (2019) reported that PTSD amongst nurses is 25%, a significantly higher proportion that is thought to be a result of witnessing trauma first-hand. Nurses see people die, they resuscitate people, they stem bleeding and they have end-of-life discussions. Nurses thus appear to be five times more likely to suffer PTSD than the general population.

Similarly, Akhtar and Aydin (2019) write that people who are most at risk of suicide and depression are those who do some of the most important jobs in society, such as doctors, childcare workers and first responders.

'Military personnel operating in a combat role have an increased likelihood of developing PTSD' (Forbes et al., 2019). Confirming Ogle et al's (2013) finding, Forbes et al (2019) also found that 'as a military career progresses, there is increased likelihood of experiencing multiple potentially traumatic events, putting individuals at greater risk of the effects of cumulative trauma exposures.'

Some occupations appear to present a greater risk of mental harm than others. In Australia, the government already recognises this, especially amongst those in public service: 'The nature of these occupation groups suggests that workers who receive compensation for a work-related mental health condition tend to be those who have high levels of interaction with other people, are often providing a public service and often doing their job in difficult and challenging circumstances' (Safe Work Australia, online).

Figure 1.4 is a timeline of a fictional person who has experienced each of the three causes of mental ill-health identified in Figure 1.3. A genetic condition (ADHD), as relates to the *person*, was inherited at birth. Being bullied at school and experiencing divorce relate to *relationships*. Finally, earning a diminishing level of income relates to *circumstances*.

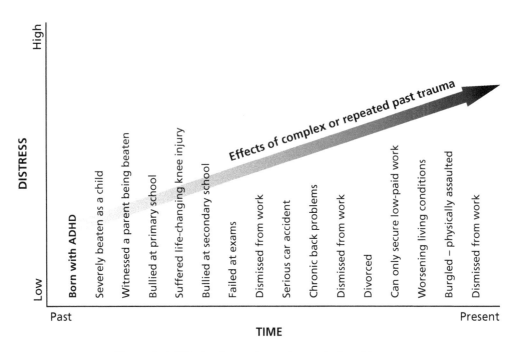

Figure 1.4 *Effects of complex and repeated past trauma*

The person whose life is illustrated in Figure 1.4 was beaten as a child. Research has found that 'cumulative exposure to *childhood violence* and *adulthood physical assaults* were most strongly associated with PTSD symptom severity in older adulthood' (Ogle et al., 2013).

Unresolved childhood trauma is an example of a past experience that might not in itself lead to emotional distress but that could do so if it is compounded or triggered later in life.

Figure 1.4 presents an example of how the *distress* illustrated in Figure 1.2 may be experienced multiple times during the course of a person's life. The example is an extreme case and intended for illustrative purposes only but it is likely that the emotional and psychological effects of such trauma may lead to post-traumatic stress disorder (PTSD), as Ogle et al. (2013) found. Ogle et al.'s study also found a direct correlation between the number of potentially traumatic events an individual had experienced and the severity of their PTSD symptoms (Figure 1.5).

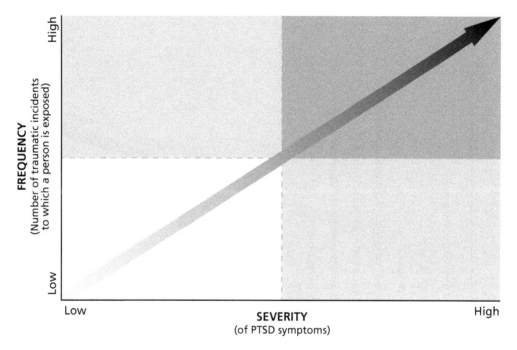

Figure 1.5 *PTSD frequency – severity matrix*

Source: Based on Ogle et al., 2013

It should also be remembered that women may experience many types of trauma that men simply will not, such as a difficult pregnancy, a difficult birth, miscarriage, stillbirth, abortion, the menopause and so on. Some women experience repeated pregnancy-related traumas, carrying these extremely emotional experiences with them for the rest of their lives. Loss and grief are common amongst women aged 30 or over. Yet in most workplaces this fact is barely acknowledged.

Bear in mind that the symptoms of PTSD may emerge later in life. Delayed-onset PTSD (D-PTSD) can occur well after a traumatic event; according to Sareen (2014), delayed-onset PTSD is defined as symptoms that meet the criteria for PTSD at least six months after the trauma.

Of course, most of the past traumatic events illustrated in Figure 1.4 relate to events occurring outside of work. However, many employees may not have issues affecting their mental health to any significant extent outside of work. Their mental health issues may result purely from work and work-related factors. Some examples of workplace factors that can undermine mental health, along with the effect these factors have on the employee, are illustrated in Figure 1.6.

A compound effect is evident. As more factors or causes are experienced, so distress increases. Some factors may persist for long periods, elevating distress levels on a continuing basis, bringing the employee closer to their resilience threshold; closer to the point where they can no longer cope.

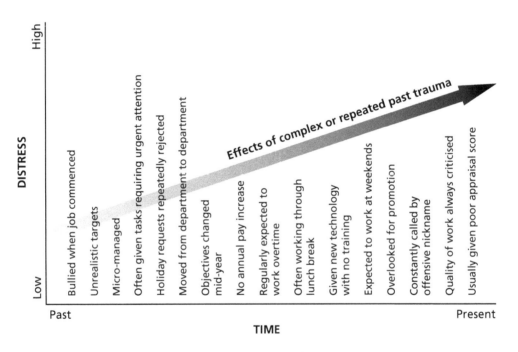

Figure 1.6 *The development of stress at work*

Each of the events depicted in Figure 1.6 may not be traumatic in and of themselves, despite causing stress or other adverse symptoms. But when compounded, the overall effect may become traumatic.

Work-related and non-work-related factors, when combined, can have an overwhelming adverse effect on the employee.

Two issues can now be seen with some clarity. Firstly, multiple traumatic events can lead to declining mental health and possibly PTSD. Secondly, the symptoms associated with PTSD may not emerge immediately. These two points indicate that *one small thing* occurring at work – for instance, stress caused by an increase in workload or a confrontation with a colleague – could trigger PTSD-like symptoms. One final traumatic event, which may be the last in a long line of traumatic events, may prove to be 'the straw that breaks the camel's back', leading an employee (with or without mental health issues) to move from a state of *coping* to a state of *distress*.

Mental Health and Employers

This book is principally concerned with the role employers play in managing the mental health of their workforce. The global impact of poor mental health on public and private sector employers is staggering. The World Health Organization (WHO) estimates that globally, depression and anxiety account for $1 trillion each year in lost productivity (WHO, 2019b).

Business in the Community (2019) found that two in five (39%) employees reported experiencing poor mental health symptoms related to work in the last year. Other studies found this to be even higher, with the CIPD (2018b) reporting the figure at 54%. However, 71% of employees still consider mental health to be a taboo subject in the workplace, so much so that 45% of employees will make up an alternative reason for being absent from work rather than report a mental health issue to their employer (Drewberry Insurance, online).

Having established that mental ill-health has a wide range of causes relating to the *person*, their *circumstance* and their *relationships,* it is, perhaps, unsurprising that 61% of employees say they have experienced mental health issues due to work or where work was a related factor (Business in the Community, 2018). In its 2019 study, Business in the Community found that 39% of employees reported having experienced symptoms of poor mental health related to work in the previous year.

It seems, then, a significant proportion of cases of mental ill-health are caused by work or work-related factors. Given that two in five employees report having experienced work-related mental ill-health in a single year, employers should take a strategic and structured approach to tackling mental health at work. The sheer scale of the issue warrants this type of approach.

However, there is a major barrier to effective workplace management of mental health. Many employers lack knowledge and understanding of mental health, so they are uncertain about what actions to take in response to the mental health issue. Figure 1.7 illustrates the possible level of *understanding* and *certainty* that employers may experience when managing physical health, age equality, gender equality and mental health.

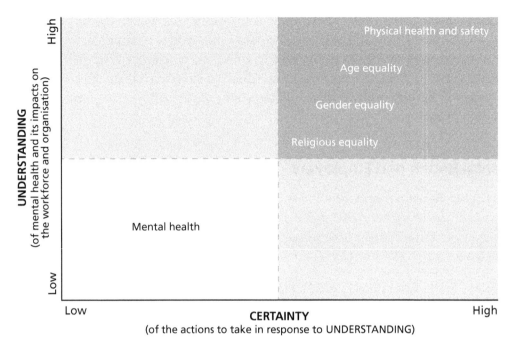

Figure 1.7 *Mental health understanding – certainty matrix*

There are three reasons that employers' *understanding* and *certainty* of how to manage mental health lag behind physical health and other aspects of management: lack of established practice; lack of a clear definition; and ambiguous third-party guidance.

Lack of established practice: Those aspects of management that have existed the longest are understood best. Employers have been managing physical health and safety for 50 years, since the Health and Safety at Work etc Act (HASAWA) was introduced in 1974, so today's practice is well-developed. By contrast, most employers would be uncertain of their own obligations under mental health-related legislation or which mental health conditions are protected by it.

Lack of a clear definition: Most of the management aspects in Figure 1.7 (eg. age, gender, religion) are defined in law. They are also defined in the workplace. Most employers have written procedures for each of them, typically in the form of an employee handbook. This means that leaders, managers and workers all understand the 'whys and wherefores' of issues such as gender equality and religious equality. Mental health and mental ill-health are generally less well defined, with far more ambiguity attached to them.

Ambiguous third-party guidance: Many third parties offer guidance to employers about health and safety, age, gender and religious equality. These third parties include regulators, legal practitioners, training organisations, consultants and so on. Because mental health has only recently emerged as a management discipline, third-party guidance is less well-developed and is thus less effective and less progressive.

Employers may even feel less likely to be able to support employees with mental health issues today than they did ten years ago. Research shows that in 2009, 90% of managers felt comfortable talking about mental health with their staff members. In 2017, this figure was just 64% (Shaw Trust, 2018). Worryingly, the suicide rate has risen in recent years. I cannot say whether there is a link between these two variables (Figure 1.8). However, if managers are less comfortable supporting employees with their mental health, perhaps this diminishing level of employer support is adding to the levels of distress being experienced by employees.

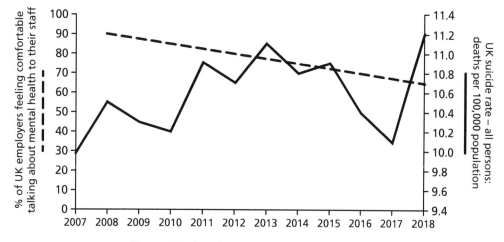

Figure 1.8 *Suicide – employer confidence trend*

Source: Office for National Statistics, 2019 (suicide rate); Shaw Trust, 2018 (employer confidence rate)

I would argue that it is possible that some employers are running the risk of making things worse for the employee with a mental health issue. This might be linked to employers' lack of understanding and confidence around:

- types of mental health condition
- the effects or symptoms that can arise as a result of each condition
- types of treatment
- which conditions are protected by law
- how to empathise with people with mental health issues
- what adjustments might be required in the workplace
- what strategic management actions to take to support mental health
- how to stop mental health stigma.

These gaps in knowledge and understanding may be slowing the progress employers are making in tackling workplace mental health issues. As a result, mental health may remain an issue for employers for many years to come.

However, slow progress is better than no progress. Third-party pressure is building, encouraging employers to act. Mind, Time to Change (TTC), Rethink Mental Illness and similar organisations are educating and training employers so they can tackle mental health in a more constructive and effective manner. Currently, employers are responding to the mental health challenge through four increasingly popular approaches: speaking out; wellbeing; mental health first aid; and building resilience.

Speaking out: The main thrust of the messages from government and the charity sector is on getting people with mental health issues to talk about their experiences. Given that the people themselves are being asked to speak out, employers are, logically, being asked to develop the ability within their organisation to listen and respond to them and take action based on what they hear. However, employees with poor mental health should only be invited to speak out when those listening are willing and able to provide effective support.

Wellbeing: Lifestyle is known to play a significant part in a person's mental health (Figure 1.9). Diet, exercise levels, use of recreational substances (such as tobacco and alcohol), along with social life, can affect mood, energy levels and wider mental health. Increasingly, employers are putting in place initiatives that support employees to live healthier lifestyles, which, in part, will help improve mental health. Evidence shows there is a link between exercise and good mental wellbeing (NHS, 2019). Wellbeing is a far broader subject than mental health. Although wellbeing can benefit mental health enormously, it can also miss some of the key elements of mental health that require specific management.

Mental health first aid: When an employee speaks out about their mental health and presents as being close to or actually distressed, some form of first aid may be required. Mental health first aid has boomed since 2010, and results appear to demonstrate awareness of mental health has improved. However, there is little evidence to support whether mental health first aid has actually benefitted the recipients of it. The HSE's (2018) review found:

- There are only a small number of published occupational studies that have addressed mental health first aid (MHFA) and these had design and quality limitations
- There is limited evidence that the content of MHFA training has been adapted for workplace circumstances
- There is consistent evidence that MHFA training raises employees' awareness of mental ill-health conditions, including signs and symptoms
- There is limited evidence that MHFA training leads to sustained improvement in the ability of those trained to help colleagues experiencing mental ill-health

▨   There is no evidence that the introduction of MHFA training has improved the organisational management of mental health in workplaces.

More recently, Mental Health First Aid England (2018) promoted the results of a study which identified numerous benefits arising from mental health first aid training. However, this later study also failed to identify the effects of mental health first aid on the recipients of it. Did mental health first aid immediately reduce symptoms of distress? Did mental health first aid reduce the need for the employee to present to public health services? Did the ongoing provision of workplace support (including mental health first aid) lead to a long-term improvement in employee mental health? Training is one thing. Helping people with mental health issues actually move from being distressed to a more preferable state (eg. coping, managing, content) is another. Employers should not utilise or rely on mental health first aid in any significant way. First aid is provided after an incident, so it is a 'post-injury' method of treatment. It is not a proactive and preventative method, and it does nothing to prevent mental health injuries arising in the first place. Chapter 3 explores physical health and safety management methods. First aid does not feature as it does not play a strategic or significant role in any physical health and safety management system. Likewise, mental health first aid shouldn't be thought of as a strategic or significant initiative in any workplace mental health management system.

Building resilience: Some proactive methods aimed at preventing poor mental health are available. Resilience training is provided by many employers, including mindfulness. According to many sources, including Cho (2016), mindfulness can provide scientifically proven benefits. Perhaps unsurprisingly, mindfulness is being widely adopted by employers as a go-to solution for workplace mental health management, and there is a perception among them that mindfulness is effective. But has mindfulness been over-hyped (Lieberman, 2018)? Some people think so. Employers usually want to establish a link between actions and results, yet some embark on mindfulness programmes without understanding them and without measuring their results, simply assuming they are doing good. However, some studies suggest there can be downsides to meditation and mindfulness (Greenwood, 2018). As Croner (online) explains: 'Some critics of mindfulness have pointed out that it does not address legitimate issues within the workplace. In some cases, mindfulness is used as a tool to help employees cope with needlessly stressful or negative situations. Mindfulness should not be a substitute for an actual solution.' Resilience training might focus on current work-related issues, such as boosting energy, coping with change and stress through improving flexible thinking, and improving workplace relationships (Figure 1.10). Its aim is to increase the resilience 'buffer'. However, such training tends to be limited in scope, and places little or no emphasis on coping with past trauma, which has been shown in this chapter to contribute significantly towards poor mental health (Figure 1.11).

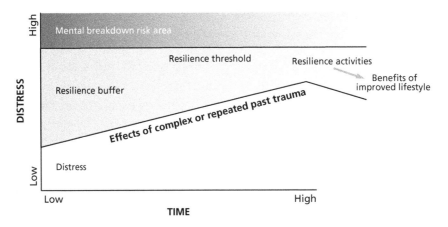

Figure 1.9 *Aim of resilience building – improved lifestyle*

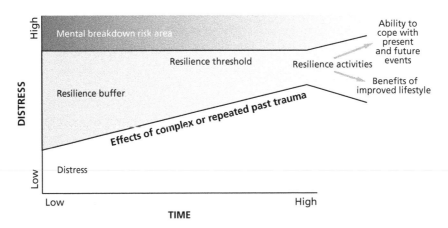

Figure 1.10 *Aim of resilience building – coping with current and future stressors*

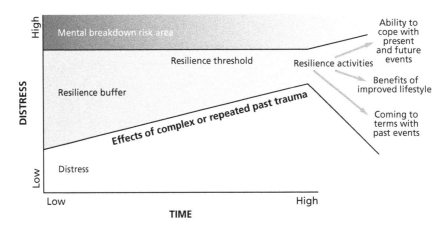

Figure 1.11 *Aim of resilience building – coming to terms with the past*

It is vital for employers to make efforts to prevent the sort of stress and mental ill-health that adversely affect employees, if the tipping point leading to *distress* is to be avoided. Employers must stop the 'one small thing' arising at work that might make the difference between mental health and mental ill-health. Getting people to speak out, wellbeing activity, resilience training and mental health first aid are all tactical responses to the mental health crisis. These measures are not strategic. They place too much emphasis on the employee, with too little emphasis being placed upon the employer.

The tactical nature of typical mental health management responses is apparent because, when we compare management methods for physical health and safety to those for mental health, it is evident that speaking out, training and first aid are tactical. They do not necessarily stem from a policy, they only form a limited part of a programme of activity and their effects appear questionable, as was found by the HSE. It is apparent – based on my review of advice and services available from government, charities, consultants and training providers – that the more strategic and preventative methods of managing physical health and safety are not currently commonly associated with methods of mental health management.

Part II of this book aims to fill this gap by providing a strategic and structured approach that will help employers to manage mental health in a similar way to physical health, and that will also complement current practices set out above.

This chapter considered the scale of the mental health problem, the four stages of mental health people experience and the causes of poor mental health, including some of those arising at work. It presented the prevalence of mental health conditions and explored repeated and complex PTSD, including issues especially faced by women. The chapter continued by exploring some of the challenges faced by employers in managing mental health and some of the contemporary methods employers are utilising in response. It concluded by suggesting employers should focus on helping employees cope with current and future stressors, develop healthier lifestyles and coming to terms with past trauma.

The main take-outs from this chapter are:

- Between one in four and one in five people suffers with a mental health issue each year.
- Globally, depression and anxiety cause $1 trillion dollars in lost productivity each year.
- People with mental health issues tend to occupy one of four states: distress; coping; managing; or content.
- The causes of mental ill-health relate to the person, circumstances and relationships.
- 61% of employees experiencing mental health issues say work was a factor, presenting a challenge for employers.

- The workforce is ageing, meaning the problem of mental health as it affects employers is growing.

- The older people get the more likely they are to have experienced mental health trauma.

- PTSD is underestimated. There is a correlation between the number of traumatic events experienced and PTSD symptoms.

- Women may suffer particular problems, for example, related to pregnancy, birth and the menopause.

- Distress arising from poor mental health can be caused by factors at work or outside of work. A compound effect can occur, with the last in a long succession of stressors causing an employee to become distressed – the 'one small thing' principle.

- Current employer responses – which include speaking out, resilience training and mental health first aid – are mostly tactical and are not considered strategic.

- The reason employers do not take more strategic action to address mental health is linked to a lack of understanding and uncertainty.

- Employers must take a more strategic approach to managing mental health.

References

Advisory Board (2019) *Why 1 in 4 Nurses Suffers from PTSD (and How to Help Them)* (online). Available at: *https://www.advisory.com/daily-briefing/2019/05/15/nurse-trauma* (accessed 3 March 2020).

AgeUK (2019) The Equality Act. *Age UK* (online). Available at: *https://www.ageuk.org.uk/information-advice/work-learning/discrimination-rights/the-equality-act/* (accessed 8 January 2020).

Akhtar, A. and Aydin, R. (2019) Some of the jobs most at risk for suicide and depression are the most important to society. Here's a rundown of mental-health risks for doctors, childcare workers, first responders, and more. *Business Insider* 14 November. Available at: *https://www.businessinsider.com/jobs-with-mental-health-risks-like-suicide-depression-2019-10?r=US&IR=T* (accessed 8 March 2020).

American Psychiatric Association (2018) What is mental illness? *American Psychiatric Association* (online). Available at: *https://www.psychiatry.org/patients-families/what-is-mental-illness* (accessed 15 December 2019).

Anxiety and Depression Association of America (online) *Adult ADHD (Attention Deficit Hyperactivity Disorder)*. Available at: *https://adaa.org/understanding-anxiety/related-illnesses/other-related-conditions/adult-adhd* (accessed 25 November 2019).

Business in the Community (2016) *Mental Health at Work 2016 Report: National Employee Mental Wellbeing Survey Findings 2016*. Available at: *https://www.basw.co.uk/resources/mental-health-work-report-2016* (accessed 6 February 2020).

Business in the Community (2017) *Mental Health at Work 2017 Report: National Employee Mental Wellbeing Survey Findings 2017*. Available at: https://www.uk.mercer.com/our-thinking/health/mental-health-at-work-2017-report.html (accessed 6 February 2020).

Business in the Community (2018) *Mental Health at Work 2018 Report: Seizing the momentum*. Available at: *https://www.bitc.org.uk/wp-content/uploads/2019/10/bitc-wellbeing-report-mentalhealthatworkreport2018fullversion-oct2018.pdf* (accessed 6 February 2020).

Business in the Community (2019) *Mental Health at Work 2019: Time to take ownership*. Available at: *https://www.bitc.org.uk/report/mental-health-at-work-2019-time-to-take-ownership/* (accessed 22 November 2019).

Carter, S.B. (2011) The hidden health hazards of toxic relationships. *Psychology Today* (online). Available at: *https://www.psychologytoday.com/gb/blog/high-octane-women/201108/the-hidden-health-hazards-toxic-relationships* (accessed 28 November 2019).

Chartered Institute of Personnel and Development (2018a) *Health and Well-being at Work*. Available at: *https://www.cipd.co.uk/Images/health-and-well-being-at-work_tcm18-40863.pdf* (accessed 28 November 2019).

Chartered Institute of Personnel and Development (2018b) *People Managers' Guide to Mental Health*. Available at: *https://www.cipd.co.uk/Images/mental-health-at-work-1_tcm18-10567.pdf* (accessed 28 November 2019).

Cho, J. (2016) 6 scientifically proven benefits of mindfulness and meditation. *Forbes* 14 July. Available at: *https://www.forbes.com/sites/jeenacho/2016/07/14/10-scientifically-proven-benefits-of-mindfulness-and-meditation/#13442bc963ce* (accessed 21 March 2020).

Croner (online) *Should Companies Offer Mindfulness Training?* Available at: *https://croner.co.uk/resources/pay-benefits/companies-offering-mindfulness-training/* (accessed 19 March 2020).

Drewberry Insurance (online) *5 Shocking Statistics About Stress & Mental Health in the Workplace*. Available at: *https://www.drewberryinsurance.co.uk/news/employee-benefits/5-shocking-statistics-about-stress-mental-health-in-the-workplace* (accessed 29 November 2019).

Everymind (online) *Understanding Mental Ill-health*. Available at: *https://everymind.org.au/mental-health/understanding-mental-health/what-is-mental-illness* (accessed 20 December 2019).

Forbes, D., Pedlar, D., Adler, A. B., Bennett, C., Bryant, R., Busuttil, W., Cooper, J., Creamer, M. C., Fear, N. T., Greenberg, N., Heber, A., Hinton, M., Hopwood, M., Jetly, R., Lawrence-Wood, E., McFarlane, A., Metcalf, O., O'Donnell, M., Phelps, A., Richardson, J. D., Sadler, N., Schnurr, P. P., Sharp, M-L., Thompson, J. M., Ursano, R. J., Van Hooff, M., Wade D. & Wessely, S. (2019) Treatment of military-related post-traumatic stress disorder: challenges, innovations, and the way forward. *International Review of Psychiatry, DOI: 10.1080/09540261.2019.1595545*. Available at: https://www.kcl.ac.uk/kcmhr/publications/assetfiles/2019/forbes2019.pdf (accessed 21 March 2020).

Greenwood, C. (2018) 7 surprising ways meditating could be hurting you. *Insider* 21 March. Available at: *https://www.insider.com/why-meditation-can-be-bad-2018-3* (accessed 19 March 2020).

Harvard Health Publishing (2019) *Past Trauma May Harm your Future Health*. Available at: *https://www.health.harvard.edu/diseases-and-conditions/past-trauma-may-haunt-your-future-health* (accessed 20 December 2019).

Health and Safety Executive (online, a) *Non-fatal injuries at work in Great Britain*. Available at: *https://www.hse.gov.uk/statistics/causinj/index.htm* (accessed 20 January 2020).

Health and Safety Executive (online, b). *Health and safety statistics: Key figures for Great Britain 2018/19*. Available at: *https://www.hse.gov.uk/statistics/index.htm?ebul=postats14* (accessed on 20 Feb 2020).

Health and Safety Executive (online, c) *What are the Management Standards?* Available at: *https://www.hse.gov.uk/stress/standards/* (accessed 5 January 2020).

Health and Safety Executive (2018). Summary of the evidence on the effectiveness of Mental Health First Aid (MHFA) training in the workplace. Available at: *https://www.hse.gov.uk/research/rrhtm/rr1135.htm* (accessed 5 January 2020).

Health and Safety Executive (2019) Work-related Stress, Anxiety or Depression Statistics in Great Britain, 2019. Available at: *http://www.hse.gov.uk/statistics/causdis/stress.pdf* (accessed 18 November 2019).

Health and Safety at Work etc Act (1974) (HASAWA) Available at: *http://www.legislation.gov.uk/ukpga/1974/37/section/2* (accessed 5 December 2019).

Lieberman, B. (2018) Mindfulness may have been over-hyped. *BBC Future* 7 May. Available at: *https://www.bbc.com/future/article/20180502-does-mindfulness-really-improve-our-health* (accessed 19 March 2020).

Mental Health Foundation (2017) *Surviving or Thriving? The state of the UK's mental health.* Available at: *https://www.mentalhealth.org.uk/sites/default/files/surviving-or-thriving-state-uk-mental-health.pdf* (accessed 28 November 2019).

Mind (2017a) *How common are mental health problems?* Available at: *https://www.mind.org.uk/information-support/types-of-mental-health-problems/statistics-and-facts-about-mental-health/how-common-are-mental-health-problems/#.XbmhHUagLIU* (accessed 30 January 2020).

Mind (2017b) *Mental Health Problems – An introduction.* Available at: *https://www.mind.org.uk/information-support/types-of-mental-health-problems/mental-health-problems-introduction/causes/#.XbqOCEagLIU* (accessed 19 October 2019).

National Alliance on Mental Illness (2019) *Mental Health by the Numbers.* Available at: *https://www.nami.org/learn-more/mental-health-by-the-numbers* (accessed 30 January 2020).

National Health Service (2019) *5 Steps to Mental Wellbeing.* Available at: *https://www.nhs.uk/conditions/stress-anxiety-depression/mental-benefits-of-exercise/* (accessed 18 December 2019).

Office for National Statistics (online). *Suicides in the UK Statistical bulletins.* Available at: *https://www.ons.gov.uk/peoplepopulationandcommunity/birthsdeathsandmarriages/deaths/bulletins/suicidesintheunitedkingdom/previousReleases* (accessed on 20 Feb 2020)

Ogle, C.M., Rubin, D.C. and Siegler, I.C. (2013) Cumulative exposure to traumatic events in older adults. *Aging & Mental Health* 18:3, 316–325. Available at: *https://www.ncbi.nlm.nih.gov/pmc/articles/PMC3944195/* (accessed 5 January 2020).

Olff, M. (2017) Sex and gender differences in post-traumatic stress disorder: an update. Available at: *https://www.ncbi.nlm.nih.gov/pmc/articles/PMC5632782/* (accessed 20 March 2020).

Plana-Ripoll, O., Pedersen, C.B., Agerbo, E., Holtx, Y., Erlangsen, A., Canudas-Romo, V., Andersen, P.K., Charlson, F., Christensen, M.K., Erskine, H.E., Ferrari, A.J., Iburg, K.M., Momen, N., Mortensen, P.B., Nordentoft, M., Santomauro, D.F., Scott, J.G., Whiteford, H.A. and Laurensen, T.M. (2019) A comprehensive analysis of mortality-related health metrics associated with mental disorders: a nationwide, register-based cohort study. *The Lancet* 394:10211, 1827–1835. Available at: *https://www.sciencedirect.com/science/article/pii/S0140673619323165?via%3Dihub* (accessed 30 October 2019).

Postpartum Support International (online). *Post-Partum Post-Traumatic Stress Disorder.* Available at: *https://www.postpartum.net/learn-more/postpartum-post-traumatic-stress-disorder/* (accessed 20 March 2020).

Robinson, L., Smith M. and Segal, J. (2019) Emotional and psychological trauma. *HelpGuide* (online). Available at: *https://www.helpguide.org/articles/ptsd-trauma/coping-with-emotional-and-psychological-trauma.htm* (accessed 23 October 2019).

Rosen, P. (online) ADHD and anxiety: what you need to know. *Understood*. Available at: *https://www.understood.org/en/learning-thinking-differences/child-learning-disabilities/add-adhd/adhd-and-anxiety-what-you-need-to-know* (accessed 2 January 2020).

Safe Work Australia (online). *Mental Health*. Available at: *https://www.safeworkaustralia.gov.au/topic/mental-health* (accessed 20 March 2020).

Sareen, J. (2014) Posttraumatic stress disorder in adults: Impact, comorbidity, risk factors, and treatment. Canadian Journal of Psychiatry 59:9, 460–467. Available at: *https://www.ncbi.nlm.nih.gov/pmc/articles/PMC4168808/* (accessed 23 October 2019).

Shaw Trust (2018) *Mental Health at Work: Still the last taboo*. Available at: *https://www.shaw-trust.org.uk/Shaw31%TrustMediaLibraries/ShawTrust/ShawTrust/Documents/Shaw-Trust-Mental-Health-at-Work-Report-2018-full_1.pdf* (accessed 29 November 2019).

Smith, H. (2017). *Benenden Mental Health in the Workplace Report*. Available at: *https://www.benenden.co.uk/media/4164/benenden_mental_health_report.pdf* (accessed 17 February 2020).

Stevenson, D. and Farmer, P. (2017) *Thriving at Work: The Stevenson/Farmer review of mental health and employers*. Available at: *https://assets.publishing.service.gov.uk/government/uploads/system/uploads/attachment_data/file/658145/thriving-at-work-stevenson-farmer-review.pdf* (accessed 28 October 2019).

United Nations (online) *Ageing*. Available at: *https://www.un.org/en/sections/issues-depth/ageing/* (accessed 18 January 2020).

Workplace Bullying Institute (2017) *2017 WBI U.S. Workplace Bullying Survey*. Available at: *https://www.workplacebullying.org/wbiresearch/wbi-2017-survey/* (accessed 28 October 2019).

World Health Organization (2019a) *Mental health*. Available at: *https://www.who.int/mental_health/who_urges_investment/en/* (accessed 4 January 2020).

World Health Organization (2019b) *Mental Health in the Workplace*. Available at: *https://www.who.int/mental_health/in_the_workplace/en/* (accessed 28 October 2019).

2

EMPATHISING WITH EMPLOYEES WHO HAVE MENTAL HEALTH ISSUES

You might find that empathising with employees who have mental health issues can be difficult and awkward. This can come from a lack of understanding, which this chapter aims to go some way to addressing.

There are suggestions half of employers view staff with mental health conditions as a 'significant risk' to their business, an increase of 10% since 2009 (Shaw Trust, 2018). Given the scale of the mental health issue identified in chapter 1, most employers will have employees with mental health issues, whether they think they do or not. Risks may not only come from people with mental health issues themselves, but from failing to properly manage and support them. Palmer (2019), writing in People Management, reports that managers are more likely to be diagnosed with mental health conditions than employees. Organisations, especially large employers, must learn to empathise with those managers and employees with mental health issues. Developing such empathy will assist in the design of effective mental health management systems that support efforts to maximise organisational performance whilst minimising related risks.

People can learn to empathise through personal experience. If somebody experiences something that you have experienced yourself, you can understand to some extent how they feel and you can behave accordingly. Empathising with someone who has a mental health condition can be a challenge if you have had no personal experience of it. How can you empathise with someone with ADHD, for example, when you do not have it yourself and have not encountered it in those close to you?

As a leader and manager, it might help if you ask four questions (Figure 2.1) when supporting an employee with their mental health.

Figure 2.1 *The four questions of workplace mental health*

If you can form some understanding of the answers to these four questions, you will be better placed to provide effective support. This chapter aims to build empathy, partly by exploring these four questions and partly by setting out four of the key challenges facing employees who have a mental health issue:

1   The mental ill-health discovery process

2   Disclosing a mental health issue at work

3   Stigma and bullying

4   The knock-on effects of poor mental health

People with mental health issues are often incredibly resourceful and determined. Many of them have an interesting story. Life can be tough, even for people without mental health issues; when you add to this a mental health condition, along with the host of adverse factors that arise as a consequence of it, then it becomes evident that someone with a mental health condition is often at a disadvantage in any given situation, compared to someone who does not. They are more likely to be on a low income, more likely to have poor living conditions, more likely to have poorly relatives and more likely to spend longer periods of time out of work. If their mental health condition is genetic, they may pass it on to their children, giving them even more to worry about. They must, out of necessity, possess enormous strength of character and courage if they are to approach life positively (case study 1). A helping hand along the way will usually be gratefully received and can make all the difference. As an employer, you are encouraged to offer such a helping hand.

Case Study 1 – Alex – IT Support Engineer

Alex is 23. He has Asperger's Syndrome and Autism. He had a troubled childhood, experiencing difficulties at home and at school. These troubles have had a profound effect upon him. Living at home with his parents and siblings has been far from straight-forward. They struggle to make ends meet. Alex recognises some people may see traits in him that indicate he may have a mental health condition. However, when applying for jobs, he is unsure whether to disclose his condition or not. If he is asked about it, Alex is always open. If he isn't asked, he won't always say. Alex has had six jobs in three years. Because of his condition, employers prefer to hire Alex on a short-term contract. Alex feels that unfair criticism from colleagues usually leads to his employment contract not being extended. As a result, he often finds himself unemployed. Alex has applied for thousands of jobs and attended hundreds of telephone and face-to-face interviews. Alex remains positive and determined. He knows some employers will value his strengths far more than they will worry about his weaknesses. He just has to keep applying for jobs until he finds them.

I am now going to explore some different perspectives to give you an understanding of the experience of the person with a mental health issue.

The Mental Health Discovery Process

The first key challenge facing an employee is the discovery process. When someone finds out they might have a mental health condition they embark on a journey of discovery that might last days, with a diagnosis coming quickly, or it might last years. It might even remain a mystery. The process can be simple and straightforward, or it can be highly complex. It can be embarked upon alone, involve one or two professionals, or it can involve dozens. Even after diagnosis, the journey may be unclear and confusing. It is unsurprising that some employers may find supporting employees with mental health conditions difficult.

This journey of mental health discovery can be daunting not only for the person affected but also for their loved ones, who may themselves develop mental health issues through worrying about their partner, parent or child. The five stages involved in the journey of discovery are presented in Figure 2.2.

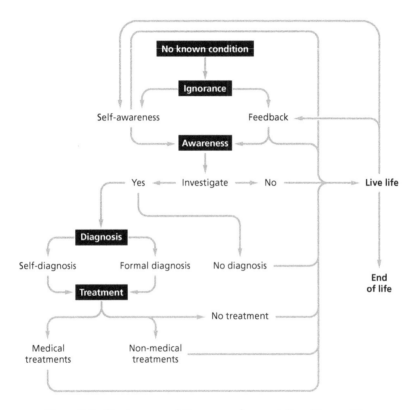

Figure 2.2 *The journey of discovery of a mental health condition*

Stage 1. No known condition: The first stage of the journey may appear obvious. Millions of people have no known mental health condition. This is not to say they do not have a condition. *No known condition* applies to people who do not suspect they have a condition and have not been told by anyone else they may have one. They do not have what would typically be described as a mental health problem and their life may not be affected adversely by their mental state. It may be the case that people included in this group have experienced past trauma but that trauma has not yet adversely affected them by crossing their resilience threshold (Figure 1.11). As identified in chapter 1, a later incident could possibly trigger delayed-onset PTSD (Sareen, 2011). People with *no known condition* go about their life in a state of positive mental health so, relatively speaking, they are content, managing or coping.

Stage 2. Ignorance: This occurs when somebody has a mental health problem that others are aware of but the person is not. It is not unusual for someone to be in denial of their condition, and it is tempting to say that a person refusing to accept a diagnosis is in denial. But a person with acute mental ill-health may not be making a conscious choice. They may have a condition called anosognosia (from the Greek, meaning to not know a disease), which causes people to have a lack of insight or lack of awareness (National Alliance on Mental Illness, online). Alternatively, the person may believe their condition is not as bad as others are making out – or they might believe it to be worse. The emphasis here is on the person, who is ignorant of their condition despite what others might think and say. If it is discussed openly, the person's conflicting perceptions may add further to their condition, and may even result in them developing paranoia.

Stage 3. Awareness: This occurs when somebody suspects they might have a condition, either because they have noticed certain behaviours in themselves or because somebody has suggested it to them. Awareness can arise suddenly, say, immediately after a traumatic event, or gradually over a long period of time. It can come before or after a mental ill-health episode, whether this is a sudden, unexpected mental breakdown that is first treated then diagnosed, followed by long-term treatment, or a slight change in behaviour that is diagnosed then treated. Some people may be aware of behaviours or feedback that suggests they have a mental health condition but choose to do nothing about it. This decision is perfectly valid and may arise for one of two reasons: 1) the condition is not affecting the person's life significantly so there is little point in treatment; or 2) the person does not wish to be labelled or stigmatised, so chooses not to explore the issue further. Some people are well placed to notice potential mental health conditions in others; for example, it is not uncommon for school teachers to suspect a child has a mental health issue and raise this with the child's parents. This is largely welcome, as schools and teachers play a vital role in identifying and overcoming barriers to a child's learning and development. However, the role of employers is less well-established and less clear. It may be that a manager suspects an employee has a mental health issue. Perhaps the employee appears agitated, forgetful or confrontational, and may not even be aware of their own behaviour. Should the manager raise their concerns? Under what conditions is it acceptable for the employer to intervene? Certainly, the employer has a legal duty to act in terms of safety. But what if safety is not an issue and the employee is actually doing a good job? Should the employer say something? Mental health may not just be a dilemma for an employee, therefore, it may well be a dilemma for the employer too. Many people have a totally different perception of their symptoms from those around them. When someone discloses a condition at work, this difference in perception can lead to problems, just as any difference of opinion can. Managers listening to people speak out about their mental health condition must understand how to handle this. Such differences in perception are often overlooked by current mental health training courses, so employers should be wary. If an employer decides to suggest to an employee that they may have a mental health condition, and that employee has no awareness of it, the employer must be prepared not only to provide guidance or assistance in arranging a diagnosis but also to support the employee at work, post-diagnosis, through their prescribed treatment. Mind provides useful guidance for employers about supporting employees at work (Mind, 2017).

Stage 4. Diagnosis: When awareness leads someone to move towards a *diagnosis*, they will face further decisions. How do they get a diagnosis? Is self-diagnosis adequate or will a professional opinion be more helpful, in which case how does the person go about arranging that? Should they see a psychologist or a psychiatrist? (There is a difference – for example, psychiatrists can prescribe medication but psychologists cannot.) There are many online sources of information, both credible and dubious, and with care these can help people form an opinion about what may be 'wrong' with them. Some people may choose to self-diagnose because of convenience and cost. The problem with self-diagnosis is self-evident; the person may reach a conclusion that might not be the conclusion a medical expert would reach. For example, Asperger's syndrome, autism and attention deficit hyperactivity disorder (ADHD) have some characteristics in common but they are distinctly different. Medical professionals have developed testing methods to be able to isolate condition traits, meaning they can tell these conditions apart where the layperson might not. Self-diagnosis may then risk misdiagnosis. Employers might also be wary of employees self-diagnosing. At the other end of the spectrum, for some people only a comprehensive diagnosis by a world-leading authority may be good enough, possibly supported by an equally authoritative second opinion. For these people, certainty and clarity, informed by expertise, is the paramount concern. No matter how they are diagnosed, however, surveys suggest that 40% of mental health patients want to be involved in the decision-making about their care (NHS England, 2017). That said, people with mental health conditions often feel less involved in the decision-making process by medical practitioners than people with physical conditions (Care Quality Commission, 2016). Involvement in decision-making may help reduce the stress and anxiety caused by a diagnosis, and people are likely to feel more in control than if they have little or no say. Being diagnosed with a mental health condition may come as a relief to some, as it may resolve a nagging doubt they have had for some time; for others it may lead to distress, and perhaps shock or worry. Indeed, people may hold many fears before, during and following diagnosis. These fears include questions such as: What's happening to me? How did I end up with this condition? How will it affect me? Will my career prospects be affected? Have I passed this condition on to my child? What treatment do I require? Are there alternatives to psycho-active drugs? Further, a mental health condition can, in itself, cause unusual behaviours, but it can also involve knock-on effects that have an equally profound impact on the person's mental state, emotions and behaviours. These knock-on effects are discussed later in this chapter. Bear in mind also that following a formal diagnosis, the rights of the employee may become more apparent and the Equality Act 2010 may become applicable if it was not thought to apply to them before diagnosis.

Stage 5. Treatment: After diagnosis, *treatment* presents the person with yet more choices and decisions. A wide range of medical and non-medical treatments are available. Non-medical treatments might involve: diet and exercise; therapy, such as counselling, eco-therapy and cognitive behavioural therapy (NHS, 2019); and training, such as resilience training, which some employers now provide for staff. Medical treatments are largely based on medication. A wide variety of drugs are available, most of which can be categorised into antidepressants, antipsychotics, benzodiazepines and mood stabilisers (Rethink Mental Illness, online). Very rarely, an operational procedure may be recommended, perhaps involving neurosurgery. Formal diagnosis can have benefits when it comes to non-medical treatment and support. It allows the person to share their diagnosis and can help in providing them with holistic care. In the case of children, sharing a diagnosis with a school can lead to the development of an Individual Health Care Plan (IHCP) for the child, which can help support their learning and development (Department for Education, 2017). In the case of employees, when they disclose their condition to their employer (which is discussed in more detail later), it may result in the development of a diagnosis and treatment plan detailing the adjustments the employer might make to help support the employee at work. Indeed, the employer may have a legal duty to make reasonable adjustments that suit the employee. Some employers may limit the adjustments they are willing to make to those required by law, but more progressive employers may make adjustments for other reasons, some doing far more for their employees than simply meeting the minimum legal requirement.

Having discussed the five stages of the mental health discovery process, it can be seen that there are many people involved in the discovery process, many decisions to be made and much doubt and uncertainty along the way. The path is far more complex than Figure 2.2 suggests and the range of emotions people can feel while they are on the journey can be equally complex. The discovery process itself can add significant pressure, stress and anxiety to an already potentially distressing situation.

It is also evident that the journey is potentially a long one with many decisions to be made along the way, some of which may prove life-changing, hopefully for the better. For these reasons, employers must manage the subject of mental health with great care. Suicide and self-harm are not in themselves mental health issues but are a person's response to their mental health issues. Employers run the risk of making mental health conditions worse, or even contributing in part towards a decision to commit suicide and self-harm, should they take the wrong course of action when dealing with an employee with mental ill-health. Given that employers discipline or dismiss 15% of workers who disclose a mental health issue at work, this risk is very real (Shaw Trust, 2018a). A later study in 2019 by Business in the Community

(2019) reported this figure as being 9%. Hopefully this more recent statistic reflects a genuine improvement in the treatment of those with mental health issues, as opposed to a difference in study methodology. Whether 15% or 9%, the statistic is still alarming. Stevenson and Farmer (2017) found in the UK, 300,000 people with a long-term mental health condition lose their jobs every year, twice as many as people with no condition. This suggests employers are not as supportive as they might be.

Mental health is becoming a more significant dilemma for employers. As awareness of mental health increases in general and as the incidence of mental health problems increases amongst workers, it follows that employers need to be more effective in the actions they take to manage mental health at work.

Disclosing a Mental Health Condition at Work

As we have seen, it is important for employers to develop a good understanding of the mental health discovery process, so they can better empathise with employees who have a mental health condition. But empathy should not stop there.

As an employer, you can develop deeper understanding and empathy for an employee who discloses a mental health condition at work by putting yourself in their shoes and looking at the disclosure from their perspective. For many people, disclosing a mental health issue is a *major* decision. Disclosing lets the genie out of the bottle and it cannot be put back in if the employee has a change of heart. The decision is lifelong (or career-long). For some people, disclosing their condition to an employer can come as a massive relief. For others, it can spell disaster and significantly worsen their situation and their mental health. Some of the considerations they face are shown in Table 2.1.

Table 2.1   *Pros and cons of disclosing a mental health condition at work*

Disclose	Don't disclose
Pros:	Pros:
▪ behaviours are better understood	▪ maintains confidentiality
▪ support is provided	▪ minimises stigma/no humiliation
▪ empathy/understanding	▪ career prospects unaffected
Cons:	Cons:
▪ reprisals	▪ have to keep up 'normal' pretence
▪ stigma/humiliation	▪ may be seen as odd anyway
▪ career-limiting	▪ no support

Approximately half of all workers would not disclose a mental health issue at work (Scott, 2017). Business in the Community (2019) found 44% of employees would feel comfortable talking to their line manager about their own mental health. This figure is even worse for younger people; an article in *Metro* reports that the student and graduate careers app *Debut* revealed that 70% of students would not disclose a mental health condition to their employer (Abgarian, 2018). This indicates that the next generation of workers may be even less trusting of their employer than the current generation.

Despite campaigning in recent years to raise awareness of mental health, no progress has been made in the drive to make employees feel more comfortable about speaking to their line manager about their mental health (Figure 2.3).

As an aside, is anyone actually monitoring this type of trend? I have found numerous annual reports, some of which reflect on prior year data, but I have yet to see comprehensive linear trend estimation or time series report which present data over the long-term. This lack of strategic analysis again demonstrates the tactical nature of workplace mental health management.

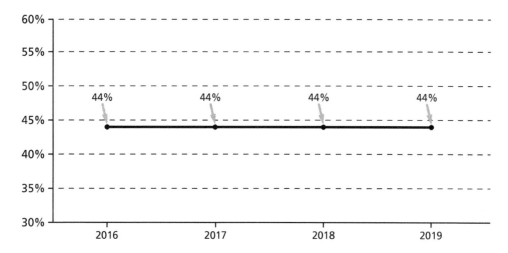

Figure 2.3 *Percentage of employees who feel quite or very comfortable talking to their line manager about their mental health*
Source: Figures collated from BITC, 2016, 2017, 2018, 2019.

Some employees are even prepared to lie to keep their mental health issues confidential. 'Of those (employees) who took mental health days, 55 per cent told their employer they were physically ill, with less than a third (32 per cent) admitting that the reasons were to do with mental health' (Churchill, 2019).

Having made the significant decision to disclose their mental health condition, the employee must now wait to see if a bomb goes off. This is exactly how it can feel. If they have limited their disclosure to a couple of senior managers, the employee will worry about whether the managers will tell others. If the employee has made their disclosure public, they will worry about whether they will be stigmatised. Whether their disclosure is confidential or public, they will worry about how others will treat them in future and whether it will affect their career. The days and weeks that follow the disclosure of a mental health condition can be incredibly nerve-racking for the employee. Perhaps with good reason.

Business in the Community's (BITC) *Mental Health at Work 2019 Report* states that 9% of people who disclosed a mental health issue at work were dismissed, demoted or disciplined, and a further 10% resigned shortly after disclosing (BITC, 2019). Across various reports, it can be seen that around 20% of employees disclosing a mental health condition at work are disciplined, dismissed or resigned shortly after disclosing. One in four people! And these statistics do not touch on those employees who suffer stigmatisation following disclosure but stay with their employer. The proportion of employees whose lives deteriorate after disclosure is far too high. Employers are to blame for this when they fail to create the right culture, fail to manage the disclosure process correctly and fail to garner support from other employees. Where this happens, it is a significant failure of leadership. Hardly surprising, then, that many people choose not to disclose a mental health condition because of the reaction they anticipate from their employer and colleagues. Business in the Community (2019) found that 27% of employees fear negative consequences if they make their mental health issues formal at work.

Decoding Stigma

The third key challenge facing an employee with a mental health issue is the possibility of stigma and bullying. Stigma can be defined as 'a sign of disgrace or discredit, which sets a person apart from others' (Byrne, 2000).

The Shaw Trust (2018b) found over half of employers are reluctant to employ someone with a mental health condition due to a fear of that person being stigmatised by co-workers (56%, up from 51% in 2009). Employers are apparently now more reluctant to employ people with mental health issues.

People with mental ill-health suffer a wide range of negative emotions that can have a profound effect upon them. The feeling of 'disgrace' Byrne (2000) talks of is only one such emotion. There may be other emotional effects of the person's mental health condition, which can compound the problem.

However, disgrace only arises if people are disgraced. Somebody must be *doing* the disgracing! People disgrace others simply because they are bullies. They tend to do so for four reasons (see Figure 2.4). None of the causes of bullying are pleasant or laudable, and none have a place in a modern, progressive organisation.

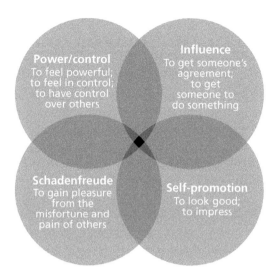

Figure 2.4 *Motives for bullying*

Bullying is a significant cause of stress at work. It was identified earlier that approximately 10% of employees suffer workplace bullying (as identified by Smith, 2017). According to the Workplace Bullying Institute (2017), approximately 60 million Americans are affected by bullying, 60% of bullies are bosses and 40% of victims develop health issues because of bullying. Bullying is a major contributor to workplace stress and poor mental health. Levels of bullying can vary from workplace to workplace.

Bullying generally arises as a result of one of four motives: i) power and control; ii) desire to influence; iii) desire to impress; or iv) to take pleasure (Figure 2.3).

Power and control over others: Where a person feels empowered by and may even gain pleasure from having control over others. Power mongers may wish to exert control of others for the sake of it, possibly to demonstrate their power to themselves and to others.

The desire to influence: The bully adopts coercive instead of collaborative behaviours to get somebody to agree to or do something. Some bullies justify their behaviour by saying they are 'just passionate' or blame the victim by saying they are 'over-sensitive'. This is a training issue, linked to the culture of the organisation. In cases of race discrimination, if the victim takes offence then the perpetrator has no defence. This should be the case with bullying as well; there is no acceptable justification for bullying behaviour.

The desire to impress: The bully brings others down in order to make themselves look good. In terms of teamworking, this is counterproductive and undermines the wellbeing of the other people in the team. It may also highlight discrimination, for example where an employee has disclosed a mental health condition only to senior managers but those senior managers do nothing to stop the bullying.

The desire to take pleasure: Finally, bullies may simply take pleasure from seeing other people suffer – schadenfreude. Such attitudes have no place in any organisation.

Nearly nine out of ten people with mental health problems say that stigma and discrimination have a negative effect on their lives (Mental Health Foundation, 2015). The negative emotions caused by bullies can be significant. If bullying is allowed, whether through action or inaction, employees may further suffer at the hands of bullies, experiencing:

Under-confidence: The person being bullied may feel in some way inferior or not good enough. Their under-confidence may hold them back from playing a full role in society as well as at work.

Anxiety: Panic attacks and other adverse symptoms, brought on by fear and other factors, are common in people with mental health conditions. Such attacks can be debilitating and can contribute towards people not being able to face the world, including the world of work.

Stress: For those who are aware of their mental health condition, worrying about how it might affect them is likely to add to their burden. In some cases, anxiety and stress may even have a more adverse effect on the person than their mental ill-health.

Asocial behaviour: As a result of under-confidence and stress, the person with a mental health condition may choose to live a more isolated life than they would otherwise, perhaps confining themselves in a way that means their condition will not have such a significantly adverse effect upon them.

As we have seen above, Scott (2017) and Business in the Community (2019) found about half of employees would not disclose a mental health condition at work. We have also seen that approximately 20% would be demoted, dismissed, disciplined or forced to resign immediately after disclosure, and that some people who stay with their employer after they reveal their mental health condition experience stigma.

Employers must look at the issue of stigma from a new angle, with a focus on the perpetrator rather than the person who is targeted. There should be no shame in having a mental health condition and those who have one deserve support. However, there *should* be shame in disgracing others, including disgracing people with mental health conditions, just as there is when somebody tries to disgrace somebody because of their race, religion, gender, age or colour.

It is sometimes the case that the values and behaviours of an organisation exclude compassion. It could be that senior managers themselves display bullying behaviour, or they may turn a blind eye to it. It is important for leaders to consider the values and behaviours their organisation aspires to, determine the culture they want their organisation to build and actively promote the behaviours that reflect that, leading by example and encouraging others to do the same. The aspirations and behaviours of leaders should include compassion towards employees, especially those in vulnerable groups, such as those with mental health issues.

Knock-On Effects of Poor Mental Health

The fourth and final key challenge facing an employee with a mental health condition considered in this chapter involves the knock-on effects of poor mental health.

There are many knock-on effects that can accompany mental ill-health, many of which might not even occur to employers. Yet people with long-term mental health conditions live with them every day. They can be inescapable and add to the 'cycle of suffering' (Figure 2.5). The three causes of mental ill-health – the *person*, their *circumstances* and their *relationships* – can be seen to be feeding the cycle in Figure 2.5.

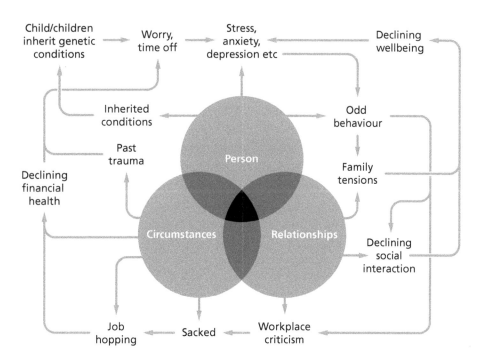

Figure 2.5 *Cycle of mental health 'suffering'*

Things like traumatic issues from the past and a genetic mental health condition can act as constant, underlying causes of mental ill-health, and it can feel like a daily struggle to cope with them. New stressors may be added on top of this, such as worrying about the health of children, issues at work, the loss of a job and pay, and financial health. The knock-on effects of poor mental health can be significant.

Employment security: People with mental health issues are eight times more likely to find it difficult to go to work, three times more likely to have deteriorating relationships with colleagues and twice as likely to need to leave their job (Thorne, 2018). The person's CV can be blighted by a large number of jobs and frequent periods of unemployment, making it increasingly difficult for them to secure employment as they get older. Issues can thus arise around securing a job, staying in employment and performing well at work. Recruiting managers may think a person with a mental health issue presents as 'odd', so dare not put them forward for a job in case their line manager questions their judgement. When the person does gain employment, the issue of job insecurity might arise, perhaps on the grounds that they do not 'fit in' rather than on grounds of performance. Leaders and managers like teams to 'gel'; they may perceive an employee with a mental health issue to be disrupting conditions that would otherwise be harmonious. The employer might think it best to 'exit' the employee. Alternatively, they could invest in developing the team's understanding of mental health so the employee in question becomes more accepted by their colleagues and their skills put to good use. The consequences of a person's mental health issue can thus lead to them struggling to secure and keep a job.

Invalidation: Once an employee discloses a mental health condition, they will at some point be treated as 'less valid' (or 'invalid' – an unpleasant term). There are individuals at work who *will* hold their condition against them. This invalidation will arise as a consequence of the responses of other people, both intended and unintended. Other people might say things like 'she only thinks that because of her condition' or 'he can't help saying that; he doesn't really mean it – it's just his condition talking'. Invalidating an employee because of their mental health is as offensive as using inappropriate language about race, religion or colour, and it is up to leaders to help eradicate it. An employee's credibility may well be questioned after they make a disclosure, and it is the leader's role to support the employee making such a disclosure. Leaders must ensure disclosing employees receive appropriate support and are not left to become 'invalid' – which will invariably harm their mental health further.

Low pay: This can be another knock-on effect of poor mental health. As Sareen (2011) states: 'Low levels of household income are associated with several lifetime mental disorders and suicide attempts, and a decrease in income is associated with a higher risk for anxiety, substance use, and mood disorders'. Mental health issues can be exacerbated by low earnings or not earning at all. Dismissal from a job will almost certainly add to the plight of a person with mental health issues. This can lead to them earning a low level of pay, with gaps in employment making them unreliable earners. Poor living conditions and an inability to support their family can result, which can add further to their worries and stress.

Family worries: It is nobody's fault when someone inherits a genetic mental health condition or passes it on to their child. As well as dealing with their own mental health condition, the person will have to help their child come to terms with theirs, and watch their child struggle at school and struggle to make friends. Some parents invest significant amounts of time in supporting their child, desperately trying to keep them healthy and happy. The last thing the parent wants is for their child, who has already inherited a mental health condition, to suffer consequential mental health issues, such as anxiety or depression, as well as possible poverty and isolation. The guilt from having passed on the condition to a child, can itself cause depression, as can the guilt of having to pass the responsibility for earning to a partner. For many, their main battle with mental health is not their own; it is their child's. It is unsurprising when some employees do not behave as others do at work, given the burdens they may carry.

Loneliness and isolation: Loneliness can be particularly taxing for people already struggling with their mental health (Matthews, 2018). When someone has significant worries and low earnings, it can be difficult to have much of a social life; with reduced means comes reduced participation. The person may feel lonely and isolated socially and appear more solitary at work. This can add to colleagues' perception that they are not a team player, do not (try to) conform or fit in, and are not a 'company' person. Commenting on a Cigna survey, the American Psychological Association (2019) states: 'loneliness levels have reached an all-time high, with nearly half of 20,000 U.S. adults reporting they sometimes or always feel alone. Forty percent of survey participants also reported they sometimes or always feel that their relationships are not meaningful and that they feel isolated'.

Troubled personal relationships: The divorce rate amongst adults with ADHD has been reported as twice as high as the average (Haupt, 2010), and reports show lower levels of marital satisfaction in couples where ADHD is present (Weir, 2012). Other mental health issues present similar problems. Partners of people with a mental health issue can find themselves having to take control of household affairs as their partner may be forgetful. If the partner with a mental health issue is the primary earner, they may become a poor provider as they may only be able to secure employment with low wages. Their partner can grow resentful of this, especially if they are financially dependent upon them. This resentment can build if the person repeatedly loses their job and struggles to provide the financial security most 'normal' families strive for. This resentment can grow because of poor living conditions or because the partner without a mental health issue has to work extra hours to make ends meet. A primary carer who has a mental health issue may present their partner with similar challenges.

Sustainability Through Compassion Towards Employees

As we have discovered, mental health problems often arise from the cumulative effect of multiple causes or repeated trauma (see chapter 1). The mental health 'cycle of suffering' (Figure 2.4) can develop a momentum of its own, often downward. Employers are in a position either to affect this cycle negatively, through harsh treatment of the person involved, or to support struggling employees to a greater extent than perhaps they do today, in line with their corporate social responsibility, sustainability and social wellbeing policies.

Here, the notion of *sustainability through compassion towards employees* arises for employers.

This notion relates to a person's ability to sustain a position in society – at home, at work and socially. In today's generally capitalist world, the ability to earn is central to quality of life.

Earning a wage allows for better wellbeing. All employees deserve 'good' wellbeing, which can be affected by their ability to earn, as this provides them with a suitable place to live, a healthy diet, exercise and, for parents, the ability to invest in their child's health, education and social activity. Employers can be in a position either to empower an employee with the ability to earn, granting them an aspirational quality of life, or to compound their mental health issues by contributing to their financial problems. An employer can also affect an employee's self-respect. People with mental health issues often see employment as a gift granted to them by their employer, for which they are more grateful than their employer will ever realise.

In this chapter, I hope I have given leaders and managers some insight into the perspectives of people with mental health issues, the journey they go on and the lives they lead. I explored the journey of discovery from having no known condition, to ignorance, then awareness, then diagnosis and treatment. I discussed the major decision of whether to disclose a mental health condition and the potential for stigma to arise from doing so. Finally, I explored the knock-on effects of mental ill-health, including how having a mental health condition can blight a person's career, leading to low wages and periods of unemployment. I touched on the possibility of other members of the family also developing mental health conditions, either from genetic causes or through witnessing and supporting a loved one with a mental health condition.

The main take-outs from this chapter are:

- People go through a five-stage discovery process (no known condition, ignorance, awareness, diagnosis and treatment), which can be short or lengthy, simple or complex.

- Employers must act with caution before suggesting to an employee they may have a mental health condition.

- Many employers see people with mental health issues as a 'significant risk', so the reticence of employees to disclose is understandable.

- Employees with a mental health condition face a major decision when contemplating whether to divulge their mental health condition to their employer. They may fear reprisals, such as dismissal. Approximately 20% of employees who disclose a mental health condition are demoted, disciplined, dismissed or forced to resign.

- Stigma arises where there is a failure of culture and leadership. Anti-bullying policies must be enforced if a pro-mental health culture is to develop.

- People with a mental health condition may suffer from numerous knock-on effects, such as passing their condition on to their child, low income levels, repeatedly being sacked, financial problems and poor living conditions. A 'cycle of suffering' can result.

- Employers may consider developing a policy of *sustainability through compassion towards employees.*

References

Abgarian, A. (2018) 'It crushes your hopes': people share bad experiences of sharing mental health issues in the workplace. *Metro*, 12 June. Available at: *https://metro.co.uk/2018/06/12/it-crushes-your-hopes-people-share-bad-experiences-of-sharing-mental-health-issues-in-the-workplace-7569419/* (accessed 11 February 2020).

American Psychological Association (2019). *Social isolation: It could kill you.* Available at: *https://www.apa.org/monitor/2019/05/ce-corner-isolation* (accessed 15 February 2020).

Business in the Community (2016) *Mental Health at Work 2016 Report: National Employee Mental Wellbeing Survey Findings 2016.* Available at: *https://www.basw.co.uk/resources/mental-health-work-report-2016* (accessed 6 February 2020).

Business in the Community (2017) *Mental Health at Work 2017 Report: National Employee Mental Wellbeing Survey Findings 2017.* Available at: https://www.uk.mercer.com/our-thinking/health/mental-health-at-work-2017-report.html (accessed 6 February 2020).

Business in the Community (2018) *Mental Health at Work 2018 Report: Seizing the momentum.* Available at: *https://www.bitc.org.uk/wp-content/uploads/2019/10/bitc-wellbeing-report-mentalhealthatworkreport2018fullversion-oct2018.pdf* (accessed 6 February 2020).

Business in the Community (2019) *Mental Health at Work 2019: Time to take ownership.* Available at: *https://www.bitc.org.uk/report/mental-health-at-work-2019-time-to-take-ownership/* (accessed 22 November 2019).

Byrne, P. (2000) Stigma of mental illness and ways of diminishing it. *Advances in Psychiatric Treatment* 6:1, 65–72. Available at: https://www.cambridge.org/core/journals/advances-in-psychiatric-treatment/article/stigma-of-mental-illness-and-ways-of-diminishing-it/EF630432A797A5296D131EC0D4D5D7AD (accessed 12 February 2020).

Care Quality Commission (2016) *NHS Patient Survey Programme: 2015 adult inpatient survey.* Available at: *https://www.cqc.org.uk/sites/default/files/20150822_ip15_statistical_release_corrected.pdf* (accessed 28 November 2019).

Churchill, F. (2019). *Workers call in physically sick to hide mental ill-health, poll reveals* (online). Available at: *https://www.peoplemanagement.co.uk/news/articles/workers-call-in-physically-sick-hide-mental-ill-health* (accessed on 22 Feb 2020).

Department for Education (2017) *Statutory Guidance: Supporting pupils with medical conditions at school.* Available at: *https://www.gov.uk/government/publications/supporting-pupils-at-school-with-medical-conditions--3* (accessed 28 November 2019).

Haupt, A. (2010) Can Your Relationship Survive ADHD? *U.S. News*, 28 September. Available at: *https://health.usnews.com/health-news/family-health/brain-and-behavior/articles/2010/09/28/can-your-relationship-survive-adhd* (accessed 5 December 2019).

Matthews, T. (2018) Tackling loneliness in people with mental health problems. *The Mental Elf.* Available at: *https://www.nationalelfservice.net/populations-and-settings/loneliness/tackling-loneliness-in-people-with-mental-health-problems/* (accessed 22 November 2018).

Mental Health Foundation (2015) *Stigma and discrimination.* Available at: *https://www. mentalhealth.org.uk/a-to-z/s/stigma-and-discrimination* (accessed 18 November 2019).

Mind (2017) *How can I help someone seeking help?* Available at: *https://www.mind.org.uk/ information-support/guides-to-support-and-services/seeking-help-for-a-mental-health- problem/helping-someone-else-seek-help/#.XbwoO0agLIU* (accessed 30 November 2019).

National Alliance on Mental Illness (online) *Anosognosia.* Available at: *https://www.nami.org/learn-more/ mental-health-conditions/related-conditions/anosognosia* (accessed 30 November 2019).

NHS (2019) *Overview: Cognitive behavioural therapy (CBT).* Available at: *https://www.nhs.uk/ conditions/cognitive-behavioural-therapy-cbt/* (accessed 20 November 2019).

NHS England (2017) *Involving People in their own Health and Care: Statutory guidance for clinical commissioning groups and NHS England.* Available at: *https://www.england.nhs.uk/ wp-content/uploads/2017/04/ppp-involving-people-health-care-guidance.pdf* (accessed 25 November 2019).

Palmer, S. (2019). *Managers more likely to be diagnosed with a mental health condition than other employees.* Available at: *https://www.peoplemanagement.co.uk/news/articles/managers-more- likely-diagnosed-mental-health-condition-other-employees* (accessed 20 February 2020).

Rethink Mental Illness (online) *Medications.* Available at: *https://www.rethink.org/advice-and- information/living-with-mental-illness/medications/* (accessed 21 November 2019).

Sareen, J. (2011) Low income associated with mental disorders and suicide attempts, study finds. *Science Daily*, 4 April. Available at: *https://www.sciencedaily.com/ releases/2011/04/110404161716.htm* (accessed 21 November 2019).

Scott, K. (2017) The law and mental health in the workplace. *Personnel Today*, 5 July. Available at: *https://www.personneltoday.com/hr/the-law-and-mental-health-in-the-workplace/* (accessed 28 November 2019).

Shaw Trust (2018a) *Is work affecting your health?* Available at: *https://www.shaw-trust.org.uk/ News/Blog/March-2018/Is-work-affecting-your-health* (accessed 20 Feb 2020).

Shaw Trust (2018b) *Mental Health at Work: Still the last taboo.* Available at: *https://www.shaw-trust. org.uk/ShawTrustMediaLibraries/ShawTrust/ShawTrust/Documents/Shaw-Trust-Mental- Health-at-Work-Report-2018-full_1.pdf* (accessed 29 November 2019).

Thorne, M. (2018) Mental health and employment – a vicious cycle? *Citizen's Advice*, 9 February. Available at: *https://wearecitizensadvice.org.uk/mental-health-and-employment-a-vicious- circle-74aaea17f644* (accessed 21 November 2019).

Weir, K. (2012) Pay attention to me. *Monitor on Psychology* 43:3, 3. Available at: *https://www.apa. org/monitor/2012/03/adhd* (accessed 5 December 2019).

Workplace Bullying Institute (2017) *2017 WBI U.S. Workplace Bullying Survey June 2017.* Available at: *https://www.workplacebullying.org/wbiresearch/wbi-2017-survey/* (accessed 28 October 2019).

AN INTRODUCTION TO PHYSICAL HEALTH AND SAFETY MANAGEMENT

This chapter offers a basic introduction to the core elements of health and safety management, so if you already have experience in health and safety management, much of it will already be familiar to you.

There are seven core elements of health and safety management, and an exploration of these should allow you to see how physical health and safety management methods can be applied to workplace mental health management. The seven core elements are:

1 The management system

2 Commitment

3 Policy

4 Risk assessments

5 The hierarchy of controls

6 Consultation

7 Reporting.

I do not pretend to provide a detailed explanation of physical health and safety here; you can find more information in the NEBOSH study book produced by RMS Publishing (2015). Instead, this chapter sets out the broad principles of physical health and safety management, so that they can be extrapolated into the field of workplace mental health management.

The seven core elements offer a simple, structured approach to the management of health and safety. Some of the principles of these core elements are shared with other management systems, such as quality management systems (QMS) and environmental management systems (EMS), such as commitment, policy and reporting. Each of the seven elements provides a ready-made framework through which physical health can be effectively managed, and they can be applied equally to mental health. These seven core elements of health and safety management are applicable in many countries. Whilst the UK acts as a focal point for this chapter, the principles presented in it will be familiar to most leaders and managers from around the world, with health and safety laws and practices being similar across country borders.

For example, UK law, the Health and Safety etc Act 1974 (HASAWA) imposes duties upon employers (Section 2) and upon employees (Section 7). In the USA, Section 5 of the Occupational Safety and Health Act of 1970 imposes similar duties upon employers and employees. The Occupation Safety and Health Administration states (OSHA, online):

Each employer —

(1) shall furnish to each of his employees employment and a place of employment which are free from recognized hazards that are causing or are likely to cause death or serious physical harm to his employees;

(2) shall comply with occupational safety and health standards promulgated under this Act.

(b) Each employee shall comply with occupational safety and health standards and all rules, regulations, and orders issued pursuant to this Act which are applicable to his own actions and conduct.

Unlike the USA's OSHA law, the UK's HASAWA does not distinguish between physical and mental health.

In the UK, the directors of any organisation have a legal duty to comply with HASAWA. The Health and Safety Executive (HSE, online, a) states:

If a health and safety offence is committed with the consent or connivance of, or is attributable to any neglect on the part of, any director, manager, secretary or other similar officer of the organisation, then that person (as well as the organisation) can be prosecuted under section 37 of the Health and Safety at Work etc Act 1974.

Recent case law has confirmed that directors cannot avoid a charge of neglect under section 37 by arranging their organisation's business so as to leave them ignorant of circumstances which would trigger their obligation to address health and safety breaches.

Today, leaders and managers have a duty to develop a strategy for managing mental health, especially given it may be a legal requirement, given recent advances in mental health management practice and given the high media profile of mental health which is driving greater awareness.

Tools, such as the HSE's (2019a) stress managements standards workbook which was updated in March 2019, provide useful guidance to leaders and managers when developing related management methods, although the limited nature of the HSE's workbook should be recognised as it only applies to stress and it only identifies six workplace stressors.

Part II of this book takes an in-depth look at the seven core elements of physical health and safety management, applying them to workplace mental health management and offering a comprehensive approach through which employers can discharge many of their obligations under health and safety law as it relates to mental health.

The Management System

A management system is a structured approach to managing any activity that runs through an entire organisation. Management systems operate in the long-term and apply to the whole organisation, so can form part of the strategic measures of success for the organisation. Health and safety, quality, and environmental management systems are among the best known management systems, with each of these often being adopted to meet a recognised accredited standard, such as those operated by the International Standards Organisation (ISO).

Figure 3.1 shows the core elements of a health and safety management system, as set out by the HSE. The core elements of the workplace mental health management system presented in Part II of this book have been based upon Figure 3.1.

Figure 3.1 *Core elements of a health and safety management system*
Source: HSE, online, c

This book takes a management system approach for a number of key reasons, including: the fact that it is established practice; it takes a strategic approach; and it takes a structured approach. Each of these three points is now briefly considered.

Established practice: Management systems have existed for decades. The OHSAS 18001 standard was introduced in 1999, and the ISO 9001 standard was introduced as long ago as 1987. More than a million organisations are certified to the ISO 9001 standard, with about 10% of this number (100,000) being accredited to the OHSAS 18001 standard. Given the length of time these standards have been available and given the number of organisations that have signed up to them, it seems logical to take an approach to mental health that a high number of organisations will easily relate to.

Strategic approach: Just like physical health and safety, any employee can be affected by mental health (whether their own or that of their colleagues), no matter the capacity in which they are employed. It was established earlier that managers are more likely to develop mental health issues than employees. As a result, any mental health management system must be strategic as it must reach every person within the organisation. Such a system will need to operate in the long-term and may form part of an organisation's most significant success criteria. There is no doubt that more stringent enforcement of mental health by the HSE is only a few years or even months away, given the scale of the current mental health crisis. When this happens, organisations will surely give mental health the same level of attention they currently give physical health and safety. This means that many employers will soon be paying much more attention to mental health than they do today. This book aims to help leaders and managers by setting out how they can pay more attention to mental health now, ahead of any such change.

Structured approach: All management systems provide a structured approach to managing an activity. Accreditation bodies look at the effectiveness of the management system and each of its components when they assess organisations against a given standard. This systematic approach has become routine for many organisations as they repeatedly go through the process of renewing those standards that are most important to them. ISO has issued more than 22,000 standards since it was formed in 1947. In 2021, it will introduce ISO 45003 (part of the ISO 45000 series, which in the UK will replace and improve upon OHSAS 18001), which will provide guidance on how to manage psychological health and safety at work.

We now see that a management system for mental health can provide many benefits; it is a well-established, strategic and structured approach that many organisations will be familiar with.

Commitment

One of the core elements of the health and safety management system is *commitment*, from leaders as well as from all employees. Organisational leaders determine and set a long-term direction; they develop and implement a strategy; and they build support for that strategic direction across the whole organisation. They create a sense of purpose, create motivation, provide direction and encourage effort. This is the meaning of *commitment*.

In this section I want to briefly explore some of the elements of *commitment*, especially: personal belief; strategic direction; goals and objectives; gaining buy-in; developing a plan; and checking progress.

Personal belief: Do members of a congregation want an atheist to run the church? Do football fans want a manager who isn't passionate about their team? Do patients want a nurse who doesn't care? Of course not. So why would employees want a leader who does not believe in a cause they promote? An atheist can hold sermons, they can say prayers and chat with the congregation, they can sing hymns and light candles, but they lack faith. Anyone can rearrange the furniture but the best parties are held by people who truly want their guests to have a great time. In the same way, the most effective leaders are those who truly believe in what they are working towards. Based on strong personal belief and a clear vision, leaders must establish a positive culture of physical health and safety, a culture that ensures health and safety is integrated into all of the processes of the organisation.

Strategic direction: A strategic initiative relates to the whole organisation, in the long-term. Typically, especially in industries such as construction, transport and manufacturing, organisations set health and safety as their number one goal, mainly because the risk of death and injury at work is higher than in other sectors. Most directors place health and safety at the heart of their organisation, so it becomes an intrinsic part of it. This is a conscious choice. In organisations that are more office-based, such as software development companies and financial services, health and safety may not play such a prominent role because the risk of death and injury is much lower than in industries such as construction. Clearly, then, the strategic direction of health and safety is linked to the risks involved; leaders must set the strategic direction of their organisation based on the aspirational level of health, safety and welfare of their employees.

Goals and objectives: Strategic initiatives are often important to an organisation and often require investment. When leaders set particular goals and objectives, they indicate the importance of the task and the standards they expect to be achieved. Given the importance of physical health and safety, leaders will want to measure performance and see a return on their investment. Physical health and safety goals often relate to aspirations such as 'zero harm' and 'every employee going home safe and well every day'. The return on investment comes from minimising death and injury. The measurement of goals and objectives is covered in the section headed 'Reporting' at the end of this chapter.

Gaining buy-in: The commitment of leaders alone is not enough. If the people at other levels of the organisation are not similarly committed, strategy cannot be turned into effective action. Everyone in the organisation must 'buy in' to the strategy. In the case of physical health and safety, there are several key drivers that help leaders encourage their staff to 'buy in'. First, it is usually employees' safety that is most at risk so they are naturally motivated to follow the health and safety 'rules'. Second, Section 7 of HASAWA places a duty on employees to take reasonable care of their own safety and that of others, which means that employees have a legal duty to follow health and safety 'rules'. Third, leaders generally set health and safety objectives for junior managers, placing health and safety performance at the forefront. There are other ways to gain buy-in, such as training and consultation, both of which are covered later in this chapter.

Developing a plan: Physical health and safety plans take many forms. Generally, they set out how the health and safety policy will be implemented, who will do what, and how progress will be measured. Typically, plans involve:

- writing, reviewing and improving policies and procedures

- training and information

- meetings to discuss performance and develop improvement action plans

- implementing new ways of working and new control methods

- innovating by developing new ways of working

- learning from outside the organisation and keeping up to date.

Health and safety plans tend to be input-based; that is to say, they describe the tasks or actions to be undertaken. The outputs are self-evident: fewer deaths and fewer injuries. The progress of the plan can be checked by monitoring whether the planned tasks and actions have been completed effectively and on time.

Checking progress: Leaders usually take a direct, personal interest in the management of physical health and safety. They do so by:

- regularly reviewing policies and procedures

- checking how the organisation is meeting its legal obligations

- reviewing the progress of the implementation of the action plan

- requesting routine and ad hoc reports

- overseeing the development of new methods to manage health and safety more effectively

- visiting sites to check that plans, policies and procedures are being implemented correctly at a local level

- presenting updates in meetings and cascading related information down the management chain

- attending consultation group meetings, to hear feedback directly from employees and ensure feedback is being appropriately acted upon

- overseeing the sharing of best practice across the organisation.

Leaders and managers have many opportunities to check that health and safety is being managed in line with their organisation's strategy and policies. When leaders are seen to place significant emphasis on health and safety, it sends a clear signal to middle managers, supervisors and employees about the importance of prioritising it.

Policy

As identified by RMS Publishing (2015), health and safety policies should be cost effective and should aim to achieve 'the preservation and development of physical and human resources and reductions in financial losses and liabilities'. A health and safety policy usefully details practical ways to manage health and safety, but it is also a legal requirement for most employers. In the UK, the HSE (online, b) states:

> *Your business must have a health and safety policy, and if you have fewer than five employees, you don't have to write anything down. Most businesses set out their policy in three sections:*
>
> ▓ *The statement of general policy on health and safety at work sets out your commitment to managing health and safety effectively, and what you want to achieve*
>
> ▓ *The responsibility section sets out who is responsible for specific actions*
>
> ▓ *The arrangements section contains the detail of what you are going to do in practice to achieve the aims set out in your statement of health and safety policy.*

The three key sections of most health and safety policies are: the *statement of intent*, which sets out the organisation's commitment; the management structure with *responsibility* for the policy and related actions; and the *arrangements*, which detail specific methods of compliance. The policy is usually signed by the organisation's managing director or other senior leader, reflecting its importance.

Statement of intent: This is where leaders state their general policy on health and safety, including an expressed commitment to their support for it. It sets out the aims of the organisation for its health and safety policy and practices. The statement is typically short, perhaps a single page, and is usually signed by the responsible person (RP). It is communicated throughout the organisation and made available to all staff online, by email and on notice boards in all of the organisation's locations. The statement should be reviewed at least annually.

Responsibility: In managing health and safety, organisations will specify a responsible person (RP) and a competent person (CP). Both roles can be taken by the same person, although larger employers might choose to have two different people. The RP should be a director, managing director or a similar leader who can take charge of the organisation of the policy. I have mentioned that the directors have a legal duty to comply with health and safety laws such as HASAWA; they are responsible and liable for any acts and omissions of their organisation in relation to health and safety. The CP should be an expert in health and safety. The person taking this role can be employed by the organisation or hired on a freelance basis as an adviser or consultant. A CP is defined as someone who has sufficient training, experience and knowledge of health and safety, in addition to other qualities (RMS Publishing, 2015). The lines of management are usually shown in the policy document, with the RP and CP clearly identified in the management structure.

Arrangements: In many health and safety policies, the *arrangements* are based on a well-established model known as 'Plan-Do-Check-Act' (Figure 3.2). This framework for managing physical health and safety is highly structured and widely utilised. In the United States, it is promoted by the American Society for Quality (online), amongst others. In the UK, the HSE has produced a useful document that outlines the sort of arrangements organisations might adopt in their health and safety policy (HSE, online, c). These arrangements might include the provision of information, training, instruction and supervision for all appropriate aspects of the organisation's work. Some of these arrangements are shown in Table 3.1 (the list is not exhaustive). Typically, a procedure for each of the relevant aspects will be included in the arrangements section of a policy, with step-by-step guidance and information on what to do, what should be avoided, what is allowed and what requires special authorisation, along with reporting, supervision and escalation procedures.

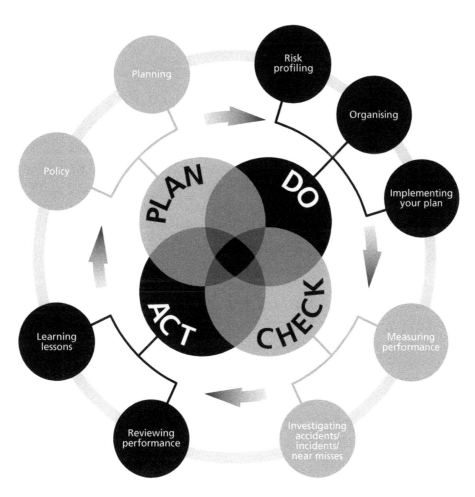

Figure 3.2 *The 'Plan-Do-Check-Act' model*

Source: HSE, online, c

Table 3.1   *Typical arrangements in a health and safety policy*

• Accidents/incidents and reportable occurrences – RIDDOR procedure	• Manual handling
• Asbestos	• Noise
• Auditing and inspection	• Permits to work
• Control of substances hazardous to health (COSHH)	• Personal protective equipment (PPE)
• Dangerous substances and atmospheres	• Respiratory protective equipment (RPE)
• Display screen equipment (DSE)	• Risk assessment
• Driving	• Safe working procedures
• Equipment – electrical, mechanical and general	• Risk rating matrix
• Electricity at work	• Safety performance
• Emergency and disaster	• Site and personal security
• Fire	• Training
• First aid	• Vehicles
• Health surveillance	• Vibration
• Home working	• Visitors and the public
	• Welfare
	• Working at height (also see permits to work)
	• Young persons and vulnerable adults

All of these procedures should be reviewed annually or more frequently if particular changes happen. The CP usually oversees the production and review of each procedure and is typically responsible for the communication and implementation of updated and amended procedures.

Risk Assessments

In the UK, organisations have a legal duty to assess risks. Under the Management of Health and Safety at Work Regulations 1999 (MHSWR), all organisations (including self-employed people) must assess the risk to the health and safety of their employees, contractors, visitors and anyone else who may be harmed or otherwise affected as a result of the organisation's work and other activities. Risk assessments are generally undertaken using the following five-step approach:

1   Identify the hazard; ask what can cause harm

2   Determine who can be harmed and how

3   Evaluate the risks and determine the most suitable control measures

4   Write up the risk assessment and implement it

5   Review the risk assessment whenever necessary.

Each of these steps is now considered.

Step 1. Identify what can cause harm. The first step is to identify all hazards, defined as anything with the potential to cause harm. This involves the CP or other suitably qualified person using their knowledge, experience and training to identify any hazards that might adversely affect people, including employees, contractors and visitors. The sources of hazard are incredibly diverse. They can include heat, dust, smoke, light and noise, as well as mechanical sources such as machinery, tools, equipment, vehicles and so on. The individual's activities must also be considered, such as lifting, climbing, twisting and bending. Patterns of work may present hazards, such as tiredness in night workers. All potential hazards must be identified and understood in order to protect anyone who is at risk.

Step 2. Determine who can be harmed and how. The next step is to identify the population at risk. This will include individuals and groups, such as those doing work, those supporting them and those passing nearby. The population might include employees, contractors, visitors, maintenance staff and cleaners. Consideration must also be given to vulnerable groups, who might include young people who lack experience, older people who are frail, and pregnant women who are advised to avoid certain hazards and tasks. The population identified may potentially risk injury when using tools, being burned when using chemicals or undertaking hot work, or suffering respiratory issues from breathing in smoke or dust. Sitting at desks and using display screens can also cause harm to necks, backs and eyesight. It is important to consider who can be harmed and how this harm might happen.

Step 3. Evaluate the risks and determine control measures. It is best to use a matrix like the one in Figure 3.3 to evaluate risks. The matrix approach assesses the likelihood and severity of the risk. Sites, areas and activities that carry both a high likelihood and a high severity of risk should be controlled to the greatest extent. Measures should be put in place that are practical but also proportionate to the risk. If the chance of death is high, significant control measures would be expected. If the chance of death is low, lesser control measures might be appropriate.

Potential severity of harm

		Slightly harmful 1	Harmful 2	Extremely harmful 3
Likelihood of harm occurring	Highly unlikely 1	Trivial 1	Tolerable 2	Moderate 3
	Unlikely 2	Tolerable 2	Moderate 4	Substantial 6
	Likely 3	Moderate 3	Substantial 6	Intolerable 9

Figure 3.3 *Risk assessment matrix*
Source: HSE, 2020

Step 4. Write up the risk assessment and implement it. Risk assessments are written documents. This allows them to be held centrally, audited and checked for adequacy, and shared as part of a package of information to help employees and others understand the hazards and control measures that help them work safely. The risk assessment is also provided to supervisors to enable them to supervise workers effectively. Some risk assessments will be provided to other groups, such as contractors, visitors and cleaners, so they too can work safely.

Step 5. Review the risk assessment. Risk assessments should be reviewed periodically, perhaps annually, when a significant change occurs, or dynamically to cope with changing conditions. Periodic reviews are common in environments that do not change from year to year, but additional reviews will be needed, for example if an extension is built, new machinery installed or new substances stored on site. If changes to the risk assessment have to be made as a result of the review, everyone affected will need to be retrained and brought up to date with the new hazards, controls and safe ways of working.

This five-step approach to risk assessments is used throughout much of the modern world, and is a good way to determine whether an organisation has fulfilled at least part of its legal obligations under MHSWR.

Hierarchy of Controls

The hierarchy of hazard controls is recognised by employers worldwide as a preferred approach to managing the risks that have been identified by risk assessments. The hierarchy of controls provides a clear, structured approach to considering how best to protect the population through the use of protective control measures.

The hierarchy of controls (Figure 3.4) operates on the principle that the main obligation is on the employer to find safe ways of working; in other words, the onus is on the employer not to expose their employees to harm.

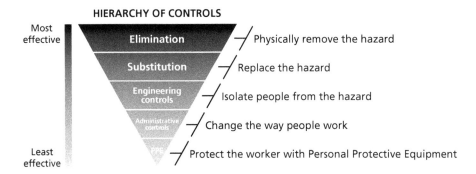

HIERARCHY OF CONTROLS

Most effective
- **Elimination** — Physically remove the hazard
- **Substitution** — Replace the hazard
- **Engineering controls** — Isolate people from the hazard
- **Administrative controls** — Change the way people work
- **PPE** — Protect the worker with Personal Protective Equipment

Least effective

Figure 3.4 *Hierarchy of controls*

Source: CDC/NIOSH, USA, online

As is shown in Figure 3.4, the hierarchy comprises five elements, although some organisations add a sixth – isolation – after substitution. At the top come eliminating risks and substituting working methods, which is how employers should and most prefer to address the issue, with personal protective equipment (PPE) the least preferred method. Between these come isolation (if adopted), engineering controls and administrative controls.

Elimination: If a task can be adapted so an employee avoids exposure to a hazard, the hazard can be said to have been eliminated. For example, if an aerial on top of a building needs to be repaired, it is safer to lower the aerial to the ground and repair it there than for the work to be done at height, with the aerial still raised. This way, any chance of the worker falling is eliminated.

Substitution: If a task can be undertaken using alternate methods that avoid exposure, those alternate methods may lead to a more hazardous approach being replaced with a less hazardous approach. For example, firefighting today is sometimes done by dropping water from aircraft rather than by human firefighters. This substitution reduces the threat of death and injury by fire. Similarly, robotic manufacturing techniques, machinery in mining and robots in rescue missions are all being used as a substitute for people, thus removing the risk of human harm.

Isolation: Included in some 'Hierarchy of Controls' models, isolation typically separates people from a hazard. Chemicals may be stored in a specially designed building, located away from hazardous sources such as heat and vehicles, with strictly controlled access. Hot works at a manufacturing facility may be done at a distance from the general workforce, so if a fire did occur the fewest people possible would be at risk. By isolating substances and activities, fewer people are exposed to the related hazards, more effectively protecting the greatest proportion of the population.

Engineering controls: Tools, equipment and machinery are often subject to engineering controls that aim to minimise the exposure of people to, say, moving parts or hazardous areas. These include guards covering moving parts, pressure pads that cut off the electrical supply, and access doors and barriers. Engineering controls may require particular actions to be taken before an item of equipment will operate. For example, two separate 'on' buttons may need to be pushed by two people to activate a machine, with both people doing pre-operation safety checks and checking each other's work; or a safety door may need to be closed before an item of machinery becomes operable; or an operator may need to stand on a pressure pedal or pad to activate the electrical supply so that, should they fall, the machine automatically switches off. Engineering controls can be built into activities, protecting workers and others in the surrounding area from harm.

Administrative controls: Authorisation to perform a task is often required. Employers typically arrange for employees to be licenced, trained and tested to perform tasks from driving a vehicle to lifting a heavy load. These authorisation processes are known as administrative controls. They are used to limit, for example, who can access dangerous areas, undertake more dangerous tasks and work with more dangerous substances. Permits to work are a common administrative control, often used when people are performing hot works, working at height and working in confined spaces. Administrative controls provide protection mainly through a system of supervision; that is to say, the risks are accepted but a supervisor checks that all the control measures designed to protect workers have been effectively implemented.

Personal protective equipment (PPE): This is the least preferred and least effective control method. After every other measure has been employed, the last line of defence is the safety equipment worn by the worker, such as gloves, goggles, safety hat and safety boots. In some environments, breathing apparatus may be used, such as that worn by fire fighters. In others, full protective suits may be required, such as when handling asbestos. PPE is used when an employee could or is likely to come into direct contact with a hazard, with the PPE preventing the employee from suffering harm. PPE must be fit for purpose, designed to withstand the hazard to which it and the employee wearing it is being exposed to.

Consultation

Consultation is a two-way dialogue between management and the workforce, and employers have a legal duty to consult their employees about health and safety. The HSE states (HSE, 2013):

> In workplaces where the employer recognises trade unions and trade unions are recognised for collective bargaining purposes, the Safety Representatives and Safety Committees Regulations 1977 (as amended) will apply.

> In workplaces where employees are not in a trade union and/or the employer does not recognise the trade union, or the trade union does not represent those employees not in the trade union, the Health and Safety (Consultation with Employees) Regulations 1996 (as amended) will apply.

Consultations should be seen as a two-way process that offers an opportunity to share information, discuss problems and solutions, and raise ideas. Some of the aims of consultations around health and safety are to:

- analyse and assess information related to health and safety, such as accident investigation reports, lost-time injury statistics and sickness absence rates
- bring forward suggestions from the workforce about how health and safety can be more effectively managed
- bring forward information from third parties about health and safety management practice from outside the organisation, such as research and other information that may help the organisation achieve and maintain best practice

- discuss and agree actions required by reports, such as inspection reports, accident investigation reports, accredited standards (eg. ISO) audits and consultant assessments

- discuss and debate changes to health and safety management practices proposed by the employer

- raise areas of concern, or specific cases of injury or illness, that the employee representatives wish to be formally investigated.

The process of consultation should be based on a shared vision and a desire to protect employees and others from harm as far as is reasonably practicable, through mutual understanding and agreement.

A layered approach can be taken when consulting the workforce. Consultation can be undertaken using a top-down or bottom-up approach. Both might be appropriate. The consultation triangle (Figure 3.5) provides a useful framework.

Figure 3.5 *The consultation triangle*

In a top-down approach, members of the leadership team and appointed and/or union health and safety representatives engage in consultation at the very highest levels of the organisation. At this level, the interests of the workforce as a whole are discussed, although individual cases still receive some attention. Employee representatives consult with front-line workers to gather information, data, experiences and observations about health and safety. The representatives then present the information they have gathered to the consultation group, justifying how health and safety can be more effectively managed.

If there are circumstances on a particular site or in a particular department that do not apply to the rest of the organisation, there may need to be consultation at the site or department level.

Middle managers may also want to consult with their team members, especially in fast-changing environments; such consultations might be more frequent and easier to organise.

It may also be worth arranging consultations with individuals to gain an insight into individual views and opinions. This approach is especially appropriate where work is unique, where workers are highly skilled, or where working conditions are especially challenging.

Consultations are an excellent way to combine the strategic interests of organisational leaders with the gritty, front-line challenges of actually doing the work. This combination can be incredibly powerful, which is, perhaps, one reason the act of consulting the workforce has been enshrined in law.

Reporting

Reporting is the final, vitally important component of the health and safety management system. There are many types of report that relate to health and safety. Some reporting must be done by law, such as reports under the Reporting of Injuries, Diseases and Dangerous Occurrences Regulations 2013 (RIDDOR). Some reports are produced after a single event or incident, such as an accident investigation report. Others are strategic and consider factors outside of the organisation, such as health and safety performance benchmarking and reports of safety innovation.

Reporting requirements: Under the Reporting of Injuries, Diseases and Dangerous Occurrences Regulations 2013 (RIDDOR), UK organisations have a legal duty to report certain types of incident to the HSE. Other country health and safety authorities, such as the OSHA in the USA and the HAS in Ireland may have similar reporting requirements. In the UK, types of incident that must be reported to the HSE include: death and specified injuries; the contracting of specified diseases; and incidents where the injured person is unable to perform their duties for seven days in a row (including weekends).

Inspection/audit reports: Inspection and audit reports are typically undertaken to make sure health and safety policies, procedures and control measures are being properly followed and effectively address the risks identified in risk assessments. A supervisor or team leader may undertake an inspection and write this up in a report; for example, a report might be produced every day after scaffolding is inspected.

Incident reports: An incident report is produced after somebody has suffered harm. The report includes details of who was involved, the time and place of the incident, what was happening at the time the injury occurred and the cause of the incident, along with recommendations to prevent it happening again.

Statistical reports: These are produced at management level to monitor performance compared to objectives and targets, and to assess performance trends. Organisational leaders will want to see a downward trend in incident rates that act as measures of health and safety performance, such as RIDDOR reportable incidents, injuries that result in lost working time, seven-day absences and so on. Statistical reports are usually prepared by the CP every month or quarter, for discussion by the directors. In smaller organisations, statistical analysis may be more difficult as the sample size of incidents may not be sufficient to provide for reliable results.

Benchmarking reports: External bodies, such as the HSE, provide statistics that employers can use to benchmark their organisation's performance (HSE, 2019b). Benchmarking allows organisations to see how well they are doing in managing health and safety compared to other organisations in the same industry that face similar challenges. If an organisation is performing poorly compared to others, it knows it must make its practices more effective. If it is doing well, it knows it should maintain its commitment and continue to drive improvements, possibly using its high-performance standard as a differentiator.

Reports take many forms; they are used both strategically and tactically, they can assess performance and chart progress, and they can provide specific details in the event of incidents.

This chapter has presented seven core elements of health and safety management: the management system, commitment, policy, risk assessments, the hierarchy of controls, consultation and reporting. These core elements provide the leader and manager with an understanding of how physical health and safety is managed. When the seven elements are combined, they provide a systematic, strategic and structured approach to managing health and safety. It follows that these elements can be extrapolated for the purposes of managing workplace mental health. The notion of managing mental health in the same way as physical health is developed and presented in Part II of this book.

The main take-outs from this chapter are:

- Health and safety is most effectively managed using an established, comprehensive, systematic and structured approach.
- The whole organisation should commit to managing health and safety effectively, with leaders establishing the culture and framework for doing so.
- The policy for managing health and safety should set out the statement of intent, the management structure through which responsibility for managing health and safety will be controlled, and the arrangements through which health and safety will be integrated into the processes of the organisation.
- Risk assessments should be undertaken using a five-step approach, so that every person who might be affected by the organisation's activities is protected as far as is reasonably practicable.
- The hierarchy of controls provides a structured approach to the planning and implementing of measures that control health and safety risks, with elimination and substitution being the most preferred methods.

- Workforce consultations, at whole organisation and local levels, can provide an effective method for sharing information, discussing and agreeing improvements, and deciding upon the best solutions to problems, so bringing together strategic aspiration with practical insight.

- Reporting health and safety incidents can be a legal requirement. It is also a way to determine the adequacy and effectiveness of control measures and a way to investigate incidents, as well as providing strategic insight into organisational performance over time and when compared to other organisations.

References

American Society for Quality (online) *What is the Plan-Do-Check-Act (PDCA) Cycle?* Available at: *https://asq.org/quality-resources/pdca-cycle* (accessed 20 December 2019).

Centers for Disease Control and Prevention / The National Institute for Occupational Safety and Health (online). *HIERARCHY OF CONTROLS.* Available at: *https://www.cdc.gov/niosh/topics/hierarchy/default.html* (accessed 20 February 2020).

Health and Safety Executive (2013) *Consulting Employees on Health and Safety. A brief guide to the law.* Available at: https://www.hse.gov.uk/pubns/indg232.pdf (accessed 5 January 2020).

Health and Safety Executive (2019a) *Construction Statistics in Great Britain, 2019.* Available at: *https://www.hse.gov.uk/stress/standards/* (accessed 28 November 2019).

Health and Safety Executive (2019b) *Construction Statistics in Great Britain, 2019.* Available at: *http://www.hse.gov.uk/statistics/industry/construction.pdf* (accessed 28 November 2019).

Health and Safety Executive (online, a) *Legislation.* Available at: *http://www.hse.gov.uk/leadership/legislation.htm* (accessed 2 January 2020).

Health and Safety Executive (online, b) *Writing a Health and Safety Policy.* Available at: *http://www.hse.gov.uk/toolbox/managing/writing.htm* (accessed 5 January 2020).

Health and Safety Executive (online, c) *Managing for Health and Safety (HSG65).* Available at: *http://www.hse.gov.uk/pubns/books/hsg65.htm* (accessed 5 January 2020).

Health and Safety Authority, Ireland (online) *Hazard and Risk.* Available at: *https://www.hsa.ie/eng/Topics/Hazards/* (accessed 21 October 2019).

Occupation Safety and Health Administration (2004). *OSH Act of 1970; General Duty Clause.* Available at: *https://www.osha.gov/laws-regs/oshact/section5-duties* (accessed 20 February 2020).

RMS Publishing (2015) *A Study Book for the NEBOSH National General Certificate: Essential health and safety guide.* Stourbridge, England: RMS Publishing.

Stevenson, D. and Farmer, P. (2017) Thriving at Work: The Stevenson/Farmer Review of Mental Health and Employers. Available at: https://assets.publishing.service.gov.uk/government/uploads/system/uploads/attachment_data/file/658145/thriving-at-work-stevenson-farmer-review.pdf (accessed 28 October 2019).

4

DIFFERENCES BETWEEN PHYSICAL AND MENTAL HEALTH

Before we go any further, we need to explore the differences between physical and mental health so we can build an awareness of why mental health management at work lags behind physical health management and begin to look at how that gap can be closed.

Mental health management at work is an emerging discipline, still in its infancy and not yet fully developed. The practices that have emerged thus far are mainly tactical ones, and management books tend to promote theories and principles rather than offering management systems (such as ISO 9001) of the sort that leaders and managers are familiar with.

The gap between mental and physical health management exists because of six key factors:

1   Lack of established practice

2   Intangibility

3   Technical ambiguity

4   Lack of commitment

5   Lack of employee engagement

6   Lack of enforcement.

I will now explore each of these factors in turn, and examine how they undermine effective mental health management in the workplace.

Lack of Established Practice

Physical health and safety has been managed effectively for more than 50 years. Practice is well-established, proven and largely seen as effective. The professional standing of health and safety practice and practitioners has improved as a result of:

▪ UK laws such as HASAWA, introduced in 1974, requires leaders to focus on taking effective physical health and safety action. In the USA, the Occupational Safety and Health Act was introduced in 1970

▪ enforcement through government bodies such as the UK's Health and Safety Executive (HSE), founded in 1975, and in the USA, through the Occupational Safety and Health Administration, established in 1971

▪ the setting of high and accredited standards such as OHSAS 18001 (established in 1999), which is internationally recognised. ISO 45001 will replace OHSAS 18001 in 2021

▪ recognition of good practice, through schemes such as that operated by the Royal Society for the Prevention of Accidents (RoSPA), founded in 1916

▪ training, such as that provided by the Institute for Occupational Safety and Health (IOSH), an internationally recognised training and certification body founded in 1945.

All of the main drivers of standards and compliance that have a significant impact upon physical health and safety practice and performance have existed for many decades. The most recent development in the discipline – the introduction of the OHSAS 18001 standard – occurred 20 years ago. The main actors involved in physical health and safety in the UK, such as the HSE, RoSPA and IOSH, are not only well-known across industry, but also recognised internationally. But where are the equivalent laws, bodies, standards and organisations for mental health management?

- Which laws relate to mental health at work?
- What mental health conditions do these laws cover?
- Does the HSE enforce the management of mental health in the workplace?
- What is the internationally recognised standard for mental health management?
- Does OHSAS 18001 apply to mental health?
- Who provides training in mental health management?
- Is the mental health training that is available as widely respected as IOSH training?
- What are the most recognised mental health achievement awards?

Mental health management is simply not as well established as physical health and safety management. There are far fewer credible organisations operating in the field of workplace mental health and safety than in the field of physical health and safety. The most notable of these organisations are charities, such as Mind, Rethink Mental Illness and the Mental Health Foundation.

Intangibility

The main difference between physical and mental health is that our emotions, our ability to work and our relationships are the main things to be influenced by our mental health (Scotland's Mental Health First Aid, online). Reflecting on this definition, it is evident that most aspects of mental health are intangible.

This intangibility means there are aspects of mental health that can be virtually impossible to quantify; even when an effort is made to do this, problems can arise because of differences in perception. These perception differences may relate to: causes; diagnosis; the nature of symptoms; the severity of symptoms; and the most suitable treatments. Just as mental health conditions are intangible, so are many of the causes and contributing factors that lead to mental health problems.

Few organisations assess mental health hazards or manage related risks in the same way as they assess physical health and safety hazards. Like mental health conditions, mental health hazards are often intangible. There are no commonly used methods for identifying mental health hazards and just as few methods of assessing the risks they represent. The notion of mental health hazards at work barely registers with most organisations.

Intangibility and poor quantifiability, along with a lack of definition, plus a lack of process and procedural design, all conspire to cause inaction.

Technical Ambiguity

Technical ambiguity exists at the macro and micro levels.

At the macro level – the national level – governments are not considering workplace mental health law; law-makers are not considering psychiatry; psychiatrists are not considering workplace management methods; and managers often have little empathy with employees. No one group within the mental health model seems to understand the whole. This may be the reason the Stevenson/Farmer Review of Mental Health and Employers (Stevenson and Farmer, 2017) and the leading mental health charities have failed to date to deliver a significant positive change in mental health outcomes. Nobody seems to be joining the macro level mental health 'dots' together. Stevenson and Farmer (2017) nearly managed it with their recommendation that government should examine what more it can do to require employer compliance with existing equalities and employment laws – but they stopped short of what was needed. Employers have a simple approach: understand the law; develop compliance methods; implement them; and review. Stevenson and Farmer (2017) failed to adequately explore the first of these steps – to understand workplace mental health law. This book aims to present some more of the macro mental health 'dots', and make an attempt to join more of them up.

At the micro level – the organisational level – the same type of ambiguity arises. Where should responsibility for mental health sit within an organisation? With the health and safety team? With human resources? On its own? Mental health may sit with the health and safety function, because it relates to health and safety. Or it may sit with human resources, because it relates to people. However, neither function is likely to be steeped in experience of managing mental health. Health and safety professionals, such as those who have a qualification from the Institution of Occupational Health and Safety (IOSH), are often very experienced in managing physical risks caused by factors such as noise, heat, power, weight, tools, machinery and chemicals. By law, employers are required to take action to prevent physical hazards causing harm to people. These health and safety managers are usually experts in physical risk management, thanks to their knowledge, experience and training. However, are they expert in mental health management? Is their knowledge, experience and training sufficient to manage mental health effectively? Recent health and safety graduates may have some knowledge, given 'wellbeing' is being added to health and safety degree syllabuses, but they may possess little experience. Can health and safety managers empathise with employees with mental health issues? Do they understand the Equality Act 2010 and the purpose of Protected Characteristics? Do they understand how to avoid mental health negligence? Similarly, do HR managers understand approaches to risk management? Can they undertake a mental health risk assessment? Do they understand the hierarchy of controls? Can they design mental health control measures? Clearly aspects of both health and safety management and HR management will be necessary when managing workplace mental health. Failure to unite health and safety and HR practices, as well as new techniques, in a cohesive mental health management system will lead to ambiguity, uncertainty and, potentially, liability. This brings me to occupational health practitioners. I have worked with several, and I know about the valuable work they do. Occupational health practitioners might have experience in or be able to provide access to suitably qualified mental health services. In terms of mental health management, the occupational health practitioner may need to work to identify causes of mental harm, either on their own or with other organisational managers. Based on their assessment, they or their colleagues will need to develop control measures in the workplace that eliminate or reduce the effects of the causes of mental harm, as opposed to simply trying to reduce employees' symptoms. The reduction of stress symptoms is still important, but this must be undertaken after efforts have been made to eliminate and reduce the causes of mental harm (see chapter 13). If occupational health managers have their role extended into areas they are unfamiliar with, such as identifying and eliminating the cause of stress, this again may create role ambiguity or even a clash of roles, say, with line managers. Appointing an occupational health manager, such as an ex-nurse, to take a leading role in the management of mental health can be a good thing, provided their role is well defined, their role fits well with other roles and their skills are developed accordingly. In large organisations, the triumvirate of human resources (HR), health and safety (H&S) and occupational health (OH) may need to work collaboratively to achieve the optimum mental health result. In smaller organisations, expertise from across these same three disciplines will need to be applied, to join the mental health 'dots' (whether through internal or external resources), if mental health is to be managed effectively.

When we look at the numbers, the scale of the issue becomes apparent. I mentioned in chapter 3 that more than a million organisations are ISO 9001 accredited and that 10% of that number (100,000 organisations) are accredited to the OHSAS 18001 standard. What proportion of those 100,000 OHSAS 18001 registered organisations can we say are competent in managing mental health at work? How many of these organisations have all three elements needed – knowledge, experience and training – to be considered competent? My view is that this can only be a small proportion. Even these organisations may not be that effective, given that mental health management practice is still emerging and has yet to be fully defined as a management standard.

My impression is that most influencers in the world of mental health management appear to be doctors, psychologists and psychiatrists, counsellors and consultants. Some in this group are advising governments and consulting on management methods. This is good news. However, within organisations, technical ambiguity between physical and mental health management is evident. There seems to be little overlap between the two disciplines of physical risk management and mental health risk management, meaning the use of methods to manage physical health are not being transferred across to manage mental health; this is the tenet of this book. This technical ambiguity is evident at many levels. How many organisations:

- have a stand-alone mental health policy? Or, failing this, how many expressly refer to mental health in their health and safety policy?

- undertake adequate mental health risk assessments? (The HSE's stress managements standards are too limited to be considered adequate in most organisations.)

- apply the 'hierarchy of controls' to mental health risk management?

- have mental health consultation groups?

- measure the effect of mental health on productivity?

Each of these practices is common when managing physical health and safety, yet all of them appear rare when managing mental health.

Wellbeing is starting to emerge as a management discipline. In some organisations, responsibility for this lies with the diversity and inclusion branch of human resources departments, mainly because wellbeing relates to people. It is a broad subject, it's true. In the NHS, wellbeing focuses very much on health interventions for employees (NHS Employers, 2018), with diet and exercise forming a key focus. As a small subset of the wider subject of wellbeing, mental health can receive little attention.

There are some organisations that rush to adopt wellbeing techniques that are thought to be good at supporting mental health and wider wellbeing. This tactical, scatter-gun approach is not ideal, however. Just as with physical health and safety, a risk-based approach is required.

This lack of focus on mental health is odd when we consider the statistics. There were 1.4 million work-related ill health cases in 2018/19 of which 0.6 million related to work-related stress, depression and anxiety (HSE, online, a). We also saw in chapter 1 that in the UK, a massive eight million employees suffer from some form of mental health problem every year. The HSE may well not be aware of the full extent of the mental health problem. Despite HSE statistics showing mental health issues are as common as physical health issues (and if Mind's figure of one in four people suffering a mental health issue each year is correct, mental health issues might be ten times as prevalent as physical health issues) it is surprising mental health receives nowhere near the same level of priority in employer organisations as physical health. It does not receive the same level of priority from the HSE either. In employers, in many cases mental health is simply tacked onto physical health and safety, even though the causes, controls and interventions are totally different. For many organisations, mental health appears to be an afterthought, as it does for the HSE.

Should mental health management sit within health and safety management teams or within human resources management? In many organisations, this simple point evidences technical ambiguity and demonstrates the uncertainty attached to managing mental health at work. There can be no doubt that responsibility for mental health lies with organisational leaders, but ambiguity is one of the reasons for the lack of commitment to mental health management.

To discuss the issue of technical ambiguity further, two more points can be considered:

■ The UK's health and safety law, HASAWA, has never distinguished between mental health and physical health. If this is true, why have so many health and safety practitioners been so late to the mental health party? Why have they overlooked mental health for so long? A key part of a health and safety manager's role is to ensure the organisation stays up to date with HSE rules and guidance. Maybe this is not their fault, of course; maybe the health and safety industry has not led or pushed them in that direction. Nevertheless, when it comes to mental health, many health and safety managers have been far from proactive. In the USA, the OSH Act of 1970 appears to purely relate to physical health and safety. The USA does not even seem to be having a mental health party. In Australia, the party is well under way.

■ In cases where health and safety managers have embraced mental health management, just how effectively have they done so? Have they demanded that leaders establish a pro-mental-health culture? Have they written a mental health policy? Have they implemented mental health risk assessments? Have they implemented a programme of mental health consultations? If yes, good for them and their employees. They really are in the vanguard. If not, why not? Mental health first aid and mindfulness alone are not sufficient. Why are the techniques used in physical health and safety management not being used to manage mental health?

Many leaders wrestle with the subject of mental health. This is understandable, given that the discipline emerged relatively recently. However, the first steps towards successful mental health management should not be that complicated. Part II of this book offers guidance, providing a high-level guide to help leaders implement a mental health management system.

Lack of Commitment

Protected Characteristics have no relationship to ability. Someone can be a good accountant or salesperson no matter if they are black or white. Someone can be a good engineer whether they are gay or straight. Someone can be a good leader whether they are a man or a woman. A person's gender, race or sexual orientation has no bearing on whether they are highly capable and effective in their role.

When it comes to mental health, however, such conditions may have a bearing – whether actual or perceived – on a person's ability to do their job. For employers, this poses a problem, and it may be part of the reason some are not sure how to tackle mental health in the workplace. Is there a risk involved in putting somebody in a certain role, because of their mental health issue? Should a manager with depression be put in charge of a sales team? Can somebody with anxiety head up operations? Should somebody with bipolar disorder be put in charge of customer relationships? Unless the person has received a clear diagnosis and has a treatment plan that is likely to minimise the effect of any mental health condition, an employer is unlikely to want to take the risk of putting that employee in a given role – or even employ them at all. Cautious leaders may not like taking risks, and employees with mental health issues may pose too great a risk. Leaders may well think, 'If in doubt, don't do it. Be sure, and protect the organisation.' The Shaw Trust (2018) has established that 56% of employers would be reluctant to recruit an individual with a mental health condition. But where does that leave the individual with mental health issues? All too often it leaves them excluded from employment, prevented from earning a living and unable to play a 'normal' role in society. This cannot be acceptable in a supposedly modern, progressive and compassionate world.

Alas, there are some employers who are anything but compassionate. As we saw in chapter 2, approximately 20% of people who disclose their mental health condition to their employer are disciplined, dismissed, demoted or pressured into resigning (Shaw Trust, 2018), yet this should be the last thing a socially responsible employer would want to happen.

In order to support employees with mental health issues more effectively, an organisation-wide level of commitment to mental health is called for, as presented in Part II of this book.

Lack of Effective Employee Engagement

Before discussing employee engagement as most leaders and managers understand it, the legal aspects of employee engagement in health and safety must be considered.

In the UK, Section 7 of the Health and Safety at Work etc Act (HASAWA) places a legal duty upon employees to take reasonable care for the health and safety of themselves, colleagues and other persons who may be affected by their acts and omissions at work. This duty, in theory, extends to mental health. Similarly, but less specifically, in the USA, the Occupational Safety and Health Administration calls for safety and health programmes to include worker participation (OSHA, online). Health and safety law in Australia specifically refers to mental health.

One key consideration for employers relates to ensuring their employees take reasonable care of their own mental health as well as that of colleagues. Employers should provide their employees with information, training, instruction and supervision in good mental health practice. They should also provide them with similar information about conduct and behaviour, to make sure there is no bullying or any of the other negative behaviours that are known to cause mental health problems. By doing this, employers are more effectively complying with their legal duty under health and safety law, such as the UK's HASAWA, as well as creating the right conditions for employees to thrive.

This is not just about the employer's legal duty; engagement with employees represents an approach to the workplace that should result in the right conditions for everyone in the organisation to give their best each day. It means everyone is committed to the organisation's goals and values, everyone is motivated to contribute to its success, and everyone has an enhanced sense of their own wellbeing (Engage for Success, 2019).

Employee engagement is often undertaken through consultation, events and surveys. More recently in some organisations, mental health awareness training is being undertaken in an attempt to break down barriers and reduce stigma. Here, concern arises relating to the effect of this training. Undoubtedly, a tick is being put in a box to state mental health awareness training has been completed. But has the state of the mental health of the workforce improved? Do employees with mental health issues feel less stigmatised? Has mental health-related absence reduced? We saw in chapter 1 the HSE's concerns about mental health first aid training effectiveness. The same question mark must be applied to mental health-related employee engagement.

As for engagement surveys, dare employers ask about mental health? Should employers ask such questions? How should questions be worded? Will answers be truthful? Employers will understandably be nervous about asking mental health questions in surveys. Few leaders will want to use words like 'bullying' in engagement surveys. More positive language related to behaviours may be preferable. Surveys might include behaviours such as empathising, understanding, compassion and caring. Over time, an increased proportion of employees should report demonstrating and witnessing these behaviours, with these positive behaviours 'crowding out' negative and undesirable behaviours. Engagement surveys related to mental health are addressed in more detail in chapter 14.

Ultimately, employee engagement related to mental health is not about training. It's about developing a culture of caring and compassion amongst employees, so that all groups – especially vulnerable groups, including employees with mental health issue – feel included, respected and valued. If only half of employees with mental health issues will disclose their mental health condition at work, if around 10% of employees feel bullied, and if stigma is still an issue, current employee engagement must be considered largely ineffective.

Lack of Enforcement

Each country has its own health and safety enforcer. The HSE is the UK's enforcer of physical health and safety law. The US's is OSHA. I established earlier in this chapter that there are eight times as many mental health problems compared to physical health injuries (eight million versus one million, respectively, each year).

In chapter 3, RIDDOR incidents, which employers must report to the HSE, were discussed. Specified injuries, illnesses and diseases must be reported. This is a mandatory requirement. However, the HSE states stress and other mental health injuries and illnesses are not reportable.

In 2018, the HSE updated its guidance on first aid to include mental health (Fox, 2018). The HSE subsequently updated its guidance, setting out more recently when it will investigate stress at work (Liversedge, 2019). The HSE (online, b) will consider investigating concerns about work-related stress where:

- *There is evidence that a number of staff are currently experiencing work-related stress or stress-related ill health, (i.e. that it is not an individual case), but*

- *HSE is not the appropriate body to investigate concerns solely related to individual cases of bullying or harassment, but may consider this if there is evidence of a wider organisational failing, and*

- *HSE would expect concerns about work-related stress to have been raised already with the employer, and for the employer to have been given sufficient time to respond accordingly.*

The HSE does not make it clear who should make such a report. Presumably employees must know of this reporting facility if they are the ones expected to make the report. It is unclear how the HSE expects employees to learn of it. The reporting of work-related stress (it does not appear that other forms of work-related mental health issue can be reported, such as anxiety) appears not to be a mandatory requirement, no matter how severe the mental harm suffered and how long-lasting its effects. Unlike physical injuries which must be reported where the employee is unable to perform their usual duties for more than seven days, employees might be absent for months with mental health issues, yet still the HSE does not require such incidents to be reported.

Additionally, the HSE is quick to point would-be complainants to other legislation and other regulators, especially in cases of bullying and harassment (HSE, online, b). Here, the HSE may be misguided. Some of the legal cases presented in chapter 5 that relate to the tort of negligence stemmed from mental health issues caused by bullying, harassment and victimisation at work. These mental health issues led to court rulings that employers had breached their duty of care by failing to provide a safe place to work. Surely, the main purpose of the HSE is to ensure employers provide a safe place to work? Additionally, no regulator supported the employee claimants. They had to bring their own private prosecutions by taking civil action. It could be argued the HSE let these employees down. Perhaps the HSE should look again at their purpose and policies.

In cases of physical health and safety, employers who fail to protect their workforce from physical harm are rightly sanctioned. The HSE issues between eight thousand and ten thousand enforcement notices for physical health and safety each year (Figure 4.1).

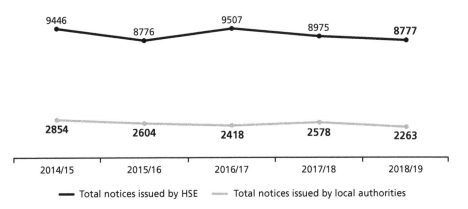

Figure 4.1 *Enforcement notices issued by local authorities and HSE*

Source: HSE, online, c

By contrast, based on a recent Freedom of Information request made when researching this book, there is 'no data available' about the number of enforcement notices issued for reportable mental health incidents, because this type of incident is not reportable. I cannot stress this clearly enough: there is no legal duty on employers to report mental health incidents, no matter what the cause and no matter how severe the effect.

Together, the HSE in the UK and the Crown Office Procurator Fiscal Service (COPFS) in Scotland issue between £20m and £50m of fines for physical health injuries and incidents each year (Figure 4.2). By contrast, there is 'no data available' about fines for breaches of law related to mental health because reporting of mental health incidents is not a legal requirement.

Mental ill-health, including stress, depression and anxiety, is thought to be responsible for 91 million lost working days in the UK each year, more than for any other illness (ACAS, 2012). We know there are eight million mental health 'incidents' at work each year compared to one million physical health incidents – so why is there no enforcement?

The HSE responded to a Freedom of Information request about mental health reporting and sanctions by saying no data was available. Some might infer from this response that the answer is zero. If there are zero enforcement notices and zero sanctions being issued because there is no requirement to report, why should employers be motivated to comply with health and safety laws as they relate to mental health?

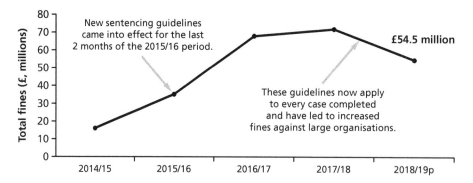

Figure 4.2 *Total fines for health and safety offences prosecuted by HSE (UK) and COPFS (Scotland)*

Source: HSE, online, c

It may be the case that a person is absent from work for months because of a mental health condition that was directly caused by work. Even with an accompanying doctor's certificate, which might clearly state that the person's work is the sole cause of their illness, no sanction of any kind will be issued against the employer, even if that employee is off sick for months, or even years, or even dismissed on grounds of incapability. It is reasonable to ask whether this is right.

Attitudes Towards Mental Health – Getting Worse Before Getting Better?

The disparity between physical and mental health management is leading to uncertainty, indecision and inaction. This is clear from the available statistics. In a 1996, in a survey commissioned by Mind, Read and Baker found that 52% of employees concealed their psychiatric history for fear of losing their job. So, about half of people would not tell their employer about their condition. Twenty years on, despite significant attention being given to mental health in recent years, only 44% of employees would feel comfortable talking to their line manager about their own mental health (BITC, 2019). If anything, the proportion of people willing to talk about their own mental health at work seems to be declining. If so, why is this?

Given that governments, charities and other groups are increasing people's awareness of mental health, we might surmise that responsibility for this decline lies with employers. What are employers doing that is making employees more likely, not less likely, to keep their mental health a secret?

The fault may not lie solely with employers, of course. But they do have a significant role to play in supporting employees with mental ill-health by making them feel included, respected and valued. Wider parts of society may also be feeling uncertain about mental health and what to do about it. Perhaps this phenomenon is not surprising. The Kubler-Ross change curve (Figure 4.3) might help us to understand it.

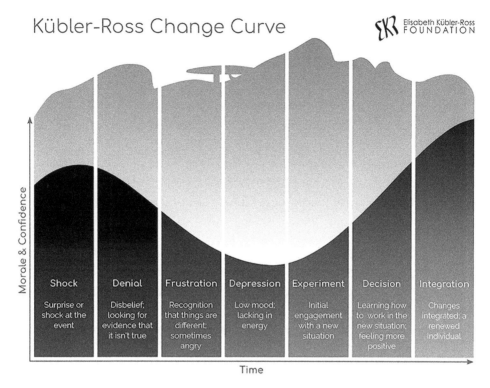

Figure 4.3 *The Kubler-Ross change curve*

Source: Based on ON DEATH AND DYING by Dr. Elisabeth Kubler-Ross. Copyright © 1969 by Elisabeth Kubler-Ross; copyright renewed © 1997 by Elisabeth Kubler-Ross. Reprinted with the permission of Scribner, a division of Simon & Schuster, Inc. All rights reserved.

The change curve originally related to the seven stages of death-related grief. It has become widely applied to other areas of change management. In the context of mental health, perhaps it is the case that now, when presented with an increasing demand for attention to be given to mental health, society, including employers, is experiencing denial, rejection, frustration and even anger at having this change imposed upon it.

Sometimes, things that have hitherto been located in people's subconscious minds move into their consciousness. In other words, people go from not really thinking about something to thinking about it. Mental health is going through this transition. Let us consider a simile in the form of Brexit. As the world watched, the UK population was asked whether it wanted to remain in or leave the EU. Yes or no? It was a binary decision. There were some people who saw this as a question of whether they wanted more or fewer immigrants in the country; a particular UKIP poster, 'Breaking Point', became infamous (Stewart and Mason, 2016).

The result of the Brexit referendum is not fully understood. Perhaps it was anti-immigrant opinion that swayed the vote; perhaps it was not. At the same time, UK nursing applicants from elsewhere in the EU were also forced to make a binary choice. They had to consider whether they wanted to live and work in a post-Brexit UK. Yes or no? 'No' was the resounding answer. The number of EU nursing applicants plummeted by more than 90%, contributing to the UK's current nursing shortage (Siddique, 2017).

Now, thanks to mental health campaigns centred on speaking out, the UK population – including employees, organisational leaders and managers – are having to consciously think about mental health and answer another binary question: are you willing to work with a person with mental health issues? Yes or no? Brexit teaches us that if the future appears uncertain and potentially problematic, the decision-making trend appears to favour a cautious approach. If a binary response is required, we must expect a 'no' answer to the mental health question.

It is for this reason that speaking out about mental health should come after the population has been properly prepared for it, making people, including employers, receptive to the idea of mental health before thrusting it upon them. The positive case for employing people with mental health issues has not yet been adequately made. The vast majority of effort has focused on trying to get people without mental health issues to accept those that have them, without any real explanation or justification. It's like trying to trade on goodwill alone. But if you have not developed the basis for goodwill, you can't expect to find much of it, hence attitudes towards those with mental health may harden – as they appear to have done.

If we see the attitudes of leaders, managers and neurotypical employees as moving into the 'trough' stage of the change curve, in which disruption takes place, it might imply that they are entering a phase of negative emotions and perceptions ahead of arriving at a more tolerant and understanding position (see Figure 4.3). If society and employers are entering or in a negative phase, which might involve worry, concern and uncertainty, this could mean things will get worse before they get better. I would suggest this is the reason the Shaw Trust (2018) found that:

- *half of employers view staff with mental health conditions as a 'significant risk' to their business, an increase of 10% since 2009*
- *more than half of employers are reluctant to employ someone with a mental health condition due to a fear of that person being stigmatised by co-workers (56%, up from 51% in 2009)*
- *in 2009, 90% of employers felt comfortable talking about mental health with their staff members; in 2017, this figure was just 64%.*

Shaw Trust's findings support the findings of BITC (2019) and together these findings indicate that the situation is indeed getting worse, not better. If we apply mental health to the Kubler-Ross change curve in Figure 4.3, it provides a possible explanation as to why this is happening. The length of the curve when it is applied to mental health is an unknown quantity, of course, so it is uncertain how much longer people with mental health issues will have to suffer the more negative attitudes of some of their leaders and colleagues.

We must hope that any hardening of attitudes is temporary and that we will all arrive at a better place, as the change curve suggests we might. However, it is unlikely this will happen without positive intervention. How long we stay in the trough of the change curve will be dictated by our combined efforts to move along the curve to a better place. My recommendations (see chapter 16) are intended to move us all along the mental health change curve far faster than might otherwise happen. The learning for employers who want to promote mental health at work is clear – prepare your management teams and workforce first, before expecting their behaviour to change in support of mental health.

Mental Health and Wellbeing

It is worth taking a moment here to reflect on the differences between mental health and wellbeing. Mental health is just one part of the broad subject of wellbeing (Figure 4.4).

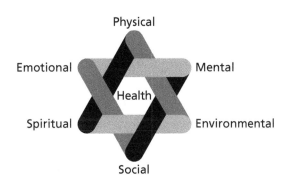

Figure 4.4 *Types of wellbeing*

Source: Image produced with kind permission of Dr Terry Davis (DC) at: TotalMSK.co.uk.

Many attempts have been made at defining wellbeing. I provide my own perspective below.

Wellbeing encompasses the whole person, their hopes and dreams, their own development, their goals and aspirations, their physical health, their faith, spirituality and mindset, their loves and their dreams, as well as their mental health and how they care for and support others (Figure 4.5).

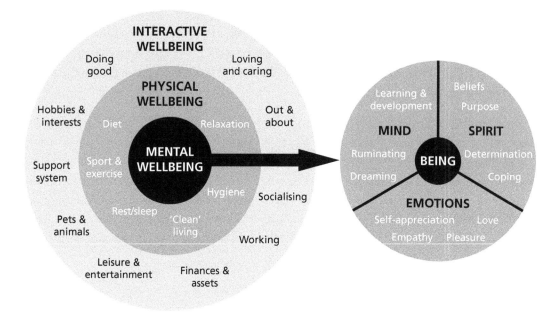

Figure 4.5 *The wellbeing bullseye*

The wellbeing bullseye comprises three interconnected elements. Each element has many aspects to it; certainly, far more than shown. Different people will feel, do and interact in different ways, making each person's bullseye unique. The inner circle – mental wellbeing – is enlarged and presented on the righthand side of Figure 4.5. In summary, the wellbeing bullseye can be described as follows:

- *Mental* wellbeing (or mental health) relates to a person's inner being.
- *Physical* wellbeing relates to the outer person.
- *Interactive* wellbeing relates to how the person interacts, connects and engages with their external environment, including relationships. It is concerned with how full and how fulfilling a life an individual leads.

Mental wellbeing: This relates to the state of an individual's mind, spirit and emotions – in fact, their very being. It relates to the innermost parts of a person, including their thoughts, feelings and beliefs. It is unique to them. It involves nobody else (we all have secret thoughts), although others can affect it. It is this state of mental wellbeing that determines how much of a commitment a person makes to their own physical wellbeing (eg. a person with low self-esteem may care less for their appearance) and to the activities typically associated with their interactive wellbeing. This 'level of commitment' issue includes a person's commitment to their work and to their employer.

Physical wellbeing: This relates to how a person looks after themselves, in terms of appearance, hygiene, diet and exercise, including whether they indulge in legal (eg. alcohol) or illegal (eg. cocaine) substance abuse. A person's mental wellbeing may directly affect their physical wellbeing. Or it may not. A person with ADHD may well benefit from good diet and exercise but these may only improve their condition by 20%. Their ADHD symptoms may still be evident and may remain disagreeable to some friends and colleagues. Improving physical wellbeing will have a varying level of effect upon mental health, dependent upon the person's condition and their responsiveness to physical wellbeing interventions.

Interactive wellbeing: How a person engages with the wider world can indicate how full their life is and how fulfilling they are likely to find it. This is interactive wellbeing. Interactive wellbeing offers the person the opportunity to engage with their environment, connect with other people and participate in activities. In so doing, they may gain positive feedback, boosting their physical and mental wellbeing, so making them feel better. Financial wellbeing may, of course, affect mental, physical and interactive wellbeing.

The wellbeing bullseye is as unique to the individual as their DNA. The size and shape of each wellbeing element will vary from person to person. Negative traits may develop within mental wellbeing, such as hate and anger, which may affect behaviours and physical and interactive wellbeing. Equally, preferences may affect people. Some people prefer being busy. Others prefer to be lazy or quiet. There is no right or wrong shape to the bullseye.

Certain aspects of physical and interactive wellbeing directly affect mental wellbeing (Figure 4.6).

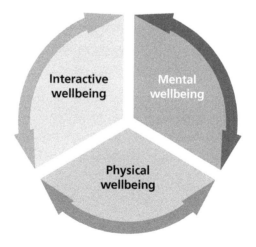

Figure 4.6 *The wellbeing cycle*

Physical exercise has been proven to improve mental health. Ecotherapy (activities in nature) is also thought to be good for mental health. Keeping a tidy house has been said to have a positive effect too. There appears to be a link between 'doing things' and mental health. The aim is to develop a cycle where the consequences of one activity positively feed an aspect of another wellbeing level, which in turn re-energises the stimulus for the activity, and so on.

It is not clear whether doing something specific causes the improvement or it is just the act of simply doing something – possibly anything – that causes it. It may be that the improvement is optimised when a person participates in activities they most like doing. Some people hate rugby; therefore, getting a person with mental health issues to play rugby may not necessarily improve their mental health, even though exercise is known to be good for people.

It is less clear how pushing somebody out of their comfort zone affects mental health. Some medical and therapeutic practitioners believe people with mental health issues might respond favourably to being challenged by taking 'safe' risks outside of their comfort zone, although employers should be wary of pushing employees with mental ill-health to step too far out of their comfort zone into potentially 'unsafe' territory.

Based on the wellbeing cycle (Figure 4.6), it seems that the more people 'do' the better they feel. But this will not be the case for everyone. If somebody has a chronic back injury but no mental health issue, for example, a good diet and exercise may ease their condition but it may not cure it. It therefore follows that if somebody has a chronic mental health condition, a good diet and exercise, or therapy and medication, may similarly ease the condition but it may not cure it. This may well be the case with genetic conditions.

All three levels in the wellbeing cycle feed each other. As the effects on mental health are different for everyone, depending on the things they prefer to do, it is evident that mental health support is not a one-size-fits all solution.

The wellbeing bullseye is a model, which provides a structure; like all models, it must be applied. The employer's task is to develop a plan to determine a course of action in which they consider their approach to wellbeing as it relates to their employees as a group and to each individual employee. A tailored, three-pathway approach is recommended:

- **Feeling:** The employer helps the employee improve the way they feel, improving their mental wellbeing.
- **Doing:** The employer arranges the employee's activities to improve their wellbeing.
- **Treating:** The employer ensures others treat the employee in such a way as to improve their wellbeing (without disclosing any mental health issue, if known).

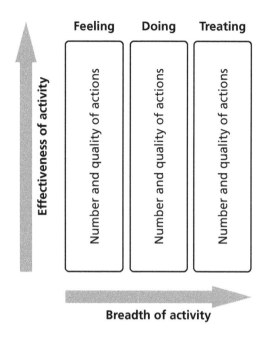

Figure 4.7 *The 'Feeling-Doing-Treating' model*

When contemplating the Feeling-Doing-Treating (FDT) approach (Figure 4.7), *every* employee should participate, for four reasons:

1   Physical health and safety management practices apply to every employee – mental health management practices should do too. Employees should not be able to opt out of programmes known to protect their physical and mental health and safety.

2   A large minority of employees have mental health issues, so it makes sense to take an organisation-wide approach.

3   Nobody likes being singled out; subjecting just employees with mental ill-health to 'FDT' support may humiliate them, harming their mental health.

4   The 'one small thing' principle (see chapter 1) means employees who have no apparent mental health issues could move from *coping* to *distressed* at any time, so including every employee builds whole-workforce resilience. No matter how resilient people appear (and appearances can be deceptive), even the most resilient of employees should be provided with support, especially as their employer may not know the employee's backstory.

With the FDT approach in mind, and having determined that all employees will participate, an Individual Activity Plan (IAP) can be developed for each employee, based on the FDT themes of feeling, doing and treating.

Every employee should be included, as established above. I recommend taking a classification approach as follows:

1   Employees with mental health issues, who have requested support
2   Employees in high-risk categories
3   Other employees.

Employees who fall into the first two categories should receive the greatest level of support, as they may face two issues: 1) they may be exposed to high-risk *circumstances*; and 2) they may be vulnerable or have a high susceptibility to mental health issues.

Feeling: It is vital for employers to make arrangements to help employees improve their mental wellbeing, through techniques such as mindfulness. However, this approach must go further. Employers must offer therapies and counselling to every employee, but especially to those in high-risk categories (see chapter 12, on risk assessments). For example, in chapter 1 we saw that nearly 5% of the population suffer from PTSD; these employees, if identified, may be more susceptible to mental injury and illness. A comprehensive approach is required for employees in high-risk categories. As a central part of the wellbeing bullseye, mental health should be the focus of the employer's attention; ideally, numerous initiatives related to it should be introduced.

Doing: Employers are good organisers. With their organisational abilities and an understanding of each individual working for them, employers are in a good position to develop Individual Activity Plans (IAPs) for all employees. Any risk-based approach suggests it is best to use tactics that limit exposure times (eg. reducing prolonged exposure to known stressors) and build resilience (eg. increasing the resilience buffer, say through mindfulness). Activities should be arranged that minimise those causing harmful effects and maximising those causing beneficial effects. Of course, this must be done within the context of the employee's role. Employers should look to make small changes to activities that have a significant effect. For example, just fifteen minutes in sunlight a few times a week can have beneficial effects (Nall, 2018).

Treating: It is important for leaders to ensure managers, supervisors, peers and co-workers all treat each other in such a way as to show high regard for their mental health. Some employees may keep their mental health issue confidential, hence the need for a 'blanket' approach. This is an issue of culture. In organisations, it is necessary to develop a far more mental-health-friendly culture in order to minimise the adverse effects of workplace stressors, such as workload, managing change, deadlines, targets, management style and toxic relationships. Positive behaviours – aimed at making all employees feel involved, respected, supported and valued – should be designed and developed, communicated and trained, role-modelled and enforced, to bring about a positive mental health culture of caring, compassion, kindness and tolerance.

An example of the FDT approach is provided at Table 4.1.

Table 4.1 *An example of the FDT approach*

Feeling	Doing	Treating
Influence of others	Exercise	Caring, compassion, kindness and tolerance.
'Me' time	Giving back (eg. charity work)	Empathising
Meditation	Ecotherapy (eg. being outside)	Listening
Reiki	Learning new skills	Respecting
Massage	Socialising	Influence of others (see Feeling)

The FDT approach is a cycle. In 'feeling', employees will be affected by how others treat them. They will also focus on managing their own feelings, through managing their own mental (feeling) and physical (doing) wellbeing. However, they too must treat others with empathy and respect, creating a cycle through which every employee looks after themselves *and* their colleagues.

Effectiveness must be at the heart of considerations when employers develop individual action plans (IAPs) for their employees.

We have established that *mental* wellbeing is distinct from *physical* wellbeing and *interactive* wellbeing. Mental wellbeing is concerned with the person's being, their mind, spirit and emotions. We have also established that *physical* wellbeing and *interactive* wellbeing can have a positive effect on *mental* wellbeing.

Currently, too much responsibility is placed on the shoulders of employees. Mindfulness, resilience, first aid and other mental health interventions require the employee to act; to learn and apply new skills. All the employer has to do is arrange these interventions. The employer's role is broader than this. My view is that the employer must take more responsibility, and a far more proactive and preventative approach.

It is appropriate at this point to demonstrate how physical health and safety management methods inform mental health management methods. Activities related to *interactive* wellbeing (eg. getting out more, socialising, personal development, loving and caring) are *control measures* (see chapter 3). The first step in the five-step risk assessment process we explored in chapter 3 is to identify the hazards (Figure 4.8). Step two is to identify who can be harmed and how. Step three is to determine *control measures*. It is apparent that the employer who, as a starting point, organises mindfulness training is entering the five-step process at step three, when they should, in fact, start at step one.

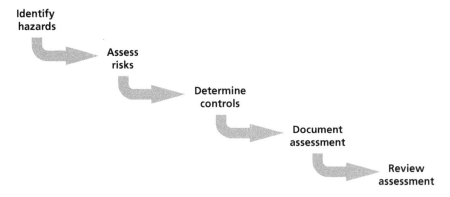

Figure 4.8 *Risk assessment process*

Based on HSE, online, d

Wellbeing hazards may include physical factors such as poor diet and lack of exercise, as well as mental health hazards related to *interactive* wellbeing, such as poor personal development and poor social interaction. All of this must be managed and, in the workplace, the primary obligation and duty for this lies with the employer. It is important for employers to adopt a risk-based approach to determining and managing workplace mental health hazards, rather than simply picking the first few initiatives that they hear of and which may be promoted to them.

When a construction manager is building a jetty at the side of a lake, he or she does not rush to put fire control measures in place. They first assess the risks (what can cause harm) and consider potential hazards, such as slips and trips, water depth and temperature, currents and eddies. They focus on who is potentially at risk of injury, hypothermia and drowning (who can be harmed and how). They may need to assess fire risks, but this might have lower priority; the construction manager would instead focus on those risks that are most *likely* and most *severe*. These same considerations – what can cause harm? Who can be harmed and how? – should be applied in exactly the same way for mental health.

Before any mental health programme is developed, the first step should be to identify hazards. After that, an assessment must be made of who can be harmed and how. Control measures should be considered only after these two steps have been completed. Mental health hazards may be more difficult to identify and control than physical hazards, but by identifying and controlling these, employers can have a far more profound effect on their employees' mental health than they would by simply encouraging them to do exercise or eat more healthily. Until risk assessments are properly undertaken it is simply not possible to know if these wellbeing practices (in other words, control measures) are justified. They may have some effect, but perhaps nothing like the effect of properly managing the hazard in the first place.

This chapter identified the six key differences between physical health and mental health. The practice of mental health management is less well established. Mental health is intangible. There is technical ambiguity in organisations, as the management methods applied to physical health are not typically adopted for use by the human resources team when managing mental health, and the health and safety team may not be sufficiently well versed in managing vulnerable groups, including those with legally protected characteristics. As a result of a lack of established practice, leaders are unsure of the type of management system to operate. Employees have a legal duty to manage their own safety and that of their colleagues, however, employers must act first. It was identified that the HSE fails to take enforcement action against organisations failing in their mental health obligations. Finally, the differences between wellbeing and mental health were considered, with an emphasis on the need for organisations to undertake hazard identification, including identification of mental health hazards, before they embark on developing and implementing a wellbeing or mental health management programme.

The main take-outs from this chapter are:

- There are significant differences between the management of mental health and the management of physical health.

- The length of time each management practice has been established has a major bearing on how it is managed today, with mental health management being less well developed than physical health and safety.

- The intangible nature of mental health can make it more difficult to understand.

- There is technical ambiguity in the management of mental health at national and organisational level.

- Organisations may be unclear about the allocation of responsibility. The resources devoted to mental health and the skills required to manage it can be inadequate.

- Mental health enforcement by the HSE seems non-existent.

- Wellbeing and mental health are different. Mental health is a part of wellbeing.

- Mental wellbeing, physical wellbeing and interactive wellbeing feed each other. Any one of them can kick-start the others or drive improvement in them.

- A Feeling-Doing-Treating (FDT) approach may ensure that work-related factors that cause or contribute towards poor mental health are properly managed.

- High risk-employees should be prioritised.

- Wellbeing activities might be used simply to try to minimise symptoms rather than address the cause (or hazard). Risk management methods must be applied.

- Wellbeing programmes can become very broad, with a loss of focus on mental health.

- Actions to improve wellbeing and/or mental health must be tailored to the individual to maximise their effectiveness.

References

ACAS (2012) *Mental Ill-Health in the Workplace is Costing UK Employers Billions*. Available at: https://archive.acas.org.uk/index.aspx?articleid=3915 (accessed 19 February 2020).

Business in the Community (2019) *Mental Health at Work 2019 Report: Time to take ownership*. Available at: *https://www.bitc.org.uk/report/mental-health-at-work-2019-time-to-take-ownership/* (accessed 11 February 2020).

Davis, T. (2018) *Stress: The individual, wellbeing, performance and the workplace (Part 1)*. Available at: https://blog.totalmsk.co.uk/2018/02/stress-and-wellbeing-in-workplace-and.html?m=1 (accessed 6 December 2019).

Engage for Success (2019) *What is Employee Engagement?* Available at: *https://engageforsuccess.org/what-is-employee-engagement* (accessed 2 December 2019).

Fox, M. (2018). Will the new HSE guidelines on workplace mental health make any difference? (online) Available at: *https://www.peoplemanagement.co.uk/voices/comment/will-new-guidelines-on-workplace-mental-health-make-difference* (accessed 12 November 2019).

Health and Safety Executive (online, a). *Health and safety at work – Summary statistics for Great Britain 2019*. Available at: *https://www.hse.gov.uk/statistics/overall/hssh1819.pdf* (accessed 18 January 2020).

Health and Safety Executive (online, b) *Reporting a concern*. Available at: *https://www.hse.gov.uk/stress/reporting-concern.htm* (accessed 20 February 2020).

Health and Safety Executive (online, c) *Enforcement in Great Britain*. Available at: *http://www.hse.gov.uk/sTATIstics/enforcement.htm* (accessed 18 November 2019).

Health and Safety Executive (online, d) *Risk – Controlling the risks in the workplace*. Available at: *https://www.hse.gov.uk/risk/controlling-risks.htm* (accessed 22 January 2020).

Liversedge, B. (2019). *HSE announces it will inspect stress "if criteria are met"* (online). Available at: *https://www.britsafe.org/publications/safety-management-magazine/safety-management-magazine/2019/hse-announces-it-will-inspect-stress-if-criteria-are-met/* (accessed 12 February 2020).

NHS Employers (2018) *NHS Health and Wellbeing Framework*. Available at: *https://www.nhsemployers.org/case-studies-and-resources/2018/05/nhs-health-and-wellbeing-framework* (accessed 20 November 2019).

Nall, R. (2018). *What Are the Benefits of Sunlight?* (online). Available at: *https://www.healthline.com/health/depression/benefits-sunlight#mental-health* (accessed on 3 Mar 2020).

Occupational Safety and Health Administration (online). *Employer Responsibilities*. Available at: *https://www.osha.gov/as/opa/worker/employer-responsibility.html* (accessed 22 February 2020).

Read, J. and Baker S. (1996). *NOT JUST STICKS AND STONES*. Available at: https://disability-studies.leeds.ac.uk/wp-content/uploads/sites/40/library/MIND-MIND.pdf (accessed 12 November 2019).

Scotland's Mental Health First Aid (online). *About Mental Health*. Available at: *http://www.smhfa. com/taking-course/about-mental-health.aspx* (accessed 18 November 2019).

Shaw Trust (2018). *Mental Health at Work: Still the last taboo*. Available at: *https://www.shaw-trust. org.uk/ShawTrustMediaLibraries/ShawTrust/ShawTrust/Documents/Shaw-Trust-Mental- Health-at-Work-Report-2018-full_1.pdf* (accessed 29 November 2019).

Siddique, H. (2017) 96% drop in EU nurses registering to work in Britain since Brexit vote. *The Guardian* 12 June. Available at: *https://www.theguardian.com/society/2017/jun/12/96- drop-in-eu-nurses-registering-to-work-in-britain-since-brexit-vote* (accessed 9 March 2020).

Stewart, H. and Mason, R. (2016) Nigel Farage's anti-migrant poster reported to police, *The Guardian*, 16 June 2016 (online) Available at: *https://www.theguardian.com/politics/2016/ jun/16/nigel-farage-defends-ukip-breaking-point-poster-queue-of-migrants* (accessed 29 April 2020).

5

MENTAL HEALTH
AND THE LAW

This chapter explores some aspects of the law that you as an employer should consider as you develop your approach to mental health management.

In this chapter, I attempt to provide sufficient legal information to provide leaders and managers with a comprehensive understanding of the key legal principles that relate to workplace mental health. I focus particularly on negligence, rather than things like discrimination and protected characteristics (such as age, disability, gender, race and religion), which you should already cover. I do not aim to provide advice. What I do aim to do is set out some of the most relevant legal considerations for employers who are contemplating their mental health strategy, system and programme. If you want to look into the subject in more depth you should investigate further or, for specific issues, seek advice from a legal professional.

This book has been designed for international distribution. It is not the aim of this book to explore each country's relevant mental health laws. Obviously, England and Wales, Scotland, Ireland, the USA and Australia each have their own laws. However, many of these laws are based on common legal principles that operate on the practice of 'common law'. For example, the tort of negligence is well established in many countries. When reading this chapter, therefore, readers are asked to concentrate on legal principles as opposed to any single country's specific laws. This focus on common legal principles makes the chapter's content relevant across countries. The laws of England and Wales provide the backbone of most of the legal references here, although I have intentionally not done this exclusively. Such references, whether based on the laws of England and Wales or not, are made to illustrate a legal principle. You, the reader, can determine if the legal principle referred to is applicable in your own legal jurisdiction. Chances are, it will be.

In this chapter, I discuss the definition of mental disability and briefly explore UK legislation, starting with the Equality Act 2010. I take a quick look at the Data Protection Act 2018, because it relates to disclosing mental health conditions to an employer. I then explore the duties of employers and employees under the Health and Safety at Work etc Act 1974 (HASAWA) and related regulations. Laws and legal rules apply to both physical and mental health, so I also take a look at the UK's health and safety enforcer, the Health and Safety Executive's (HSE) guidance on mental health. Finally, I give some considerable time to the tort of negligence, as this law is most likely to apply to claims of mental health negligence against employers.

In England and Wales, people with a mental health condition have rights and protections against discrimination. Mind (2018a) states that these rights and protections are provided through the following laws:

- Equality Act 2010
- Mental Capacity Act 2005
- Care Act 2014 (applicable in England)
- Social Services and Well-being (Wales) Act 2014 (applicable in Wales)

- Human Rights Act 1998
- Data Protection Act 2018.

In the United States, Mental Health America (online) provides useful guidance on mental health rights. It refers to the National Mental Health Act (1946), specifically to:

- liberty and autonomy
- protection from seclusion and restraint
- community inclusion
- access to services
- privacy.

Readers outside England, Wales and the United States, should refer to legislation and related material in their own country, such as:

- Model Work Health and Safety Act (Australia)
- Safety, Health and Welfare at Work Act 2005 (Ireland)
- The Mental Health (Scotland) Act 2015.

The *Irish Journal of Psychological Medicine* (Cronin et al., 2017) provides insightful reading for anyone who wants to explore differences in mental health legislation between countries.

In addition to the UK laws listed above, the UK's Health and Safety at Work etc Act 1974 (HASAWA) also makes provisions that directly affect how employers manage the mental health of employees. Health and safety laws that relate to other jurisdictions (eg. Australia, Ireland, United States) should be considered when contemplating workplace mental health management outside the UK. Significantly, health and safety laws are often left out of lists of laws relating to mental health, despite health and safety law playing a vital role in the management of mental health. This demonstrates disjointed thinking amongst even the most eminent UK mental health advocates.

I mention this wide variety of laws simply to draw the reader's attention to the many laws that apply to mental health. Most employers in the UK will be familiar with three particular laws as they apply to them: the Equality Act 2010, the Data Protection Act 2018 and they should also be very familiar with HASAWA. I do not discuss the other laws listed above because they tend to apply to state mental healthcare provision in general, rather than specifically to employers. I begin by exploring the definition of 'mental disability'.

The Meaning of 'Mental Disability'

In chapter 1 it was identified that one in four people in the UK suffers from some form of mental health problem each year, with this figure being one in five in the USA. The UK has a population of 65 million people and the USA has a population of 330 million, so this would indicate that approximately 80 million people in the UK and USA will experience a mental health issue in any given year. A proportion of this 80 million can be considered to have a mental disability.

It is important for us to have a definition of 'mental disability' because it determines a person's entitlement to public services, such as healthcare, social care, disability allowances and so on. A definition is also required in law, to protect people from discrimination because of their mental disability, although this definition is often different and broader than the definition used to establish whether people are entitled to public funds.

So, when is a mental health condition defined as a mental disability? The GOV.UK website (online) states that:

> A mental health condition is considered a disability if it has a long-term effect on your normal day-to-day activity. This is defined under the Equality Act 2010.
>
> Your condition is 'long term' if it lasts, or is likely to last, 12 months.
>
> 'Normal day-to-day activity' is defined as something you do regularly in a normal day. This includes things like using a computer, working set times or interacting with people.

Ambiguity arises with this definition. If a person suffers a bout of mental illness for a few months and it then abates, and the condition recurs every few months but never lasts for more than 12 months, does this condition fall within the definition of 'long term'? On this point, Ashtons Legal (2020), a well-respected UK law firm, states: "The test is whether the particular effect is likely to recur (para 2(2), Sch. 1, EQA 2010). Conditions with effects which recur only sporadically or for short periods can still satisfy the definition of 'long term'."

Similarly, what constitutes 'normal day-to-day activity'? What if a person is able to work, rest and play 'normally' but is repeatedly dismissed from employment because of factors related to their mental health? This situation is typically faced by people with conditions such as ADHD and autism, for example. In such cases, could it be said that the person's condition is adversely affecting them 'day-to-day', especially if they experience far longer and/or far more numerous periods of unemployment than would otherwise be expected? It would seem that the law protects people with long-term mental health conditions that lead to them being unable to undertake short-term tasks but offers no protection to people unable to undertake long-term tasks. This point is supported by Ashtons Legal (2020), who comment: "It is generally the case that 'day to day activities' are the carrying out of daily tasks – getting dressed, cooking, cleaning, doing shopping, driving, watching television – as opposed to tasks related to the specific employment itself. I am not sure that a 'tendency to be fired for one's health problems' would make someone 'disabled' in and of itself, although of course the reasons behind their being fired repeatedly may well do so." Based on the guidance of Ashtons Legal it appears the law may currently fail to recognise the effect a person's long-term mental health condition has on their *long-term* activities, such as getting and keeping a job which, for those desiring to work, should constitute part of their normal day-to-day life.

The law may be clearer to some people – perhaps solicitors, judges and even some employers – than it is to others, such as employees with mental health issues and other employers. Critically, the identification of whether someone is disabled under the Equality Act 2010 is a legal decision that only a judge can make.

To help readers grasp some of the key legal principles related to workplace mental health, several landmark mental health negligence cases are considered later in this chapter. In the meantime, let us consider mental health discrimination.

Equality Act 2010

Under the Equality Act 2010, the minimum legal requirement for employers to support an employee with mental health issues is that the employee must have a long-term condition that affects their ability to carry out day-to-day activities. The employer can choose to support employees who fall outside this strict definition, of course, and I would encourage them to do so.

Rethink Mental Illness (online) provides a useful introduction to the Equality Act 2010. It states:

> *The Equality Act 2010 protects disabled people from unfair treatment. This includes many people with a mental illness.*

> *If someone has treated you unfairly because of a mental illness that could be discrimination.*

> *The Equality Act 2010 explains what a disability is. If you match this definition, you could be protected from discrimination, harassment and victimisation by the Act.*

> *You may have the right to get your employer to make changes to your job due to your disability. These changes are 'reasonable adjustments'.*

> *The Equality Act protects you from discrimination at work. It also protects you when you are applying for jobs.*

> *The Equality Act also protects you when you use services. This includes when you try to get housing, education or any other services.*

> *The Equality Act can also protect carers of people with a mental illness.*

This UK Act means that, generally, claims are brought by employees against employers on the grounds of:

- direct discrimination
- indirect discrimination
- harassment
- victimisation
- something arising out of a disability
- issues related to 'protected characteristics'.

In the UK, to support employees who have some form of disability, employers have a duty to make 'reasonable adjustments.' In Australia, the Victorian Equal Opportunity and Human Rights Commission (online) states that reasonable adjustments are changes to the work environment that allow people with a disability to work safely and productively. Under the Australian Equal Opportunity Act 2010, 'disability' includes:

- physical, psychological or neurological disease or disorder
- illness, whether temporary or permanent
- injury, including work-related injuries.

Mind (2018b) provides some useful examples of the type of 'reasonable adjustments' employers might make to accommodate employees with a mental health condition. These include:

- changing the times when events happen
- changing the places where services are delivered
- arranging for an advocate to support the employee
- allowing more time for a face-to-face interview
- offering clear written information.

There is no limit, however, on what might constitute a reasonable adjustment. Other adjustments employers could make above and beyond those recommended by Mind might include:

- changes to working patterns (eg. flexible working)
- changes to processes
- changes to working environment (eg. quiet room/different desk space)
- provision of specialised equipment.

Based on this information from Mind and Rethink Mental Illness, it is clear they expect the employee to disclose their mental health condition to their employer and ask for the protection and/or reasonable adjustments the employer is required to provide under the Equality Act 2010 (as opposed to the employer proactively finding out about it).

This employee-led approach puts the burden on the employee to speak up first, possibly after they have already experienced some form of mental injury or harm in the workplace. As I mentioned earlier in this book, however, it is employers who should take a proactive and preventive approach so that employees do not suffer harm in the first place.

With certain mental health conditions, the employee will have no problem raising their condition with their employer. But what if the employee does not wish to do so or is even unaware they have a mental health condition?

A useful insight comes from Loch and Edmonds (2014), who suggest the employer has a responsibility to act in accordance with the law where the employer has *knowledge of an employee's mental health condition*. As a side issue, Loch and Edmonds also acknowledge that some employees may not be aware of their own mental health condition. Here, Ashtons Legal believes it is possible for an employer to indirectly discriminate, even where the employer has no knowledge of a mental health issue.

Employment solicitor David Whincup (2019) of law firm, Squire, Patton Boggs (UK) LLP, writes: "...the Equality and Human Rights Commission Code states that where it doesn't know, an employer must do 'all it can reasonably be expected to do' to find out, including proactively enquiring of the employee where there are signs that something is amiss." This appears to place a duty on employers to take proactive steps to identify the causes of, and to take steps to prevent, discrimination, harassment, victimisation and bullying.

No such proactive general obligation appears to exist in the UK regarding negligence, however, this point is thought to be under legal review. Based on Whincup's (2020) input, it appears that in negligence cases, it can be argued that employers in the UK do have an obligation to join up the mental health 'dots' where the employer has been provided with medical certificates or related oral disclosures, or where there are out-of-character behaviours on the part of an employee. In other words, the employer's proactive duty applies where there are signs that something is amiss.

In any case, what constitutes 'knowledge of an employee's mental health condition'? What constitutes 'ought reasonably to know'? To many employers, it may appear that an employer is only considered to have knowledge of an employee's mental health condition when the employee tells the employer about it. This is not the case. Ashtons Legal (2020) recommend considering case law around the principle of 'constructive knowledge', especially the case of *A Ltd v Z, 2019*. In personal correspondence to me, Ashton Legal (2020) stated although the employee did not expressly tell her employer of her mental health issues, the judge found the employer did have knowledge of it, based upon the following circumstances:

- *the GP and hospital certificates amounted to clear evidence that the claimant had experienced significant deterioration in her mental state and there was a real question about her psychiatric health*

- *the claimant's silence on her mental health could not be taken as conclusive, especially taking into account that mental health problems often carry a stigma which discourages people from disclosing such matters*

- *in the circumstances, taking into account the size and resources of the respondent, it was incumbent upon the respondent to enquire into the claimant's mental wellbeing*

- *the respondent's failure to do so precluded it from denying that they ought to have known that she had a disability.*

Based on *A Ltd v Z, 2019* it appears feasible that circumstances might arise where evidence accumulates that indirectly informs the employer of an employee's mental health condition, and that can later be used in court.

Whincup adds: 'There must be some triggers for the employer's enquiry in the way the employee behaves (assuming no express disclosure)'. In the case of *A Ltd v Z, 2019*, it appears that the 'triggers' Whincup refers to were (or certainly included) the GP and hospital certificates. Employers take note. If any of your employees have been signed off with work-related stress or other work-related mental health issues, and you have a file note saying so, you should consider such a note as providing you with actual positive knowledge of a condition that you are compelled to do something about. Holding such notes and doing nothing to support the employee is likely to amount to negligence.

There is no need to read the full case notes of *A Ltd v Z, 2019* to understand the context of these circumstances. The analysis of this case by Ashtons Legal (2020) demonstrates that employers can be regarded as having knowledge of a mental health condition without being expressly told about it. It appears from the above case analysis that the larger the employer, the more effort courts will expect them to make to proactively determine the mental health of employees. Here, larger employers should take note.

Without question, the definition of an employer's obligations as they relate to mental health and the law will continue to develop over time, as legal Acts are updated and new precedents emerge. The Occupational Health and Safety Management – Psychological Health and Safety in the Workplace Guidelines (ISO 45003), due to be published in 2021, may provide further clarity about what practices can be expected of employers. Until then, employers are certainly expected to do something to identify the state of their employees' mental health. Doing nothing will not meet the test of 'all it can reasonably be expected to do'. Doing nothing will almost certainly create a liability for the employer, as it is likely to increase the chances of a case that is brought by an employee against their employer succeeding.

So, what can you as an employer be reasonably expected to do to identify employee mental health? Again, as when trying to determine whether a person has a mental disability, only a judge will be able to decide. But the above case of *A Ltd v Z* provides some insight.

For the purposes of this chapter, you should first consider, based on everything you know about the employee, whether he or she is likely to have or have had a mental health condition. For example, if you know that one of your employees is ex-military, has experienced combat, may have witnessed trauma and may suffer from PTSD, you can reasonably be expected to suppose that they could be under significant mental pressure. The same is true for an employee who is experiencing financial difficulties, or has a family member with severe ill-health, or who has raised concerns with you about their workload. Knowing these circumstances should act as an indicator or warning signal for employers. Such employees might be considered more vulnerable and be at higher risk of mental health issues. If multiple such circumstances are being experienced by a single employee, they might be considered at very high risk.

From this point, employers might be advised to consider the circumstances surrounding an employee's employment. Some of the circumstances that might indicate that the employer should have concerns and may, indeed, already – as far as the law is concerned – have knowledge of an employee's mental health condition might include:

- recruitment information (eg. a pre-employment health questionnaire (CIPD, 2018)) where the employee has stated they have a mental health issue

- conversations between the employee and a colleague (eg. a 'line' or other manager)

- frequent or prolonged absences on the grounds of poor mental health

- provision of a 'fit note' or 'sick note' on the grounds of poor mental health

- the employee is known by the employer to be accessing aspects of the Employee Assistance Programme for stress-related or other mental health support through the occupational health department.

These types of circumstances may lead to the employer, wittingly or unwittingly, having knowledge of the employee's poor state of mental health, with a legal obligation to do something about it.

Although of course there are legal implications to all of this, the point of clarifying the level of proactivity an employer can be expected to demonstrate is really all about employee support. As identified in chapter 1, just *one small thing* at work might prove to be a tipping point for an employee, leading them to move from *coping* to becoming *distressed*. If the law and the employer's obligations were clearer, better understood and better known, employers might put more effort into preventing *one small thing* arising and thus reduce the risk of the employee becoming distressed.

In the case of physical health and safety, the onus is on the employer to determine proactively what can cause harm and who can be harmed, and to take preventative steps by putting in place appropriate control measures. The same logic applies to mental health.

Clearly, employees do not have to divulge information about their private lives, and they may not want to. However, in future, employers will find they are increasingly being held account-able in cases where work and work-related factors – such as low pay, a heavy workload and workplace bullying – are identified as stressors within their workplace. Where an employee confides in colleagues that they are coping with sick relatives, financial issues, chronic con-ditions such as back problems or other stressors outside of work, and if the employer is not specifically told about it, the employer is unlikely to be found culpable, at least unless there is other evidence giving the employer 'knowledge'. A good line manager, one who is in tune with their workforce and operates a caring and compassionate culture, might be expected to develop a close and open relationship with their employees and so might learn of such circumstances. If the line manager is told of such circumstances, even in confidence, they will almost certainly have a duty to act.

There are advantages for employers in taking this sort of proactive, preventative approach. Responding to requests for support from employees with mental health issues will not on its own lead to the development of a positive mental health culture. However, by being pro-active, as suggested here, you will be judged by your employees to be more caring, which will in turn create a more positive environment and one that is more likely to achieve the levels of productivity and other benefits that result from the effective management of workplace wellbeing and mental health.

Data Protection Act 2018

The Data Protection Act 2018, and an employer's obligations under the General Data Protection Regulation (GDPR), sets out how employers should manage data relating to employees. Employers should be well-versed in this aspect of law. This section only very briefly considers some rights and obligations surrounding the disclosure of a mental health issue.

Employees may or may not choose to divulge medical information to their employer. The choice is exclusively theirs. Should they choose to do so, they may do this:

- during the recruitment process
- once they are employed by an organisation.

During any recruitment process, applicants are not required by law to divulge any medical or health information whatsoever. However, if employees do disclose a medical condition during this process, the employer's duties under the Equality Act 2010 will apply, in terms of discrimination and reasonable adjustments. The employer may be asked to make reasonable adjustments to the recruitment process itself, and the employee should disclose any mental and physical health issue to the employer that might affect their suitability for the role.

Even if an employer provides an applicant with a medical questionnaire to complete, the employee can refuse to complete it or may choose to effectively lie on it, saying they do not have a mental health condition when in fact they might. The law is biased towards the employee's rights of confidentiality, although if they do not complete the questionnaire honestly and the employer could never have known about the disability, the employee may not receive the protection they are entitled to under the Equality Act 2010 – for example, in cases where the applicant fails to disclose a mental or physical impairment that makes them unsuitable for the role.

In chapter 2, you as an employer were encouraged to show empathy towards employees who have issues with their mental health. It seems timely to return to the subject of empathy.

If an employee openly refuses to complete a medical health questionnaire, what message does that send to the employer? That the applicant is difficult? That they have a condition but do not wish to disclose it? If the applicant is hiding a condition, does that mean they are likely to be a burden on their employer and, for example, need a significant amount of time off work? Of course, the employer may argue that the purpose of the medical questionnaire is solely to determine how they might make any 'reasonable adjustments' if necessary and that they would never use the information to discriminate in any way. Heaven forbid! Some applicants might choose to lie on the medical questionnaire, secure the job and, should their employer learn of their mental health condition, argue that the employer had no right to the information in the first place. If an employee does this, however, they risk their dishonesty being held against them, which could possibly lead to disciplinary action on grounds of a breach of trust (although such action by an employer could be risky if the employee is disabled under the Equality Act 2010). Despite this risk, an employee might still think it preferable to lie to secure the job, hoping to 'get away with it', as opposed to telling the truth about their mental health issue, have their condition held against them and not secure the job.

For further information about the issues faced by employees and job applicants when they are contemplating telling an employer about their mental health condition, see chapter 2.

Whether an employee has a mental health issue before commencing employment that the employer exacerbates, or whether they have a mental health issue that has been caused at work, how does an employer determine if they may be held liable by an employee? I now provide a reasonably comprehensive explanation of the tort of negligence, as this aspect of law as it relates to workplace mental health may be less clear than, say, law relating to mental health discrimination.

The Tort of Negligence

Employees will want to understand the circumstances under which they can bring a claim of mental health negligence against an employer; and employers will want to understand how to protect against such claims. Laws relating to the tort of negligence will almost certainly apply.

According to Thomson Reuters Practical Law (online), a tort is:

> *The name given to the branch of law that imposes civil liability for breach of obligations imposed by law. The most common tort is the tort of negligence which imposes an obligation not to breach the duty of care (that is, the duty to behave as a reasonable person would behave in the circumstances) which the law says is owed to those who may foreseeably be injured by any particular conduct.*

In other words, a tort of negligence is a breach of the duty a person or party owes to another person or party, not to cause them injury, harm or loss. A claim may arise where injury, harm or loss occurs through negligence. A claim of negligence will only succeed if certain points of law can be established. For tort liability, four tests must be met, as listed by the Legal Information Institute (online):

1   *the existence of a legal duty that the defendant owed to the plaintiff*

2   *defendant's breach of that duty*

3   *plaintiff's sufferance of an injury*

4   *proof that defendant's breach caused the injury (typically defined through proximate cause).*

Looking at those circumstances that must exist for an employee to bring a successful case of mental health negligence against an employer, and which an employer would probably wish to protect against, two cases in particular provide guidance:

- the decision of the Court of Appeal in *Sutherland v Hatton* in 2002
- the House of Lords decision in *Barber v Somerset County Council* in 2004.

In respect of *Sutherland v Hatton*, the case is also referred to below as *Hatton v Sutherland*, the differing terms simply reflecting the stage the case was at in the legal process.

Beyond the 'duty of care' considerations, both of these cases, like most cases of negligence, required: a) the claimant (the employee) to have suffered mental harm; b) for *causation* to be clear; c) for there to be *foreseeability*; and d) for there to have been *negligence*.

To help readers grasp the relevant legal principles, the above four tests of negligence as it relates to the workplace are now explored.

Foreseeability is a key component of the tort of negligence. For a negligence claim to be successful, the harm suffered by an employee must have been reasonably foreseeable by the employer. This issue of foreseeability is dealt with throughout the examination of these four tests.

Leaders and managers should bear these four points in mind when designing a mental health management programme, so that such a programme, amongst other things, minimises the risk of employees bringing mental health negligence claims against them.

I will now explore the four points in detail.

1) The Employee is Owed a Duty of Care by Their Employer

Employers owe their employees (and others affected by their activities) a duty of care. The GOV.UK website (online) states, under Section 2 of HASAWA:

2.   *General duties of employers to their employees.*

   (1) *It shall be the duty of every employer to ensure, so far as is reasonably practicable, the health, safety and welfare at work of all his employees.*

   (2) *Without prejudice to the generality of an employer's duty under the preceding subsection, the matters to which that duty extends include in particular—*

   (a) *the provision and maintenance of plant and systems of work that are, so far as is reasonably practicable, safe and without risks to health;*

   (b) *arrangements for ensuring, so far as is reasonably practicable, safety and absence of risks to health in connection with the use, handling, storage and transport of articles and substances;*

   (c) *the provision of such information, instruction, training and supervision as is necessary to ensure, so far as is reasonably practicable, the health and safety at work of his employees;*

   (d) *so far as is reasonably practicable as regards any place of work under the employer's control, the maintenance of it in a condition that is safe and without risks to health and the provision and maintenance of means of access to and egress from it that are safe and without such risks;*

   (e) *the provision and maintenance of a working environment for his employees that is, so far as is reasonably practicable, safe, without risks to health, and adequate as regards facilities and arrangements for their welfare at work.*

Considering the points in the above quote: (1) covers the general duty of the employer to ensure the health, safety and welfare of employees, which includes mental health; (2c) requires the employer to provide employees with information, instruction, training and supervision so as to protect the workforce's mental health; and finally, (2e) requires the employer to ensure the working environment is without mental health risks, as far as is reasonably practicable.

There can be no doubt that employers owe a duty of care to employees. Furthermore, the law requires employers to be proactive in preventing mental harm to their employees.

2) Has the Employer Breached Their Duty of Care?

US law firm, Walker Morgan (online) states:

> A breach of the duty of care occurs when one fails to fulfill his or her duty of care to act reasonably in some aspect. There are a variety of different situations in which one party owes a duty of care to another, therefore there can be a variety of situations in which such a duty is breached. Generally, if a party does not act in a reasonable manner to prevent foreseeable injuries to others, the duty of care is breached.

The second test of tort is whether the employer breached their duty to their employee. Loch and Edmunds (2014) and Whincup (2019) outline the circumstances that determine whether an employer has breached their duty and explain that if the employer has knowledge of a mental health issue, or ought reasonably to know about it, they have a duty to act.

Establishing whether the employer has such knowledge and has acted reasonably on that knowledge is key. Here, employees suffering mental harm at work might be obliged to declare it to their employer if their employer is to be considered to have knowledge of the employee's condition.

Lawyers Slater Gordon (online) write:

> In the case of Hatton v Sutherland, the Appeal Court placed the burden of proving this on the shoulders of the employee. In brief, the following principles emerged:
>
> - The individual is in charge of his/her own mental health
> - The individual can gauge whether the job was doing him/her any harm
> - The individual can then do something about it.
>
> The fact is, employers can effectively sit blinkered to the health of their employees; it is up to the employee to make it obvious that there was 'a sufficient indication of impending harm to health arising from stress at work which was plain enough for any reasonable employer to have realised, so as to trigger a duty to do something about it' (LJ Hale in Sutherland v Hatton 5/2/02).

Employers wishing to defend against a claim of mental health negligence will almost certainly look to the *Sutherland v Hatton* ruling for part of their defence.

Walker Morgan suggest that liability will arise where an employer fails to fulfil their duty of care to their employees if it fails to prevent foreseeable injuries, presumably including mental health injuries. Employers will attempt to avoid liability on the grounds of a lack of knowledge and the inability to foresee potential mental harm.

In proving harm was suffered, the employee must also establish that the harm was foreseeable.

Notably, in the *Sutherland v Hatton* case above, the judge, LJ Hale, made the landmark statement that is still relied upon today: 'The *test (of foreseeability) is the same* whatever the *employment: there are no* occupations which should be regarded as *intrinsically dangerous* to mental health' (Steele, 2007).

This statement appears to be in conflict with the research I presented in chapter 1, which indicated that, for example, nurses and other occupations are at greater risk of PTSD. I will return to this point later in this chapter and again in chapter 16.

There will always be debate as to what constitutes the 'reasonably practicable' measures an employer should take to prevent mental harm and what they can reasonably be expected to 'foresee'.

Commenting on a recent legal ruling in the case of *Dean & Chapter of Rochester Cathedral v Leonard Debell, 2016*, the England-based Forbes Solicitors (2017) stated:

> ... *the judge had to apply the concept of reasonable foreseeability taking a 'practical and realistic approach'. Just because a risk is foreseeable, it should not result in automatic liability.*

> ... *the law has to 'strike a balance between the nature and extent of the risk on the one hand and the cost of eliminating it on the other'.*

Two points are particularly relevant to employers here. Writing in IOSH Magazine, Bridget Leathley (2016) comments:

- *If you engage in a business activity, you are expected to be able to foresee more than the 'reasonable man' in relation to that activity.*
- *Failure to heed warnings or advice from the authorities, employees or others or to respond appropriately to 'near misses' arising in similar circumstances may be factors indicating greater foreseeability.*

The *Rorrison v West Lothian* case (Scottish Courts and Tribunals, 1999) provides an example of foreseeability. Although the employee suffered psychological harm, and that harm was caused or exacerbated by the employer, the harm suffered was not reasonably foreseeable, so the employee's case failed.

In summary, employers have a duty to foresee mental harm. This duty requires employers to take a proactive and preventative, but reasonably practicable, approach. Employers are likely to be expected to have more knowledge of the risks created by their activities than a 'reasonable man'. Ignoring employee warnings (and, possibly, other indicators or triggers) of risks may increase the chances of an employer being found liable for negligence.

3) Has the Employee Experienced Mental Harm or a Mental Health Condition?

In cases where an employee is trying to prove their employer caused mental harm through negligence, the employee will be required to prove they have suffered mental harm.

This may not be as easy as it sounds.

According to ClaimsAction (2019):

> In the world of personal injury claims the process of claiming for psychological injury is exactly the same as claiming for a physical injury. In order to pursue a claim for mental injury this must have been caused by a traumatic incident which was the fault of a negligent third party. Very often we will see physical and psychological injuries wrapped up in the same claim but many people are under the misapprehension that claiming for psychological injuries alone is not permissible.

The third test of a tort of negligence requires the employee to have suffered mental injury or harm. A doctor's certificate stating the type and cause of injury may suffice; it is not uncommon for employees to be signed off sick with 'work-related stress'.

However, proving a mental health condition may not be straightforward. On the face of it, doctors and GPs often write notes giving employees medical grounds for taking time off work on the grounds of poor mental health. Some symptoms can be identified by medical practitioners. These symptoms might relate to PTSD, adjustment disorders and depression. Particular symptoms might include: nightmares and flashbacks after witnessing a traumatic incident; insomnia; anxiety; panic attacks; hypervigilance; agoraphobia; and suicidal thoughts.

An employee will be required to provide evidence of professionally diagnosed mental health issues before they can progress a claim of mental health negligence against an employer, including significant medical records. This proof of mental injury or harm (eg. a formal diagnosis), along with the cause of that mental harm, will almost certainly need to be clear-cut.

Even then, the employer may argue that other non-negligent factors caused or significantly contributed towards the employee's mental health condition, such as financial worries, a troubled home life, sick relatives the employee is worried about, and so on.

If such medical evidence is available from a GP, a court may give some weight to that evidence, as was established in the *J v DLA Piper UK LLP, 2010* case.

Proving mental harm is one thing. Proving that work was the cause of it is another.

4) Did the Employer's Negligence Lead to the Harm Suffered by the Employee?

Causation establishes the link between a cause (an act or omission) and an effect (the effect of that act or omission on an employee's mental health).

If somebody did something they should not have done or did not do something they should have done (in other words, they acted negligently) and their negligence caused harm, the person whose acts or omissions caused harm can be held liable.

Causation relates to the fourth of the four tests of a tort. This requires the employee to prove that the employer breached their duty of care to them and caused the harm they have suffered. In cases where an employee brings an action against an employer, the employer must be shown to have caused the harm suffered by the employee through negligence.

Negligence can arise because of a number of factors.

Slater Gordon (online) write:

> You must be able to prove that the injury was the fault of the employer, and could have been avoided. For instance, doubling the workload of an employee without providing additional support or resources could well mean that the employer has failed in their duty of care.

In this example, it seems the employer may have no regard for the impact of doubling the employee's workload.

In a number of judgments culminating in the decision in *Hatton v Sutherland*, the Court of Appeal underlined the importance of foreseeability in personal injury claims arising out of stress at work. Foreseeability was addressed earlier in this chapter. Suffice it to say here that if the employer fails to foresee risks they would reasonably be expected to foresee, this may well contribute to them being found negligent.

In essence, for an employer to be found negligent, it is likely to have to establish that:

- the employer knew the employee may be at risk of harm (eg. had knowledge of a mental health issue, or should have reasonably foreseen the risk of mental harm)
- the employer failed to take action to address that risk of mental harm.

Globally, employers are being found liable for mental/psychological harm, and for acts and omissions related to it. They are also being found to be failing in their duty of care to their employees where mental harm arises.

- In Australia, *Wearne v State of Victoria, Keegan v Sussan Corporation and Hayes v State of Qld* provide examples where an employer's duty of care as it relates to mental health led to courts finding against employers (Rigby Cooke Lawyers, 2019).
- In Ireland, employers were found liable in various cases, especially relating to mental health and to an employer's duty of care, including: *McCarthy v ISS Ireland Ltd, Glynn v Minister for Justice Equality and Law Reform and Hurley v An Post (Rush, 2018).*
- In the UK, Hatton v Sutherland, Majrowski v Guy's & St Thomas' NHS Trust, Barber v Somerset County Council and Rorrison v West Lothian, provide useful guidance.

In many of the above cases, an employee's mental health issues led to the initiation of a claim against the employer. However, in many instances, the cause of the employees' mental health issues became the point of focus for the courts. For example, several employers were found to have known about bullying and harassment, and the consequential effects of these, but failed to address them. In so doing, they breached their duty of care to the bullied employee, with a failure in their duty of care being the deciding factor in the courts' judgement, as opposed to mental health negligence. In cases where a breach of the duty of care arises, the employee does not have to prove that the employer's negligence contributed towards their mental ill-health, making it easier to establish the employers' culpability.

It may be the case that courts will consider an employee's susceptibility to mental harm plus any pre-existing mental health issues the employee may have. A court may also consider the steps the employee took to look after their own mental health, as suggested earlier, where, in the case of *Hatton v Sutherland*, the Appeal Court stated that employees must be held responsible for their own mental health.

I end this section on the four tests of the tort of negligence by pointing out that, in the UK, the case of *Hatton v Sutherland, 2002* is still the leading authoritative case. The 16 points arising from it (see Appendix 5.1) should always be considered in related claims. In the *Barber v Somerset County Council* case, Lord Walker referred to the ruling in *Hatton v Sutherland* and the 16 'Hatton Propositions' that emerged from it as providing useful guidance, but stated that the propositions should not be regarded as an absolute rule (Sanders & Countouris, 2016). This means that the legal issues arising in any claim today between an employee and their employer will need to be viewed on a case-by-case basis, with generalisations being difficult to make. That said, it appears the 'Hatton Propositions' are often rigidly applied (BC Legal, 2014). So where do employers and employees stand? It appears neither will find out until they get to court.

Writing in The Law Society Gazette, considering number three of the Propositions ('An employer is usually entitled to assume that the employee can withstand the normal pressure of the job unless he knows of some particular problem or vulnerability'), Allen (2005) wrote:

> This was refined in Barber by Lord Walker, who stated: 'it is only if there is something specific about the job or the employee or the combination of the two that he (the employer) has to think harder in terms of foreseeability'.

I said earlier that I would return to the statement by LJ Hale that there are no occupations that are more intrinsically dangerous to mental health than others. In stating that the 'Hatton Propositions' are not absolute, Lord Walker appears to be suggesting there may in fact be circumstances where foreseeability might be required of an employer where an occupation is known to be more dangerous to mental health, such as nursing (chapter 1). Unsurprisingly, in law, more ambiguity arises for employers and employees, and perhaps for lawyers too.

One consideration arising from the *Hatton v Sutherland* case relates to the employee being in charge of their own mental health (Slater Gordon, online). On this point, is it realistic to expect employees to look after their own mental health? Not only is it realistic but there also appears to be a legal duty placed upon employees to take care of their own mental health, which I now explore.

Employee Legal Obligations Related to Mental Health

The practice of health and safety management was covered quite extensively in chapter 4, including the employer's duty towards their employees under health and safety law (eg. HASAWA, Section 2). It is also helpful to consider the employee's legal duties when looking at the Appeal Court comments I covered in the previous section. The GOV.UK website (online) states, under Section 7 of HASAWA:

> 7. *General duties of employees at work.*
>
>   *It shall be the duty of every employee while at work —*
>
>   *(a) to take reasonable care for the health and safety of himself and of other persons who may be affected by his acts or omissions at work; and*
>
>   *(b) as regards any duty or requirement imposed on his employer or any other person by or under any of the relevant statutory provisions, to co-operate with him so far as is necessary to enable that duty or requirement to be performed or complied with.*

It is evident from this that all employees must look after their own mental health, look after the mental health of their colleagues and comply with their employer's efforts to protect mental health in the workplace. Just how the law expects employees to take care of their own mental health appears unclear, however. Some of the ways an employee might be expected to comply with these duties, as far as is reasonably practicable, are shown in Table 5.1, although the list is not exhaustive.

Table 5.1   *Employee workplace mental health compliance*

Compliance requirement	Compliance actions
Employee to look after their own mental health	• Have a healthy diet • Exercise • Avoid substance abuse • Rest properly (eg. sleep)
Employees to look after the mental health of others	• Check on other employees • Tell management if a colleague appears to be struggling with their mental health • Do not bully others, or otherwise cause or compound mental health issues
Employees to comply with the mental health actions of their employer	• Follow the information, instruction and training provided • Participate in mindfulness, resilience and other training

As Table 5.1 shows, employees might be expected to care for their own wellbeing, including their diet and exercise, and other aspects of their mental health. Employees would also have a duty to participate in any training provided by their employer, such as resilience and mindfulness. And they should look after the mental health of colleagues, for example by checking on them and by not behaving unacceptably towards them (eg. bullying them).

In cases of mental health negligence, a court may well contemplate whether the employee has done all they could have been reasonably expected to do to take care of their own mental health. If the employee has done so, yet has still suffered harm to their mental health through the employer's negligence, the case against the employer may be strengthened.

Sections 2 and 7 of HASAWA make clear the obligations employers and employees have in law. But what if an employer breaches its legal duties and does not fulfil its duty of care to its employees as that duty relates to mental health? What then?

HSE and Mental Health Enforcement

As I revealed in chapter 4, fines amounting to approximately £20m to £50m are issued by the HSE for poor physical health and safety practice each year. However, no data was available about fines issued for poor mental health practice, from which we can only infer that no such fines were issued. Why is this, when the HSE's own guidance says employers have a legal duty to manage mental health? Is it the case that every single employer is managing mental health well? That seems unlikely. In fact, there have been many successful civil cases of negligence brought by employees against employers, suggesting that against the lower 'burden of proof' requirement in such cases, employers are being found to be in the wrong. As for non-enforcement by the HSE, why is the HSE not bringing employers to court to be held to account when civil cases against employers are succeeding?

To start with, it is appropriate to ask if the law is enforced in such a way that mental health is treated the same as physical health. It appears that, as things stand today, there is certainly a greater chance of an organisation facing a sanction for negligence in respect of physical health than mental health. But why is that?

The HSE provides the following guidance regarding mental health (HSE, 2019):

> *This guidance talks generally about work-related stress but where such stress is prolonged it can lead to both physical and psychological damage, including anxiety and depression.*
>
> *Work can also aggravate pre-existing conditions, and problems at work can bring on symptoms or make their effects worse.*
>
> *Whether work is causing the health issue or aggravating it, employers have a legal responsibility to help their employees. Work-related mental health issues must be assessed to measure the levels of risk to staff. Where a risk is identified, steps must be taken to remove it or reduce it as far as reasonably practicable.*
>
> *Some employees will have a pre-existing physical or mental health condition when recruited or may develop one caused by factors that are not work-related factors.*
>
> *Their employers may have further legal requirements, to make reasonable adjustments under equalities legislation.*

Three important points arise here:

1   The HSE recognises that work can directly cause and contribute to poor mental health.
2   Employers have a legal obligation to protect the mental health of their employees.
3   Some employees will have a pre-existing mental health condition.

The HSE's guidance establishes the first of the four tests of the tort of negligence (Legal Information Institute, online): that the employer owes its employees a legal duty to protect their mental health.

However, the HSE (2013) states that 'stress is not reportable as an occupational injury, even when accompanied by a medical certificate stating it is work-related, because it does not result from a single definable accident'.

This statement answers the question posed earlier in this chapter about why the HSE issues no sanctions (eg. notices, fines) when organisations breach health and safety laws as laws relate to workplace mental health management. It is not mandatory for employers to report mental health breaches, so no sanctions are issued.

The HSE's position appears incongruent. On one hand, it says that employers have a legal responsibility to manage the mental health of employees. On the other hand, it imposes absolutely no duty upon employers to report cases related to stress (and presumably other incidents related to mental health) and it issues no sanctions for breaches to laws as laws apply to workplace mental health.

The HSE states quite emphatically that mental harm '...does not result from a single definable accident'. The HSE's statement seems absolute. It infers that other non-negligent causes of mental harm must always exist and must have played a contributory role in causing an employee's poor mental health. In other words, the HSE assumes that the employee suffering mental harm must have had pre-existing mental health issues caused by factors other than the employer's negligence. Based on this position, the HSE appears to assume it is impossible to establish the fourth test of a tort of negligence – that the employer's negligence caused the mental harm the employee suffered.

Sufficient legal analysis has been provided earlier in this chapter to demonstrate there can be grounds for an employee to bring a case of mental health negligence against an employer. The HSE's position may appear at odds with the writings of legal experts such as Ashtons Legal. But, in fact, it is not. As Whincup (2019) says: 'There is a difference between managing it [mental health] negligently, which is relatively common, and managing it demonstrably criminally poorly'. It seems the test in law to prove guilt under UK health and safety law (eg. criminal law) is so high as to render the HSE toothless in respect of mental health. You will probably be familiar with these different legal tests:

- Criminal law test: beyond all reasonable doubt
- Civil law test: on a balance of probabilities.

In the UK, health and safety law is criminal law. The test, therefore, is of guilt being proven *beyond all reasonable doubt*. The HSE provides a useful summary of the two types of law (HSE, online).

However, in respect of the high legal test for HASAWA, I have a concern. I identified previously that there may never have been a sanction issued against employers for breaching health and safety laws as they relate to mental health (chapter 4). Is it the case that there has never, ever been a single incident where an employer has harmed the mental health of an employee, as would meet the test under criminal law? I cannot believe this to be the case. If, as I suspect is the case, some employers are criminally negligent in managing mental health, surely the HSE should be doing something to identify the culprits. With employers having no obligation to report mental health incidents to the HSE, in effect, the HSE is not even looking. Employers seem to be able to break criminal health and safety law, as it relates to mental health, with impunity.

If the HSE feels it cannot protect employees against employers under health and safety legislation because the test in law to establish guilt cannot be met, employees will have to suffer in silence or continue to bring civil claims on the grounds of negligence against their employer. But are employees likely to bring such claims? And what chances of success do they have?

Employee Mental Health Negligence Claims Against Employers

Just because the HSE does not enforce poor mental health management, it does not mean employers are off the hook or that employees have no protection. Employees are protected through several other routes, namely the Equality Act 2010 and HASAWA, which were discussed earlier in this chapter, and through the law of tort, especially negligence.

Baska (2019) reports that there has been a dramatic rise in the number of discrimination claims being brought by employees against employers on grounds of mental health. Writing in *People Management*, she writes: 'The number of disability discrimination claims brought before employment tribunals rose to 6,550 in 2018, a 37 per cent increase on the previous year' (Baska, 2019).

And it is not just discrimination claims that are on the increase. Baska's assertion that claims are rising is borne out by personal injury specialists, ClaimsAction (2019), operated by JF Law Limited, who state that the number of personal injury cases for stress, depression and anxiety per 100,000 workers has increased over the past four years (Figure 5.1).

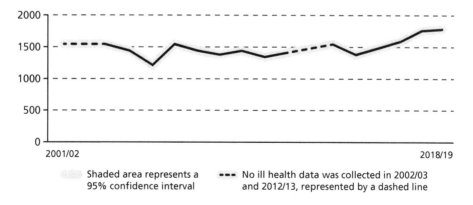

Figure 5.1 *Personal injury claims for stress, depression and anxiety per 100,000 workers*

Source: ClaimsAction, 2019

You can speculate whether you think the number of cases against employers for discrimination and mental health negligence will continue to rise.

The increasing profile of mental health, the growth of public pressure related to it, and the introduction of the new mental health management standard (ISO 45003) in 2021, appear likely to combine to clarify and reinforce employers' responsibilities. It is also likely that new legal precedents will be set through further court rulings. These developments will certainly empower employees.

These circumstances are also likely to reduce ambiguity in future by creating increasingly clear conditions and tests that employers must satisfy in order to prove they have not caused mental harm through negligence.

However, the likely effects of some of these future developments may not be clear. Although they are not legally required to sign up to it, one million organisations are accredited to the ISO 9001 international quality management standard. By comparison, only 100,000 organisations are accredited to the Occupational Health and Safety Management OHSAS 18001 standard, yet health and safety management is a legal requirement and has been for 50 years. Clearly, OHSAS 18001 has not proved to be so popular. How successful will the psychological health and safety management standard (ISO 45003), due for implementation in 2021, be? Readers can only wonder.

For now, the principle of causation and the failure to apply it to cases of mental harm (this failing by the HSE being most significant) presents the single most significant barrier to achieving a more equitable balance in the employer-employee mental health relationship.

In cases against them, employers will consider making numerous arguments in their defence. Some of the arguments likely to be put forward by employers are outlined here.

The four tests of the tort of negligence would require employers to establish in their defence that:

- the employer did not owe the person suffering harm a duty of care
- the employer did not breach any duty of care they owed to the person suffering harm
- the employee did not actually suffer harm
- the harm suffered by the employee did not arise through the employer's negligence (eg. the harm was not reasonably foreseeable).

Considerations related to these defences might include that:

- the employer's conduct was not culpable in the first place
- causation (the link between the cause and effect of harm) cannot be proven with certainty

- all work creates some form of stress and the stress created through work was not unreasonable

- the employee failed to tell their employer about their poor mental health and how their employer could support them

- the cause of the harm suffered was not reasonably foreseeable, whether or not the employee told their employer of their mental health condition

- the employee failed to look after their own mental health, so contributed to their own condition

- the employee was unduly susceptible to mental harm and/or had pre-existing mental health issues (eg. worries about their physical health, finances, sick relatives) that contributed towards their poor mental health, for which the employer cannot be held liable (although this may not affect liability per se, it might affect damages).

These are powerful arguments that most courts will almost certainly consider. However, as stated earlier in this chapter, if a court finds that work or work-related factors played a material part in causing or exacerbating mental harm that the employer failed adequately to foresee and address, the employer may be held liable, possibly for the full extent of the harm suffered, including harm caused by non-negligent factors.

To protect against this eventuality, employers should establish an effective mental health management programme, like the one set out in Part II of this book.

Conclusion

In this chapter, I explored legal considerations relevant to employers contemplating their mental health programme and I broadly argued that the 'system' tends to be biased against mental health sufferers. I provided a definition of mental disability and briefly explored the Equality Act 2010, finding that it afforded some level of protection to employees with mental health issues. I considered the Data Protection Act 2018 and found that it protects the right to confidentiality for job applicants and employees, and prohibits employers from insisting on the provision of mental health information. I explored the tort of negligence, and found that there is a difference between physical health and mental health in terms of the way they are managed and enforced in law, with there being much less chance of employers being prosecuted for poor mental health management than for poor physical health management. Finally, I considered the duties of employers and employees under the Health and Safety at Work etc Act 1974, and found that employers have a legal duty to protect the mental health of employees, while employees have a legal duty to look after their own mental health and that of colleagues.

The main take-outs from this chapter are:

- The term mental disability as defined in the Equality Act 2010 relates to somebody who has a mental impairment that has a substantial effect on their lives, lasting in the long-term (12 months or more) and that affects their ability to perform day-to-day activities.

- The Equality Act 2010 protects people with a mental disability when they are at work and in receipt of goods and services.

- The Equality Act 2010 and the law of tort as it relates to negligence can be used by employees to bring claims against their employer.

- There is no obligation upon people with a mental disability or other mental health issues to tell their employer about it, unless it relates to their suitability to do the job.

- HASAWA places a legal duty upon employers to manage the mental health of their employees.

- A new management standard related to mental health, ISO 45003 which relates to psychological health and safety, is due to be introduced in 2021.

- In the UK, the HSE is unlikely to prosecute employers under health and safety legislation as the test in law to prove guilt is high (beyond all reasonable doubt, as well as causation proving difficult to establish).

- The number of civil claims against employers for mental health negligence has risen in recent years.

- Landmark legal cases have proven that employees can successfully bring claims against employers, even where non-negligent causes of poor mental health have been apparent, with, in some cases, the employer being held liable for the full extent of the harm caused to an employee, even where the employer alone was not responsible for all of the harm suffered.

- Aspects of the law are under review, which, if amended, may see more claims for mental health negligence being brought against employers.

- Employers can defend claims against them by using a number of defences, including: the employer having no knowledge of the employee's mental health condition; not being able to foresee the harm suffered; and not being able to establish the link between the cause and effect of harm.

- Employers should put in place an effective mental health management system to minimise mental health negligence liabilities.

APPENDIX 5.1
THE 16 'HATTON PROPOSITIONS'

The leading authoritative case in terms of negligence is *Hatton v Sutherland 2002*, 2 AER 1 (also known as *Barber v Somerset County Council*). This is an edited version of the 16 propositions arising from the case.

1   There are no special control mechanisms applying to stress claims. The ordinary principles of employers' liability apply.

2   The injury to the particular employee must have been reasonably foreseeable. An injury to health (rather than knowledge the employee was under pressure) that is attributable to stress at work must be reasonably foreseeable by the employer.

3   An employer is usually entitled to assume that the employee can withstand the normal pressures of the job unless they know the employee has some particular problem or vulnerability. A mental disorder may be harder to foresee than a physical injury, but may be easier to foresee in a known individual than in the population at large.

4   There are no occupations which should be regarded as intrinsically dangerous to mental health. The test of foreseeability is the same whatever the employment.

5   The 'threshold' question:

    a   Consider the demands of the employee's work:

      ▪   Is the workload more than normal for that job?

      ▪   Is the work more emotionally/intellectually demanding for this employee?

      ▪   Are the demands unreasonable, compared with others?

      ▪   Are other employees suffering or experiencing abnormal levels of absenteeism?

    b   Signs from the employee:

      ▪   Have they previously had problems or vulnerabilities?

      ▪   Have they had uncharacteristic absences?

      ▪   Have there been complaints or warnings from him or others about stress?

6 The employer is generally entitled to take what the employee tells him or her at face value. They do not generally have to make searching enquiries of the employee or seek permission for further information from healthcare providers.

7 It must be plain enough to the reasonable employer that they should do something about an impending harm to health.

8 The employer is only in breach if they have failed to take reasonable steps in the circumstances to avoid harm to the employee. Factors to assess reasonableness include the gravity of harm that may occur, and the costs and practicability of preventing it.

9 The scope and size of the employer's operation is relevant to the test of reasonable steps to take to prevent harm (eg. redistribution of duties will be easier in a larger organisation).

10 The employer can only reasonably be expected to take steps that are likely to do some good. The court is likely to need expert advice on this (eg. from a psychiatrist).

11 An employer who offers a confidential advice service (with potential for referral to counselling and treatment) is unlikely to be found in breach of duty.

12 If the only reasonable and effective step to prevent harm was to dismiss the employee, the employer will not be in breach of duty in letting a willing employee continue in his or her job.

13 In all cases, the employee must identify what steps the employer could and should have taken to prevent the breach of duty.

14 The employee must show that the breach of duty has caused or materially contributed to the harm suffered.

15 Where the harm has more than one cause, the employer should only pay for that proportion attributable to him or her, unless the harm is truly indivisible.

16 The damages will take into account any pre-existing disorder or vulnerability, as well as the chance that the employee may have succumbed to the disorder in any event.

Source: http://www.workstress.net/sites/default/files/Legal-Update-Workshop-Handout.pdf (accessed 21 March 2020). Faithfully reproduced with the kind permission of Irwin Mitchell Solicitors.

References

Allen S. (2005) Personal Injury Law. *The Law Society Gazette* 18 February. Available at: *https://www.lawgazette.co.uk/law/personal-injury-law/3588.article* (accessed 21 March 2020).

Ashtons Legal (2020) Personal correspondence, 14 February 2020.

BC Legal (2014) *Claims for Occupational Stress, Bullying and Harassment – An Overview.* Available at: *https://www.bc-legal.co.uk/images/pdf/Journal1* (accessed 21 March 2020).

Baska, M. (2019) Number of disability discrimination cases growing eight times faster than other tribunal claims. *People Management* (online.) Available at: *https://www.peoplemanagement.co.uk/news/articles/disability-discrimination-cases-growing-eight-times-faster-other-tribunals* (accessed 20 January 2020).

Chartered Institute of Personnel and Development (2018) Pre-employment check: guidance for organisations. *CIPD* (online) Available at: *https://www.cipd.co.uk/knowledge/fundamentals/emp-law/recruitment/pre-employment-checks-guide* (accessed 5 December 2019).

ClaimsAction (2019) Key statistics financial year 2018/2019. *ClaimsAction* (online). Available at: https://www.claimsaction.co.uk/health-and-safety-in-the-workplace-statistics-2018-19/ (accessed 20 January 2020).

Cronin, T., Gouda, P., McDonald, C. and Hallahan, B. (2017) A comparison of mental health legislation in five developed countries: a narrative review. *Irish Journal of Psychological Medicine* 34: Special Issue 4, 261–269. Available at: https://www.cambridge.org/core/journals/irish-journal-of-psychological-medicine/article/comparison-of-mental-health-legislation-in-five-developed-countries-a-narrative-review/1043291DBE9B8D24480D738D47E1BAD6/core-reader# (accessed 15 January 2020).

Forbes Solicitors (2017) *Court of Appeal Clarifies 'Reasonable Foreseeability Test'* (online). Available at: *https://www.forbessolicitors.co.uk/news/37582/court-of-appeal-clarifies-reasonable-foreseeability-test* (accessed 20 January 2020).

GOV.UK (online) *When a Mental Health Condition Becomes a Disability.* Available at: *https://www.gov.uk/when-mental-health-condition-becomes-disability* (accessed 2 January 2020).

Health and Safety Executive (online) *How do Civil Law and Health and Safety Law Apply?* Available at: https://www.hse.gov.uk/voluntary/when-it-applies.htm (accessed 12 March 2020).

Health and Safety Executive (2013) Reporting injuries, diseases and dangerous occurrences in health and social care: Guidance for employers. *HSE Information Sheet No 1 (Revision 3)* (online). Available at: http://www.hse.gov.uk/pubns/hsis1.pdf (accessed 2 December 2019).

Health and Safety Executive (2019) Mental health conditions, work and the workplace. *HSE* (online). Available at: *https://www.hse.gov.uk/stress/mental-health.htm* (accessed 2 December 2019).

Leathley, B. (2016) F is for foreseeability. *IOSH Magazine* (online) Available at: *https://www.ioshmagazine.com/article/f-foreseeability* (accessed 20 January 2020).

Legal Information Institute, Cornell Law Institute (online) *Negligence*. Available at: *https://www. law.cornell.edu/wex/negligence* (accessed 2 December 2019).

Loch, P. and Edmonds, J. (2014) Employees with attention deficit disorder: practical and legal tips. *Personnel Today* (online). Available at: *https://www.personneltoday.com/hr/employees-with-attention-deficit-disorder-practical-and-legal-tips/* (accessed 2 January 2020).

Mental Health America (online) *Mental Health Rights*. Available at: *https://www.mhanational.org/ issues/mental-health-rights* (accessed 15 January 2020).

Mind (2018a) Mental Health Act 1983. *Mind* (online). Available at: *https://www.mind.org.uk/ information-support/legal-rights/mental-health-act-1983/#.XcEwL0agLIU* (accessed 20 January 2020).

Mind (2018b) Discrimination in everyday life. *Mind* (online). Available at: *https://www.mind. org.uk/information-support/legal-rights/discrimination-in-everyday-life/reasonable-adjustments/#.XeSPGeigLIU* (accessed 5 December 2019).

Rethink Mental Illness (online) *Discrimination and Mental Health*. Available at: *https://www.rethink. org/advice-and-information/rights-restrictions/mental-health-laws/discrimination-and-mental-health* (accessed 5 January 2020).

Rigby Cooke Lawyers (2019) *Mental health issues in the workplace and the employer's duty of care*. Available at: *https://www.rigbycooke.com.au/mental-health-issues-in-the-workplace-and-the-employers-duty-of-care/* (accessed 20 March 2020).

Rush, S. (2018). *Ireland: Recent case law on an employer's duty of care in PTSD/psychological injury cases*. Available at: *https://www.lewissilkin.com/Insights/Ireland-Recent-caselaw-on-an-employers-duty-of-care-in-PTSDpsychological-injury-cases* (accessed 20 March 2020).

Sanders, A. and Countouris, N. (2016) *Yapp v Foreign & Commonwealth Office*. International Labour Law Reports Online, 35. Available at: *http://eprints.lse.ac.uk/101843/* (accessed 21 March 2020).

Scottish Courts and Tribunals (1999) *Angela Rorrison v West Lothian College and Lothian Regional Council*. Available at: https://www.scotcourts.gov.uk/search-judgments/ judgment?id=dc778aa6-8980-69d2-b500-ff0000d74aa7 (accessed 6 March 2020).

Slater Gordon (online) *Occupational Stress: An overview of the issues surrounding claims based on stress caused in the workplace*. Available at: https://www.slatergordon.co.uk/ media/402239/occupational-stress.pdf (accessed 28 February 2020).

Steele, J. (2007) *Tort Law: Text, cases and materials*, fourth edition. Oxford: Oxford University Press. Available at: https://books.google.co.uk/books?id=WW8sDwAAQBAJ&p-g=PA323&lpg=PA323&dq=lj+hale+sutherland+hatton+the+test+is+the+same +no+job+intrinsically+dangerous&source=bl&ots=4HPh0ffG7 l&sig=ACfU3U1aXN2yc18vskUuYD5rRY8Zi8KDVA&hl =en&sa=X&ved=2ahUKEwjwpNqq5ljoAhUGTsAKHRtaAUcQ6AEwAXoECAgQAQ#v= onepage&q=lj%20hale%20sutherland%20hatton%20the%20test%20is%20the%20 same%20no%20job%20intrinsically%20dangerous&f=false (accessed 6 March 2020).

Thomson Reuters Practical Law (online) *Tort*. Available at: *https://uk.practicallaw. thomsonreuters.com/6-107-7397?transitionType=Default&contextData=(sc. Default)&firstPage=true&bhcp=1* (accessed 2 December 2019).

Victorian Equal Opportunity and Human Rights Commission (online) *About the Commission: Who we are and what we do*. Available at: *https://www.humanrightscommission.vic.gov.au/ about* (accessed 18 January 2020).

Walker Morgan (online) *Breach of the Duty of Care*. Available at: *https://www.walkermorgan.com/ negligence-breach-of-the-duty-of-care/* (accessed 20 January 2020).

Whincup, D. (2019) The A-Z of when you ought to know about disability (UK). *Employment Law Worldview*. Available at: *https://www.employmentlawworldview.com/the-a-z-of-when-you- ought-to-know-about-disability-uk/* (accessed 20 January 2020).

Whincup, D. (2020) Personal correspondence, 23 February 2020.

THE POSITIVE CASE
FOR MENTAL HEALTH

In this chapter, I offer an explanation as to why it is so valuable for leaders and managers to commit to addressing mental health as it affects their organisation and their employees. The rationale for doing this is based on four arguments: legal, moral, technical and commercial. Each of these is now explored.

Before I make the case for employing people with mental health issues, I want to consider some of the reasons people give for not employing them. These include the fact that:

- about half of employers view staff with mental health conditions as a 'significant risk' to their business, an increase of 10% since 2009 (Shaw Trust, 2018)
- some employers believe that people with mental health issues may:
  - give the wrong impression to customers
  - take significant time off work
  - adversely affect other workers
  - create a liability for the organisation.

The Shaw Trust (2018) found that more than half of all employers are reluctant to employ someone with a mental health condition due to a fear of that person being stigmatised by co-workers (56% in 2018, up from 51% in 2009). In the same 2018 survey, 42% of employers stated that people with mental health conditions were less reliable, nearly double the 2009 figure.

It seems there is widespread fear amongst employers. They are less likely to hire a person with mental health issues today than they were ten years ago. This shows social injustice is increasing, not improving, with Figure 4.3 offering an explanation why. Action is required.

Employers can make a significant difference, both to their own organisation and to the lives of those with mental health issues. Employers may already employ people who are doing a good job but feel they must hide their mental health issue in case it affects their employer's attitude towards them.

The four key arguments employers might consider – legal, moral, technical and commercial – are now explored.

The Legal Argument

In the USA, the OSH Act of 1970, Section 5., states employers: 'shall furnish to each of his employees employment and a place of employment which are free from recognized hazards that are causing or are likely to cause death or serious physical harm to his employees' (OSHA, online). This duty appears to expressly apply to physical health only, seemingly excluding mental health. If this assessment is correct, the law must be changed to reflect mental health.

In Australia, Safe Work Australia (online), states: 'Organisations and their duties – The harmonised work health and safety (*WHS*) laws require that organisations that employ paid workers ensure, so far as is reasonably practicable, the physical and mental health and safety of its workers, including volunteers.' In Australia, health and safety laws relate equally to physical and mental health.

At least in some countries, there is a clear legal basis for employers to invest in good mental health management practices. The legal justification for doing so in the UK arises from the tort of negligence, the Equality Act 2010 and the Health and Safety at Work etc Act 1974 (HASAWA).

Tort of negligence: Negligence was explored extensively in chapter 5. Suffice it to say, here, employers owe their employees a duty of care. That duty extends to providing employees with a safe place to work. Bullying, harassment and intimidation have been found to breach the duty of care requirements, with the victim's poor mental health often leading to the initiation of related claims. Failing to provide employees with a psychologically safe place to work may expose employers to a claim of negligence.

Equality Act 2010: Most employers, of course, want to ensure their employees are treated in a non-discriminatory way and are aware that they must comply with the Equality Act 2010. Despite much media coverage in recent years, and despite the efforts of Mind and others to get those with mental health issues to speak out, however, there are reports that managers were actually less inclined to hire people with mental health problems in 2018 than they were in 2009 (Shaw Trust, 2018). In 2017, 52% of employers had a mental health policy, 30% higher than in 2009. Of those employers who had adopted mental health policies, 60% said they had done so to avoid litigation (up from 27% in 2009). Despite increased awareness of mental health at work, employers have a growing lack of confidence in discussing mental health matters with their employees. In 2009, 90% of employers felt comfortable talking about mental health with their staff members. In 2017, this figure was just 64% (Shaw Trust, 2018). Employers seem to be steering clear of employing people with mental health issues for fear of litigation. Perhaps it is unsurprising, therefore, that the proportion of people willing to disclose their mental health condition is in decline (see chapter 4). This research suggests there is now a higher chance that employers may be found to have discriminated against someone with a mental health issue than there was ten years ago. Notably, mental health discrimination claims against employers are more often succeeding today; this could be because case law is making it increasingly easy for people to be successful in bringing this type of claim (Charlton, 2016). Leaders and managers must make sure they treat people from all parts of the community fairly, including those with mental health issues, otherwise they face what should be avoidable liabilities and bad publicity, and could develop a reputation that undermines their efforts to become an employer of choice amongst job applicants, employees and the wider community.

HASAWA: In the UK, Health and safety legislation and related regulations place three responsibilities upon an employer:

1   They have a duty of care towards their employees
2   They have a responsibility to take steps that are reasonably practicable
3   They have a responsibility to keep up to date.

HASAWA does not specifically refer to physical or mental health. It sets out general provisions, duties and obligations about health, safety and welfare.

Mental health is a rapidly emerging management discipline, which employers have an increasing legal obligation to address. In keeping up to date, one key area employers should monitor is that of newly emerging hazards. For example, employers now have to meet the challenge presented by display screens, as regulations on display screen equipment were introduced in 1992. In 2018, the HSE updated its guidance on first aid to include mental health (Fox, 2018). Just as employers need to keep up to date with display screen regulations, so they need to keep up to date on regulations covering mental health. Stevenson and Farmer (2017) make several recommendations in *Thriving at Work*, their review of mental health and employers. One of these suggestions was that the HSE should update its guidance to employers regarding mental health. The HSE subsequently updated its guidance, setting out more recently when it will investigate stress at work (Liversedge, 2019). This new standard extends an employer's duty of care, especially in respect of causes of workplace stress, and increases what is considered reasonably practicable for employers to do when addressing mental health hazards. If employers do not take steps to improve how they manage mental health at work, proving they are staying up to date with HSE guidance and prevailing market practice, they run the risk of falling foul of the law. Employers must continually strengthen their mental health management practices if they are to remain compliant with HASAWA.

Throughout many developed countries, laws exist relating to negligence, as was discussed in chapter 5. In the UK, HASAWA and the Equality Act 2010 also provide a legal basis for UK employers to manage mental health effectively. Doing so will ensure higher standards of legal compliance and a reduced chance of litigation and sanction.

The Moral Argument

Many employers have been interested in, and may have invested in, the area of social responsibility (SR) since the 1950s, when the notion of doing social good became more popular. Since then, SR has evolved, firstly into corporate social responsibility (CSR) and more recently towards the more progressive practice of social wellbeing. At each phase of its evolution, the notion of doing social good has broadened. Today, more progressive organisations may align their social wellbeing activity with the 17 Sustainable Development Goals set out by the United Nations in 2015 (Figure 6.1).

Figure 6.1 *United Nations' sustainable development goals*

Full details of the UN's sustainable development goals can be found at:
https://www.un.org/sustainabledevelopment/sustainable-development-goals/.

Employers who care about sustainability might think about taking their lead from the UN. As these 17 goals demonstrate, sustainability is about every aspect of society, including good health and wellbeing and reduced inequality, including the disadvantaged, such as those people with poor mental health.

Until recently, actions around sustainability tended to focus on 'green' sourcing, energy-efficient operations, recycling materials and the disposal of waste. Today, many employers also focus on local job creation and providing local economic benefits. These employers are following the lead of localised public procurement initiatives, for example, which specify that suppliers should create local jobs, source locally and develop local economic activity. Steven/Farmer (2017) make such a recommendation regarding mental health. Many organisations also have partnerships with charities, through which they provide benefits to chosen aspects of the community. These charitable partnerships are often developed in conjunction with the organisation's employees, forming part of the employee engagement and social wellbeing programmes.

Some employers are also making efforts to reduce long-standing inequality issues, such as those related to gender. Pay parity has become a hot topic, particularly since the introduction in the UK in 2017 of gender pay gap reporting. Today, it is evident that many employers are making a conscious effort to address the gender pay gap, although there is still a long way to go. Employers are making similar efforts regarding their workforce's ethnic and religious mix and the UK Government is also exploring the introduction of ethnicity pay reporting. But what of mental health?

It seems that far fewer employers are addressing the mental health gap. Only four in ten organisations (39%) have policies or systems in place to support employees with common mental health problems (Stevenson and Farmer, 2017). Many employers appear to be over-looking their own workforce when it comes to mental health, and we might even accuse some of them of hypocrisy. What is the point of creating jobs through a local economic development partnership then dismissing employees when they disclose a mental health condition? (see chapter 2). How does disciplining or dismissing employees, or forcing them to resign, help society address the mental health crisis? Doing so perpetuates the 'cycle of suffering' (again, see chapter 2).

Employers can do social good, however, by recruiting and retaining people with mental health problems. This group certainly needs support; as we saw in chapter 2, people living with mental health issues typically:

- live in the lowest household income bracket

- are more likely to be out of work

- are more likely to get fired or resign because of their mental health issues or stigma.

Those people with poor mental health may or may not be able to contribute to an organisation in every traditional sense, however they may well be able to emotionally, spiritually, intellectually (see below) and socially, as well as practically. Here, there is a strong moral case for employing them, as was made earlier.

Some types of mental health condition clearly limit people, and there is a strong moral case to be made for employers developing a compassionate policy. If employers really want to develop their social wellbeing 'reach', they will offer employment, support and compassion to people with mental health issues.

The Technical Argument

Employing people with a mental health condition may present employers with a perceived or actual burden. However, there are also benefits to doing this.

Some research suggests there is a correlation between intelligence (as measured in IQ tests) and mental health conditions, and that those who score highly in IQ tests have a higher propensity to developing mental health issues (Hambrick, 2017). Additionally, A large number of studies in the past few decades support a link between creativity and mental illnesses (Sussman, 2007). Employing people with mental health issues may add a particular sort of brainpower to an organisation. The development of strategy requires analytical and creative thought, for example, and some people with a high IQ may excel in this. People with mental health conditions may thus improve the organisation's ability to plan and execute on its strategic intent, and may be valuable on particular sorts of teams, including executive leadership teams.

In today's fast-paced, ever-changing world, new ideas are essential if an organisation is to remain competitive. The process of innovation benefits from people who are more creative. Those with ADHD, for example, have been found to be valuable at work (Lavelle, 2018) as they tend to be more creative and have an enhanced ability to think 'outside the box' (Sarkis, 2011). Similarly, people who have a schizotypal disorder or autism appear to be more likely to come up with new ideas than those who do not (Perina, 2017); and people with autism and attention deficit disorder (ADD) have been found to have an ability to 'hyper-focus', enabling them to zero in on an activity with ultra-intense concentration, often for hours at a time (Bittner, 2017). Because of these 'superpowers', some organisations have invested in employing people with mental health issues. These include software companies, who have discovered that employees with autism can make excellent computer programmers (Dayan, 2017).

People with a mental health issue do not need to have a 'superpower' to have a positive effect at work, however. Many people with mental health conditions keep it to themselves, managing their condition effectively and still performing well at work, presenting no burden whatsoever to their employer. In fact, some people with mental health conditions try harder, possessing a strong desire to perform well so as to ensure they effectively mask their condition from their employer. Chas Howes, former Chief Financial Officer of the UK-based clothing and fashion retailer Superdry, led the company's growth over a ten-year period, increasing its sales nearly ten-fold. During this time, Chas Howes appears to have suffered with depression. His condition appears not to have held him or his employer back (BBC Radio 4, 2019). Quite the opposite, perhaps. Some people with a mental health issue seem determined not to be held back by it. Chas Howes is far from unique. Inside Out (2020, online) is a well-known UK mental health charity. It operates what it refers to as its 'Leader Board'. This Leader Board contains details of numerous organisational leaders who have declared publicly they have some form of mental health issue or have personal experience of supporting somebody with a mental health issue. It is apparent from this Leader Board that directors and senior managers can be active and effective in very demanding senior roles, with their mental health issue doing little to mar their performance. In many cases, their condition may even help them perform better.

It seems, therefore, that people with a mental health condition are often eager to play a role in organisations and can even offer particular advantages. But for this to work, their colleagues must be willing to accept them. In one study (Shaw Trust, 2018), the majority of respondents stated that they were willing to work with someone with a mental health condition; but it is concerning that 31% of senior managers responded that they would not be willing to do so and 56% of employers stated they would not employ an individual with a mental health condition. The InsideOut Leader Board provides evidence that some employers are open-minded to employing people with mental health issues and that doing so may not be as risky as some may fear.

In terms of an organisation's policy on mental health, who better to take a key role in its development than employees with mental health issues themselves? It is likely that they will be able to empathise with other people in the same situation more effectively than other members of the organisation, so should be able to play a significant role in developing policies around mental health.

The main point I want to bring out here is that mental health sufferers are not always a burden. They can be of great benefit, if given the opportunity.

The Commercial Argument

There is significant evidence to suggest organisations gain a financial advantage by investing in supporting the mental health and wellbeing of their employees.

Increased productivity: Mental health can have a significant effect on workplace productivity. Employees can be absent because of poor mental health; or they can attend work but be less productive than they are when they are well. Only two in five employees work at peak performance (Deloitte, 2017). A clear link has been established between productivity and mental health (Stevenson and Farmer, 2017). Oswald et al. (2015), found that when made happier, the productivity of employees increased by approximately 12%. Events causing sadness (eg. bereavement, family illness) were found by Oswald et al. to correspond with reduced productivity. In fact, Professor Dame Carol Black, expert government advisor on health and work, believes that 'improved wellbeing in the workplace can improve productivity by up to 25%' (Politics Home, 2019). It is becoming increasingly important for organisations to develop the management expertise required to improve employee happiness and reduce employee sadness. Your organisation's mental health Competent Person (CP) should possess this expertise. Focusing on the mental health element of wellbeing, improvements in productivity have proven to be even more effective. In the United States, the 'Be Well at Work' mental health improvement initiative recorded a 50% reduction in at-work productivity loss, known as 'presenteeism' (American Heart Association, 2018). It seems clear that by looking after its employees' mental wellbeing, an organisation will find that staff morale and loyalty will increase, as well as its innovation, productivity and profits (Deloitte, 2017).

Reduced sickness absence: Poor mental health is the most significant cause of long-term sickness absence, accounting for 23% of all such absences (Chartered Institute of Personnel and Development, 2019). This excludes stress, which accounts for another 20%.

Some employers are now trying to tackle the growing issue of mental health-related sickness absence. The most commonly recognised achievement of health and wellbeing activity undertaken by employers is better morale and engagement. A third of employers reported that these activities lead to a healthier and more inclusive culture, while just under a third report it has lowered their sickness absence (CIPD, 2018). Other studies have suggested such activities might have an even greater impact; in the United States, the 'Be Well at Work' mental health improvement initiative recorded a 50% reduction in absence due to mental health sickness (American Heart Association, 2018).

Increased staff retention: As we saw in chapter 2, approximately 20% of people who declare a mental health condition at work are disciplined, demoted or dismissed, or forced to resign. In light of these figures, it is evident mental ill-health is contributing towards employee turnover. Organisations might also be losing staff where leaders fail to create psychologically safe environments (Christiansen, 2019). For example, safe environments allow opinions to be expressed without negative or adverse repercussions; but if a leader allows one employee to admonish another (say, for making an 'out of the box' suggestion, as we established some employees with ADHD or autism might), stress can arise and workplace relationships deteriorate. We saw in chapter 1 workplace relationships have been identified as a major cause of stress at work. It is therefore up to leaders to create a positive mental health culture, thereby minimising the adverse effects of stress on employees and encouraging them to remain loyal to the organisation. This will improve staff retention and reduce the costs (both direct and indirect) of high staff turnover, as well as driving other benefits, such as those related to productivity and innovation.

Cost-benefit analysis of mental health interventions: Studies consistently show that employers financially benefit from their investment in improving mental health and wellbeing at work. Researchers have found that absence and lost productivity as a result of depression cost employers more than four times the cost of employee medical treatment (World Federation for Mental Health, 2017). Other studies are equally encouraging, with investment in mental health treatment in general shown to be cost-effective. The American Heart Association (2018) has found that many evidence-based mental health treatments can save $2 to $4 for every dollar invested in prevention and early intervention. In the UK, Deloitte (2020) found an average return of £5 for every £1 spent on mental health. Again, this indicates that up to a four-fold or five-fold return on investment may be available to employers, justifying investment in mental health and wellbeing.

Organisations must consider the legal, moral, technical and commercial arguments for employing people with a mental health condition. It is not always about cost-benefits; the moral argument is also important. The arguments can be weighed using the expertise–need approach presented in Figure 6.2.

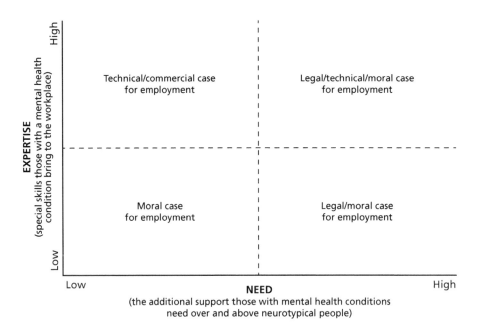

Figure 6.2 *The mental health expertise–need matrix*

Employing people with mental health issues appears to be a dilemma for employers. This is unsurprising, as the arguments are so nuanced. Yes, the moral case for employing them may be strong, but other cases may support the moral consideration, making some employment decisions easier than others. The matrix in Figure 6.2 can help with the decision-making process:

- The decision to employ high-expertise-low-need people should be quick and easy to arrive at. A person with mental health issues who offers high benefits with low needs is a 'keeper'. They may require little more support than the average employee, yet may offer greater advantages. Hire today!

- With high-expertise-high-need people, the expertise they provide may be of strategic importance, say, in product innovation or information systems development. In this case, satisfying the employee's needs may be more than justified by the expertise provided and the employment decision should again be obvious and swift. If the equation is not so obviously in favour of hiring, then moral considerations may tip the balance towards hiring.

- With low-expertise-low-need people, the moral case is strong, but so is the commercial case. An employer can do social good by hiring a person who offers lower than average expertise but does not require heavy investment because they have low needs. Such employees can play a valuable role at work, when tasked in a suitable manner, given clear instruction, and effectively supported and supervised.

- Low-expertise-high-need people are the most special of cases, and deserve special consideration. They may have long-term conditions that impact their daily lives. It is in such cases that the moral case is most strong. Employers should extend their social wellbeing 'reach', open their hearts and bring these individuals into their organisation out of nothing more than compassion. These people merit the support of employers, as they should appeal to the employer's sense of social wellbeing and social justice. In time, customers and wider community members may think it strange, even socially unacceptable, that employers do not employ people with more severe mental health issues.

Nobody likes the idea of pigeonholing vulnerable people. However, as many managers have been found to be reluctant to employ those with mental health issues (chapter 4), it makes sense to help these managers develop a more progressive approach to employment decisions. It may be useful to provide managers with a rationale and framework within which to make recruitment decisions, especially when this helps managers better relate to the social wellbeing beliefs and values the organisation holds. The 'expertise–need' matrix in Figure 6.2 may help managers to justify hiring a person with a mental health issue. By providing managers with this matrix or similar guidance, leaders are effectively giving hiring managers permission to do so, rather than leaving managers to apply any prejudices, consciously or subconsciously, during any recruitment process.

As we can see, then, by addressing mental health issues effectively, employers can benefit from increased productivity, reduced sickness absence and increased staff retention. There is a strong cost-benefit argument for doing so but this should not be the only consideration; in addition to the commercial case, employers should weigh the legal, moral and technical reasons for investing in better mental health at work. Perhaps most powerfully, instead of benefiting society through initiatives outside the organisation (such as supporting charities), organisations should also do so *inside* the organisation by employing people from particular groups, such as those with mental health issues. The arguments combine to make a compelling case that I think most investors, leaders and managers will agree more than justifies why the organisation should consider investing in an effective workplace mental health strategy.

This chapter presented the positive case for employing people with mental health issues based on the legal, moral, technical and commercial arguments. It provided much evidence in support of each of these cases. The chapter continued with the notion of assessing potential employees based upon 'expertise–need', partly as a means of overcoming potential management hiring prejudices. Finally, it called for employers to develop a social conscience when considering the most vulnerable of people with poor mental health.

The main take-outs from this chapter are:

- There is a positive case for considering employing people with mental health issues.
- This case includes legal, moral, technical and commercial arguments.

- There is a legal argument that people with certain mental health conditions are pro-tected from discrimination in law. HASAWA also places duty-of-care obligations upon employers.

- The moral case suggests that organisations with strong social values, which want to increase their social wellbeing 'reach', might consider employing people with mental health issues. Instead of just supporting external mental health charities, a commitment to mental health can be shown by employing people with poor mental health.

- The technical case considered the 'superpowers' of some people with mental health issues. For example, people who have autism, a schizotypal disorder or ADHD might prove to be highly creative, have the ability to hyper-focus or be good at problem solving.

- The commercial case shows how investing in wellbeing and mental health can increase productivity (by up to 25% in some cases), increase employee retention, reduce sickness absence and reduce related costs.

- People with mental health issues can be assessed as potential employees by using a 'expertise–need' matrix. Although it feels clumsy to pigeonhole people, this framework may help encourage and guide managers when making recruitment decisions.

References

American Heart Association (2018) *Mental Health – A workforce crisis*. Available at: *https:// ceoroundtable.heart.org/wp-content/uploads/2018/12/Mental-Health-Full-Report-March-25-2019.pdf* (accessed 29 November 2019).

BBC Radio 4 (2019) *The Highest Hill in the Cotswolds*. (Podcast.) Available at: https://www.bbc. co.uk/programmes/m0008p3b (accessed 22 February 2020).

Bittner, J.R. (2017) *Autism, ADD, and Hyperfocus*. Available at: *https://seriouslynotboring. com/2017/03/13/autism-add-hyperfocus/* (accessed 2 January 2020).

Charlton, J. (2016) Are 'discrimination arising from disability' claims an easy route to employment tribunal wins? *Personnel Today*, 5 October. Available at: *https://www. personneltoday.com/hr/are-discrimination-arising-from-disability-claims-an-easy-route-to-employment-tribunal-wins/* (accessed 29 November 2019).

Chartered Institute of Personnel and Development (2018) *Health and Well-being at Work. Survey report May 2018*. Available at: *https://www.cipd.co.uk/Images/health-and-well-being-at-work_tcm18-40863.pdf* (accessed 28 November 2019).

Chartered Institute of Personnel and Development (2019) *Health and Well-being at Work. Survey report April 2019*. Available at: *https://www.cipd.co.uk/Images/health-and-well-being-at-work-2019.v1_tcm18-55881.pdf* (accessed 29 November 2019).

Christiansen, J. (2019) 8 things leaders do that make employees quit. *Harvard Business Review*, 10 September. Available at: *https://hbr.org/2019/09/8-things-leaders-do-that-make-employees-quit* (accessed 29 November 2019).

Dayan, Z. (2017) 3 reasons autistic children excel at computer coding. *Codemonkey*, 8 October. Available at: https://www.codemonkey.com/blog/3-reasons-autistic-children-excel-at-computer-programming/ (accessed 16 January 2020).

Deloitte (2017) *At a tipping point? Workplace mental health and wellbeing*. Available at: https:// www2.deloitte.com/content/dam/Deloitte/uk/Documents/public-sector/deloitte-uk-workplace-mental-health-n-wellbeing.pdf (accessed 22 November 2019).

Deloitte (2020) Poor mental health costs UK employers up to £45 billion a year (online). Available at: *https://www2.deloitte.com/uk/en/pages/press-releases/articles/poor-mental-health-costs-uk-employers-up-to-pound-45-billion-a-year.html#* (accessed 21 March 2020).

Fox, M. (2018). Will the new HSE guidelines on workplace mental health make any difference? Available at: *https://www.peoplemanagement.co.uk/voices/comment/will-new-guidelines-on-workplace-mental-health-make-difference* (accessed 12 November 2019).

Hambrick, D.Z. (2017) Bad news for the highly intelligent. *Scientific American*, 5 December. Available at: *https://www.scientificamerican.com/article/bad-news-for-the-highly-intelligent/* (accessed 2 January 2020).

InsideOut (2020). *The InsideOut LeaderBoard for 2019*. (Online). Available at: *https://inside-out. org/leaderboard/* (accessed on 20 Jan 2020).

Lavelle, D. (2018) 'People with ADHD can be incredibly valuable at work'. *The Guardian*, 18 March. Available at: *https://www.theguardian.com/society/2018/mar/18/people-with-adhd-incredibly-valuable-at-work-diagnosis-support* (accessed 29 November 2019).

Liversedge, B. (2019). HSE announces it will inspect stress "if criteria are met" (online). Available at: *https://www.britsafe.org/publications/safety-management-magazine/safety-management-magazine/2019/hse-announces-it-will-inspect-stress-if-criteria-are-met/* (accessed 12 February 2020).

Mental Health Foundation (online). *How to support mental health at work*. Available at: https://www.mentalhealth.org.uk/publications/how-support-mental-health-work (accessed 12 December 2019).

Occupational Safety and Health Administration (online). *OSH Act of 1970 – General Duty Clause*. Available at: https://www.osha.gov/laws-regs/oshact/section5-duties (accessed 22 January 2020).

Oswald, A. J., Proto, E. and Sgroi, D (2015) *Happiness and productivity*. Journal of Labor Economics, 33 (4). pp. 789-822 (online). Available at: https://wrap.warwick.ac.uk/63228/7/WRAP_Oswald_681096.pdf (accessed 3 March 2020).

Perina, K. (2017) The mad genius mystery. *Psychology Today*, 4 July. Available at: *https://www.psychologytoday.com/gb/articles/201707/the-mad-genius-mystery* (accessed 2 January 2020).

Politics Home (2019) Solving the wellbeing puzzle. *Politics Home* 16 February. Available at: https://www.politicshome.com/news/uk/social-affairs/opinion/british-safety-council/101886/dame-carol-black-solving-wellbeing (accessed 9 March 2020).

Safe Work Australia (online). *The Essential Guide to Work Health and Safety for Organisations that Engage Volunteers*. Available at: https://www.safeworkaustralia.gov.au/book/essential-guide-work-health-and-safety-organisations-engage-volunteers (accessed 12 February 2020).

Sarkis S.A. (2011) Is the ADHD brain more creative? *Psychology Today*, 13 June. Available at: *https://www.psychologytoday.com/gb/blog/here-there-and-everywhere/201106/is-the-adhd-brain-more-creative* (accessed 2 January 2020).

Shaw Trust (2018) *Mental Health at Work: Still the last taboo*. Available at: *https://www.shaw-trust.org.uk/ShawTrustMediaLibraries/ShawTrust/ShawTrust/Documents/Shaw-Trust-Mental-Health-at-Work-Report-2018-full_1.pdf* (accessed 29 November 2019).

Stevenson, D. and Farmer, P. (2017) *Thriving at Work: The Stevenson/Farmer review of mental health and employers*. Available at: *https://assets.publishing.service.gov.uk/government/uploads/system/uploads/attachment_data/file/658145/thriving-at-work-stevenson-farmer-review.pdf* (accessed 28 October 2019).

Sussman, A. (2007) Mental illness and creativity: a neurological view of the 'tortured artist'. *Stanford Journal of Neuroscience* 1:1, Fall. Available at: *https://pdfs.semanticscholar.org/892c/aa15e19b00cc0e56ae825959ce905d2fed94.pdf* (accessed 3 January 2020).

United Nations (online) *About the Sustainable Development Goals*. Available at: *https://www. un.org/sustainabledevelopment/sustainable-development-goals/* (accessed 24 February 2020).

World Federation for Mental Health (2017) *Mental Health in the Workplace: World Mental Health Day 2017*. Available at: *https://wfmh.global/wp-content/uploads/2017-wmhd-report-english.pdf* (accessed 28 November 2019).

7

CHALLENGES
FOR EMPLOYERS

We have discovered in Part I of this book that approximately half of all employees do not disclose their mental health condition to their manager. Just think about that for a moment. Why should this be the case?

Perhaps it has to do with the individual themselves. Perhaps they have feelings of shame, low self-esteem, low self-appreciation or guilt for being different from 'normal'. Perhaps they feel confident enough but just want to keep their personal matters confidential…just in case.

Perhaps it has to do with the employer. Perhaps the person with a mental health condition is fearful (it must be called 'fear') about how their manager and colleagues will react if they disclose their condition. Whatever the organisation's policies say, the employee will quickly learn through the grapevine how they can expect to be treated. Perhaps they know that 20% of employees who disclose their mental health condition to their employer are demoted, disciplined, dismissed or forced to resign. This is the type of reaction they may fear, together with the danger of becoming stigmatised. Perhaps employees fear speaking out because employers do not take mental health seriously. 'Just 51% of employers currently have a mental health policy in place (Robert Walters, online).

For those who choose to keep their condition confidential, it may mean keeping up a pretence. They may do all sorts of things to protect their secret, such as lying on job application forms and about the cause of sickness absence. Many employees invent a physical illness as the cause of their sickness absence, rather than admitting it is because of a mental health issue (see chapter 2). This cannot be right. No self-respecting employer should want their employees to hide an illness or feel so fearful of reprisals that they are compelled to lie. A culture of lying and deceit can only undermine productivity and performance.

The first step employers should take in finding a better way to deal with this has nothing to do with getting employees to talk about their mental health condition. I established in chapter 4 that without preliminary work, this would be wrong, contrary to current popular belief. The first step is for employers to plan and implement support measures so they can provide appropriate support to employees when they do choose to disclose a mental health issue. After all, an employer puts in place physical health and safety controls *before* an employee undertakes any activities. Mental health should be no different. Employers should therefore plan and implement an appropriate mental health management system that is suitable for their activities and their workforce, before expecting employees to disclose mental health issues.

Leaping ahead for a moment, once the employer has put in place an appropriate mental health culture and management system, a key consideration arises: how are employees to learn about the culture and intent behind the management system? There are two routes to this: employees can largely find out for themselves, or their employer can tell them about it. This sounds obvious. But as Figure 7.1 shows, a perception gap can easily arise between leaders and employees regarding perceptions of any mental health management system.

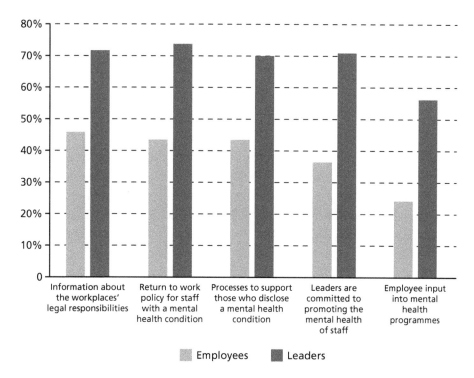

Figure 7.1 *Leader/employee perception of the organisation's mental health culture*

Source: Consult Australia / BeyondBlue, 2014

The dilemma of any employee facing the decision about whether to disclose their mental health condition was discussed in chapter 2. But there are some important additional aspects for the employer to consider which might affect an employee's decision.

An employee will decide whether to disclose a mental health condition based upon a number of judgements they must make about their employer. These judgements are about things like the culture of the organisation, the example of leaders and what precedents have been set through the treatment of other employees.

Culture: What is the culture in the organisation as it relates to mental health? Is it proactive and supportive? Are there numerous initiatives in place (like those in Part II of this book) to support good mental health at work? Do its leaders really try to ensure all employees are caring, compassionate and supportive towards those colleagues with mental health issues? If the answers to these questions are mostly positive, an employee may feel that their employer will be supportive of their condition should they choose to disclose it. The chance of support might feel high, with the risk of reprisal feeling low. On the other hand, if the answers to these questions are generally negative, the employee will almost certainly remain silent about their condition and may even be minded to resign, in the hope of finding a more supportive employer; one who they do not just feel comfortable working for, but one they feel proud to work for.

Leadership example: There is a simple acid test question here: what proportion of the most senior people in the organisation – say the top 10% of earners – have a mental health issue they talk about openly? Some of the senior leaders will have mental health issues. Managers are just as likely to have mental health issues as other employees; in fact, according to Palmer (2019) they are more likely to do so. If these leaders – who are ultimately responsible for hiring and firing decisions, and who set the culture of the organisation – feel uncomfortable or unable to talk openly about their own mental health, what signal does that send to employees, especially employees with mental health issues themselves? And if none of the top 10% earners in the organisation have a mental health issue, does that suggest a glass ceiling is operating, preventing those with mental health issues from reaching the top? Leading by example is a powerful tool for organisational leaders, which they can use to demonstrate a supportive mental health culture. If they remain silent on the matter, leaders may inadvertently reveal the organisation's true culture, despite what else it might say and do about mental health.

Precedent: Employees talk to one another. They talk about workload. About pay. About management. About each other. They talk openly and, sometimes, in confidence to one another. They may even talk about how people with mental health issues have been treated by management. This can provide further powerful evidence about the reaction an employee can expect should they choose to disclose a mental health condition. And just as one swallow does not make a summer, so one favourable case does not offset ten adverse cases. Too often an employer makes a token gesture in an attempt to demonstrate a positive orientation and garner support. However, if in the eyes of employees, the reality is that the majority of people who disclose a mental health condition are not treated well, word will spread, employees will fear the worst and those with mental health conditions will remain silent. Depressed productivity, poor employee retention and high sickness absence will prevail.

Employees will make their own minds up about whether to divulge their mental health condition. They will weigh up various factors before deciding. With such a high proportion of employees not revealing their mental health condition and lying about the reason for their sickness absence, it is evident employers have a long way to go before they establish high levels of employee confidence in their mental health culture. How to develop employee confidence, through demonstrating and developing commitment, is the subject of chapter 10.

Establishing a Positive Mental Health Culture

There is an alternative to allowing employees to come to their own conclusions about the mental health culture of an organisation. Employers can instead ensure employees know their workplace and its people are tolerant, understanding and supportive by creating a supportive mental health culture and operating an effective mental health management system.

When considering the above three factors of *culture*, *leadership example* and *precedent*, employers should not simply design and implement a mental health management system. They need to develop a *culture* of proactive and compassionate mental health support as well. This culture must not be allowed to become simply a tick-box exercise. It requires leaders to bring to life in the organisation a level of understanding, a level of empathy and a level of support that is tangible to all employees, whether or not they have a mental health issue. Employees should be able to see it, feel it and grasp it, in a physical and emotional sense. When employees speak about mental health, they should do so in a positive manner, with respect for the employer's culture, policies and practices.

Such a positive mental health culture will only emerge if leaders set an example. In fact, they need to set examples in two respects: lived experience and the treatment of others.

Lived experience: Leaders should openly discuss their own mental health issues and experiences at work. There is much talk today of lived experience becoming a currency on social media. Bloggers and vloggers share their stories online, gaining followers and likes (as well as criticism) from doing so. And so it should be with leaders. They, too, should leverage the currency that is attached to lived experience by sharing with employees their own stories about their mental health, along with anecdotes about how they themselves have been supported by the employer. Leading by example and engaging employees on a personal, almost intimate level, may prove the most effective of tools when shaping the organisation's mental health culture. In terms of demonstrating lived experience, leaders will need to possess two qualities: courage and confidence.

Courage, because he or she might feel embarrassed, reticent and awkward when they publicly reveal a mental health issue. This comes partly from the fact that many generations have taught their offspring to put on a brave face, not to be a burden, to keep issues that might hold them back to themselves and to fit in as best they can. It is only natural for the leader to feel apprehensive, given the decades of 'covering up' that has preceded them.

Confidence, because, as we have seen, revealing a mental health issue can lead to demotion, disciplinary action or dismissal, so the leader must feel confident they have the support of those above them (eg. directors, shareholders) and their peers (eg. fellow leaders and managers). If a leader's peers do not support them under such circumstances, it will demonstrate intolerance and undermine all efforts to establish a positive mental health culture. This will undermine optimum productivity, which in turn will depress the organisation's financial performance. Only a vote in favour of mental health will help the organisation achieve optimum financial performance.

Treatment of others: Leaders should not just encourage other employees to treat employees with mental health issues with care and compassion; they should also do so themselves. Leading by example literally demonstrates the level of care and compassion all employees are expected to show towards employees with mental health issues. The more cases where leaders demonstrate care and compassion towards employees with mental health issues, the more established a positive mental health culture will become. On the same point, there is no reason to exclude employees with mental health issues from promotion opportunities. Somebody with depression can function at a senior level, as the InsideOut Leader Board in chapter 6 demonstrated. Equally, somebody with anxiety can be good at operations management or accountancy. A mental health condition does not necessarily limit somebody. In some cases, it can empower them (see chapter 6). When leading by example, leaders have the opportunity to demonstrate they are 'mental-health-friendly' by promoting employees with mental health issues. Not doing so may well reinforce the belief that a glass ceiling operates in the organisation, so preventing such employees from securing senior roles. This may be interpreted as demonstrating that there is one rule for employees and another for leaders. This cannot be a desirable state of affairs in any organisation. In a meritocracy, employees with mental health issues can have merit too. Leaders must allow for this to come to the surface and recognise it when it emerges. In an organisation that is 'mental-health-friendly', all employees will be lifted up, not put down.

Coming to Terms with Perceived Risks

Having considered employees' disclosure dilemma and how leaders can develop a positive mental health culture, the question of potential problems arises.

Employees with mental health issues are often, by their very nature, complex. Their condition might make their behaviour unusual, unpredictable or even offensive. Should employers be concerned about the risks and challenges associated with employing people with mental health issues?

Chapter 6 considered the positive case for employing people with mental health issues. The legal, moral, technical and commercial cases were put forward. However, some employers may still feel that employees with mental health issues pose too significant a risk, one that may not be worth taking. To many people, this may be fair consideration. But is not taking positive action the answer?

In chapter 6, we established that investing in mental health can lead to an improvement in productivity of up to 25%. We also established that employers can support employees as part of their efforts to 'do social good'. So, what else might be holding employers back?

Stepping out of a comfort zone: Given the lack of established practice in the field of workplace mental health management, leaders and managers may lack understanding of the issue and lack certainty in knowing what to do about it (Figure 1.7). They may experience a level of discomfort around the subject. This is the same sort of anxiety people often feel before undertaking significant, high-profile tasks for the first time. Things like public speaking, the launch of a new product or IT system, or participation in competitive sports usually provide a mixture of sensations: a rush of adrenaline and a moment of euphoria, combined with anxiety or even dread. These sensations are typical when stepping out of a comfort zone into something new. Because of the lack of 'standardisation' in managing mental health, it would be surprising if leaders and managers did not have concerns about the potential problems associated with mental health management, and at the same time fail to recognise possible benefits. They may feel mental health is a 'lose-lose' scenario. If they do try to approach mental health positively, it may lead to numerous problems. If they do not, they may be criticised. As with all the other endeavours that cause anxiety, the key to success often lies in planning and preparation. If rigorous planning is undertaken and significant effort is put into preparations, when it comes to the event itself, the participant can face the challenge with confidence and even with a sense of ambition. They will know, with a high level of certainty, what they will do and how they will do it, and some may even be confident enough to predict the outcome. The same should be the case with workplace mental health management.

The reality, not the perception: When people think of mental health, their thoughts are often negative. In their mind's eye they see a child with ADHD being unruly, someone with bipolar disorder attempting suicide or a person with Tourette syndrome, swearing. How can there possibly be any benefits from managing workplace mental health? Actually, doing so may not be as problematic as some leaders and managers fear. Not by a long way. The vast majority of all people with mental health issues are, naturally, in work. They may have a higher desire to work than many, and are usually grateful of employment. They often show their appreciation through hard work. In many cases they want to repay their employer simply for employing them. And that's even before the employer has offered to support them. Just think how appreciative and hardworking they might be if their employer supported them as well! The reality is that employees with mental health issues are likely to pose less challenges for employers than they might think. Sure, they might need more time off, say, to see a therapist, and they may say or do the wrong thing from time to time, but on the whole, they will pose few challenges to the employer who has properly planned and prepared for managing mental health in the workplace. As we have seen, when a positive approach is taken to wellbeing, productivity can increase by up to 25%, employee retention rates can increase and sickness absence rates fall. Any worries about the problems mental health may pose would seem to be most relevant to workplaces in which mental health is poorly managed. Where workplace mental health is well managed, the benefits may well offset any adverse effects. For more information about employing the most challenging of people with mental health issues, charities such as Rethink Mental Illness may be able to offer guidance.

How Employers Can Gain Advantages From Managing Mental Health

Mental health may represent a real opportunity for employers who manage their employees' mental health well. As is the case with significant social challenges, the public sector often leads the way, and it is starting to do so with regard to mental health. Twenty years ago, when Black and minority ethnic (BME) groups and people with disabilities were excluded from certain aspects of society, the public sector stepped up. Its procurement policies changed, introducing the notion of 'inclusion' to private sector contractors bidding for work. These contractors were required by public bodies to state during the tendering process what percentage of their workforce was a member of a BME group and what percentage had disabilities, how that compared to the communities in which the contractor worked and what the contractor was doing to increase the workforce mix to better reflect those communities. Contractors changed. They put into practice new diversity and inclusion (D&I) policies that changed the composition of their workforce, reducing the barriers to gaining employment faced by particular groups. Some incredibly progressive contractors did far more, establishing disabled-only assembly plants, which supplied public body customers with materials during the construction phase of building contracts. Now, twenty years on, with mental health as an emerging crisis of the twenty-first century, the same position is developing. Public procurement policies are increasingly demanding that contractors provide information about their position, policies and practices as they relate to mental health. Private sector contractors can get on the front foot by taking a proactive approach to mental health, so increasing their chances of winning highly prized public sector contracts, further improving the payback on any investment made in managing mental health. Clearly, governments have a role here, by demanding in their tender documents that diversity and inclusion-related submissions have a strong mental health element.

As the mental health 'market' develops, employers face a choice – a classic marketing choice. When to enter the market? Should they sit back and wait for the market to develop, to identify with certainty how the market will operate in future, so they can enter the fray with clear intent and a clear plan of action? Or, should they take a 'first mover' position, set the pace, gain an early advantage and become renowned for being a thought leader? There are three considerations here:

1   **Legal requirement:** The UK's health and safety law does not recognise the difference between physical and mental health. Employers have a legal duty to protect *all* aspects of the health, safety and welfare of their employees. Not doing so sees employers run the risk of a claim against them, on the grounds of negligence, discrimination or health and safety (possibly related to a breach of their duty of care).

2   **Low-cost:** Many of the initiatives presented in this book are already being undertaken by employers, albeit not for mental health – writing policies, undertaking risk assessments and consulting with the workforce, for example. It would cost little extra to add the subject of mental health to these processes.

3   **Strong payback case:** Given that it offers potential productivity gains of up to 25%, and potentially other commercial advantages, it may make sound financial sense to employers to take a decisive, proactive and positive approach to mental health.

To sum up, mental health management is a legal requirement, certainly for all UK organisations. It represents a low-cost initiative that may pay back in the short-term and potentially yield financial advantages through productivity and commercial gains.

Employer Concern That an Employee Has a Mental Health Issue

Before concluding this chapter, I want to return to one of the dilemmas that employers may find themselves facing: whether a manager should say something to an employee about a suspected mental health issue. Here, employers have four options (see Figure 7.2).

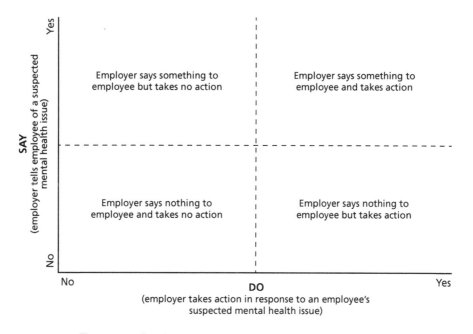

Figure 7.2 *Employer mental health concern response matrix*

Each of these options is now briefly considered.

Say nothing, do nothing: If nobody's safety is at risk, the employee is going a good job and nobody else is being adversely affected, the manager might decide to say nothing but keep the situation under review. They might make a note in the employee's file so that other appropriate people (such as human resources managers) are kept informed, but otherwise take no action. How notes are kept will depend on the employer's systems, but should be done sensitively and, where appropriate, confidentially.

Say something, do nothing: This is not an option for the progressive employer. No employee should be expected to deal with this type of situation alone, especially if the employee's poor mental health is being commented on, and possibly affected by, the employer. As with physical health and safety, the employer and the employee both have legal mental health management obligations under Sections 2 and 7 of HASAWA. Both have a responsibility: the employer to look after the mental health of their employee, and the employee to look after their own mental health.

Say nothing, do something: If an employer has suspicions that an employee may have a mental health issue, they can feasibly take action without saying anything to the employee. For example, if the employer is aware of stressors in an employee's life and can make a conjecture about the effects of these on the employee, they can make adjustments to address these. For instance, they may notice that an employee with autism has become possessive over a stapler, which should be a shared item, and is arguing over it with other employees. Without saying anything, the supportive manager provides the autistic person with their own stapler, labels it for them and ties it to their desk. Minor adjustments such as these can make a big difference. What may be a minor issue to most employees may be a major issue to an employee on the autism spectrum. *Say nothing, do something* may be thought of as the employer being the 'guardian angel' of employees' mental health. No fuss. No big deal. Just getting on with caring for employees' mental health without the need to talk about it. Of course, employers must still pay attention to the formal side of things, such as the risk assessment process and writing up.

Say something, do something: Sometimes, circumstances lead to the employer deciding they must say something to the employee, whether about their suspicion that the employee has a mental health condition or at least about their behaviour. This would be the correct course of action for the employer to take when there is any unacceptable behaviour in the workplace or the employee is clearly barely coping or in a state of distress. Having decided to intervene, the employer cannot then expect the employee to manage the situation alone. The employer must take some responsibility, and they are legally required to do so. They must satisfy themselves that all of the most preferred mental health control measures (eg. elimination) are in place and operating effectively. They must work with the employee to explore the causes of their unacceptable behaviour or distress. And where they can, employers should act before the employee does; only once the employer has exhausted all reasonably practicable control measures should the employee be expected to take action. And even then, the employer may be required to determine the best course of action for the employee to take. After all, employees do not determine what personal protective equipment (PPE) to wear when it comes to physical health and safety – it is the employer who determines the best PPE through risk assessments and consultation. The same should be the case with mental health.

Employers should have a clear policy around the subject of giving feedback to employees about a suspected mental health issue. Employers certainly won't want to make matters worse, embarrass the employee or create a negative atmosphere. Doing so could further harm an employee's mental health; hence the need for a policy and for a structured and supportive approach.

This chapter began by considering why employees might not tell their employer about their mental health condition. It speculated that this might be because of the employee themselves or their fear about their employer's response. Things an employee might consider before disclosing their condition were explored, including culture, leadership example and precedent. If these factors are favourable, an employee might disclose, trusting their employer to do the right thing. The chapter went on to show that leaders and managers either let employees reach their own conclusions about these factors or take a more proactive approach to influencing employee attitudes. In being more proactive, leaders were found to require courage and confidence, especially related to sharing their own lived experience of mental health, and were encouraged to come out of their comfort zone as it relates to mental health, and to act with confidence and ambition. They were also asked to ignore perceptions of mental health and learn about the realities of the subject and people with mental health issues. The chapter concluded by suggesting investing in mental health would help support efforts to ensure continuing legal compliance, this would be relatively low-cost and may even represent a strong financial case.

The main take-outs from this chapter are:

- Employers face the challenge of establishing a positive mental health culture. Given the news headlines, their workforce will at least expect it and probably demand it.

- Establishing a positive mental health culture should include making arrangements so that employees do not feel the need to lie and keep their condition a secret.

- Employees may be encouraged to disclose their condition if they believe their employer's culture is positive towards mental health. Before disclosing, employees will judge elements of the culture (eg. policies, procedures and training), the examples set by leaders in speaking out about their own experience, and the precedents leaders have set in how they have treated other people who have disclosed their condition.

- Speaking about their own lived experience is regarded as one of the most powerful things the directors of an organisation can do. These same leaders must also ensure, through their own actions and through the actions of other leaders and managers, that other employees who speak out are treated fairly.

- Leaders are encouraged to look at the facts, not the perception, when contemplating employing people with mental health issues. Of course, there are risks, as there are with all recruitment decisions. There are also many justifications (legal, moral, technical and commercial) and many opportunities (improvements in productivity). On balance, the justification appears strong, and most of the risks appear manageable and potentially acceptable.

- Employers should think about the best course of action to take should they suspect an employee might have a mental health issue. Generally speaking, employers have four options: 1) say nothing, do nothing; 2) say nothing, do something; 3) say something, do nothing; 4) say something, do something. Employers should take care not to make the situation worse.

References

Consult Australia / Beyond Blue (2014). *State of Workplace Mental Health in Australia.* (Online). Available at: *http://www.consultaustralia.com.au/docs/default-source/skills/striving-for-mentally-healthy-workplaces---web.pdf?sfvrsn=28* (accessed 28 November 2019).

Palmer, S. (2019) Managers more likely to be diagnosed with mental health issues than other employees. *People Management,* 8 October. Available at: *https://www.peoplemanagement. co.uk/news/articles/managers-more-likely-diagnosed-mental-health-condition-other-employees* (accessed 5 January 2020).

Robert Walters (online). *The important of mental health strategies in attracting top talent. https:// www.robertwalters.co.uk/hiring/campaigns/the-importance-of-mental-health-strategies-in-attracting-top-talent.html* (accessed 21 March 2020).

PART II

8

WHY A MANAGEMENT SYSTEM APPROACH?

In Part I, I gave readers an understanding of the mental health problem, developed the reader's empathy with people with mental health issues, introduced the principles of health and safety management, and explored differences between physical and mental health management. I went on to explore the law as it relates to mental health and the positive arguments for employing people with mental health issues, before concluding by explaining some of the challenges employers might face when implementing a mental health programme.

In Part II, I explore why employers might take a management system approach to mental health, before going on to discuss the '7 Principles' of workplace mental health management: 1) the management system; 2) commitment; 3) policy; 4) risk assessments; 5) the hierarchy of controls; 6) consultation; and 7) reporting. I follow this with a 10-point plan in which I make recommendations that are intended to improve mental health across society by developing laws and tightening the regulatory system. A summary of Parts I and II brings the book to a close.

In this chapter, I explore the rationale for taking a management system approach to the management of workplace mental health. This notion may not sit comfortably with some, and might feel too bureaucratic and impersonal, so I use some analogies to explore this point, such as looking after new-born babies and primary school children. Here, the need for compassion is perhaps at its greatest. I also reflect on what is normal working practice in most organisations.

Having considered the justification for the use of a management system approach, I then introduce the seven principles of the mental health management system and briefly describe and justify each of them. I conclude the chapter by setting out some of the advantages of taking a management system approach to mental health, which includes creating clarity and certainty in a field that may otherwise appear unstructured, complex and ambiguous.

Rationale for a Management System Approach to Mental Health

Why take a management system approach to mental health, which at its heart requires understanding, compassion and support? Surely a management system is too impersonal, too bureaucratic and too dispassionate? A management system approach is incongruent with the care and empathy that employees with mental health issues require, right?

These are fair points. Mental health is a highly sensitive matter. Employees with mental health issues may want their employers and colleagues to show them the utmost empathy. The last thing they would want is for mental health to become a tick-box exercise. And they would be right. It must not become that.

Before banishing the idea of a management systems approach, however, we need to reflect on some other health and welfare issues, for just a moment.

To begin, consider the most vulnerable of all groups, to whom the highest levels of compassion should be shown: new-born babies. Think of the management of new-born babies in a hospital delivery ward. Is a management system approach utilised here? In short, the answer is 'yes'. Access to maternity wards is strictly controlled. There are stringent documented control procedures regarding the care of new babies and their mothers. There are procedures relating to health observation checks for mother and baby, the control and provision of medication, the provision of sustenance, the control of visitor arrangements and to discharge procedures. Even care arrangements for the baby in their home will be assessed. Every measure possible to ensure the health, safety and welfare of mother and baby is designed and implemented through a comprehensive management system approach.

Let us now turn to another issue and another vulnerable group: child safety and welfare in primary schools. Children are one of the groups we care for the most. It is only right that their welfare and safety are given the highest priority. So, is a management system approach taken towards child protection in schools? The answer, again, is 'yes'. A highly bureaucratic process is in place in primary schools. Each primary school's governing body sets out its policies, overseeing and supervising the school's safeguarding and child protection policies. A specific governor may be assigned to head up this aspect of the school's operations. The governing body usually makes the school head responsible for implementing the safeguarding and child protection policy. The head writes procedures, issues these to staff and makes sure they are understood. He or she arranges training to ensure that all related policies and procedures operate effectively, and supervises practice to ensure teachers and other staff follow these policies and procedures correctly. Teachers working in schools and visitors to schools are usually required to undertake checks (such as a PVG Disclosure check in Scotland and a Disclosure and Barring Service (DBS) check elsewhere in the UK) before they are allowed to take on roles working with children. School heads rigorously enforce this process. Schools also operate strict policies about who can leave the school premises, when, and under what circumstances. In primary schools, children are rarely allowed out of school grounds at break time, for example, and if they must leave, they are required to be met by a known parent or guardian. The hand-over of the child to the carer is controlled by a school staff member who must follow a strict protocol. In primary schools, a highly bureaucratic management system approach is taken to child protection. The comprehensiveness of the management system and the rigidity of its implementation provide for the highest levels of child protection.

I now consider a third example: everyday workers, going about their everyday jobs, in everyday life. How are millions of hardworking people protected? Is a management system approach in operation? A comprehensive answer to this was offered in chapter 3, which set out the health and safety management system approach commonly employed by most large employers. First, the law demands that employers take a management system approach; in the UK, the Management of Health and Safety at Work Regulations apply (UK Government, 1999). Second, the enforcing authorities of governments around the world espouse a management system approach; the UK's Health & Safety Executive (HSE) expects employers to operate in accordance with HSG65 or similar (HSE, 2013). Third, expert advisers (eg. consultants, lawyers, trainers) also promote a management system approach. Finally, most organisations actually manage the health, safety and welfare of their workers using a management system approach similar to that set out in chapter 3. There is an almost perfect alignment – at least in terms of intent – of the law, of enforcement, of advice and of practice. In everyday life, physical health and safety is managed using a management system approach. Not only this, but the law, enforcement, advice and practice all recognise and accommodate the special circumstances of vulnerable groups, such as young adults and pregnant mothers (HSE, online).

Why should the management of workplace mental health be any different to the management of physical health or the management of other vulnerable groups?

A workplace mental health management system should seek to protect vulnerable groups, such as those with mental health issues, just as a physical health and safety management system seeks to protect the young and pregnant mothers. There should be no difference between physical health management and mental health management. Both should utilise a management system approach.

When we reflect on these three examples, it is evident that a management system approach is always employed with regard to some of the most vulnerable groups in society – when compassion and caring must be at their height. This is *because* of the need for the highest levels of compassion and caring. Nobody wants to see even one mistake being made. Everybody concerned wants to make sure the right thing is done for those being protected. A management system provides the highest level of certainty that the right thing will be done, first time, every time. Management systems are usually comprehensively designed and rigorously operated. Given the intangible and complex nature of mental health, a management system approach provides the highest level of certainty when considering how to manage it.

Having identified the near perfect alignment of laws, enforcement, advice and practice in respect of physical health and safety, does the same alignment exist for mental health? Chapter 4 explored this point, considering the various differences between physical and mental health management. It found the law to be ambiguous, enforcement non-existent, advice patchy and practice confused. Because of this lack of clarity and certainty, workplace mental health, in this early stage of its development, *must* be managed using a management system approach.

When viewed in this way, taking a management system approach to workplace mental health management makes sense. If the preferred approach is to use a management system, then, the next question is how such a management system might be structured.

Structure of a Workplace Mental Health Management System

It has been established that employers are likely to have a less developed understanding of mental health than physical health and will probably be less certain about what to do about mental health (see Figure 1.7). This, in itself, might make designing a workplace mental health management system difficult. However, this need not be the case.

As identified in chapter 5, it is a legal requirement for companies to provide for the health, safety and welfare of their employees. UK law does not distinguish between physical and mental health. As a result, and as a starting point, physical health and safety management practices can be extrapolated for the purposes of managing mental health at work. This approach creates clarity and certainty in the minds of leaders and managers, as they understand the methods of physical health and safety management. The core methods (corresponding to the '7 Principles') are:

1 The management system framework

2 Commitment

3 Policy

4 Risk assessments

5 Hierarchy of controls

6 Consultation

7 Reporting.

This book uses these seven physical health and safety management methods to create a framework for managing mental health. In Part II, I set out the seven core elements – the '7 Principles' – for managing mental health at work. Each of these is now introduced.

Principle 1: The management system. A management system requires a structured approach to be taken. The structured approach proposed for workplace mental health is based on the core elements of the management system used in the management of physical health and safety. This system comprises the management system and the other six elements (or principles) listed here, which form the structure of the management system. This structure provides for clear plans and actions. It creates a common purpose, ease of understanding and, generally speaking, provides for sure-footed implementation. A management system approach typically makes for rigorous control, allowing the intent of leaders to be executed as envisaged. This approach should also be easy to implement, as leaders and managers will already be familiar with management systems. The UK's best-known management system is ISO9001, a quality management system that was first published more than 30 years ago. There are now more than one million organisations in the UK certified to the ISO9001 quality management standard. This is just one example of employers long being familiar with a management system approach. In short, a management system approach creates clarity and certainty, along with ease of implementation.

Principle 2: Commitment. A high level of commitment is usually needed if an organisation is to be successful in any aspect of its activities. Mental health is no different. Given that approximately half of employers would prefer not to hire somebody with a mental health issue and a third of leaders would not wish to have somebody in the senior management team with mental health issues, gaining the commitment of all employees is even more vital. Prejudices must be overcome. Discrimination must be stamped out. Only through strong leadership, and ensuring that everyone buys into it and is committed to it, will mental health improve – and for some organisations this will even become a differentiator. Those organisations with strong mental health strategies will become employers of choice, able to attract the very best talent. As we saw in Part I, in the average company only two in five employees currently perform at their optimum levels. Strong mental health provision can improve this ratio, enabling progressive employers to increase productivity and gain other advantages over their rivals, increasing the chances of organisational success.

Principle 3: Policy. Most employers are legally required to have a written health and safety policy – and bear in mind that UK law does not distinguish between physical health and safety and mental health and safety. Typically, policies should be designed to set out an organisation's statement of intent, the organisation and management structure as it relates to mental health, along with the arrangements that will be put in place to implement the policy. The utilisation of policies in organisations is a well-established practice that is well understood by leaders and employees alike, and has been proven to be highly effective. Policies are communicated through a variety of methods to every employee in the organisation. They are reviewed regularly and as required, to ensure they remain effective and up to date. Policies provide leaders with a familiar, ready-made way to set out a course of action for mental health. Through such a policy, leaders can make a commitment to mental health, demonstrating leadership and allocating resources, as well as providing operational methodologies through procedures included in the policy's arrangements section. The mental health policy plays a vital role in setting out the organisation's commitment to mental health. Either an express commitment to mental health should be made in the existing health and safety policy, or a separate mental health policy should be adopted. Either way, mental health must be given its own focus.

Principle 4: Risk assessments. UK law requires employers to undertake risk assessments. At the risk of repeating myself, the law does not distinguish between physical and mental health management. Employers therefore have a legal duty to undertake workplace mental health risk assessments. In the United States, the Occupational Safety and Health Administration (OSHA) recommends a five-step approach to risk assessments (US OSHA, online, a): 1) identify hazards; 2) identify who can be harmed and how; 3) evaluate the risks and determine control measures; 4) write up the risk assessment and implement it; and 5) review the risk assessment. In the case of mental health, the first step in this risk assessment process may immediately pose challenges for employers. Exactly what mental health hazards exist in the workplace? These hazards are often invisible and intangible, they are not commonly under-stood, and their identification and measurement can be subjective. In chapter 1, several work-related causes of poor mental health were identified. My research of studies has led to the development of a mental health hazard model comprising the 12 standard mental health hazards along with 12 workplace mental health hazards. These mental health haz-ards are presented in chapter 12, to give leaders and managers a ready-made answer to the question 'What mental health hazards should I assess?'. This standardised set of hazards will guide employers, providing them with a starting point when they are identifying mental health hazards. The chapter then presents an already well understood approach to assessing hazards based upon *likelihood* and *severity*. Those hazards with the highest likelihood and severity require the greatest control. Control measures should be developed based on the 'hierarchy of controls' approach.

Principle 5: Hierarchy of controls. The hierarchy of controls is a world-renowned method of managing workplace risks, used throughout many countries including the United States (US OSHA, online b). It provides a structured approach in which the most preferred methods of risk control are put in place first. These are the methods that relate to the elimination and substitution of mental health risks. Only once these most preferred methods of risk con-trol have been implemented are further risk reduction methods employed. These further methods include engineering controls (physical safeguards), then administrative controls (administrative and supervisory procedures). Finally comes personal protective equipment (PPE), the least preferred method of risk control. In mental health terms, PPE equates to providing mindfulness and resilience training. Employers must recognise that this sort of training is the least preferred approach to mental health management, and should not think that employee training alone is adequate, although clearly it has a role and can have a ben-eficial effect. A far more strategic, broader approach is required, and mental health-related training should be supplemental to the central methods adopted. In principle, the hierarchy of controls first places the burden of responsibility for managing risk on the employer. Only after the employer has taken all reasonably practicable steps should the employee's responsibili-ties be considered. When we look at it this way, we see that the burden of responsibility is on the employee when it comes to most contemporary workplace mental health interventions, such as speaking out and resilience training. Employers have a duty to eliminate and reduce risks before expecting the employee to act.

Principle 6: Consultation. In the UK and Australia, employer organisations are required by law to consult with their workforce in respect of health and safety. In most countries, doing so is regarded as good practice. Given the scale of the issue and the significance of its impact, it seems wise to consult the workforce on mental health. The formal, two-way process of consultation that is most familiar to leaders and managers was established in the second half of the nineteenth century, when trade unions arranged for workers to be represented in consultations with employers. Today, most organisations consult their workforce on health and safety. Many also consult their workforce on other activities, such as new product development, information technology systems and, perhaps most obviously, pay and terms of employment. Consultation gives leaders the opportunity to find out about their employees' perspective. It may present the opportunity to test new ideas, jointly assess information from third parties (eg. reports on new equipment or techniques), discuss statistical data and trends, reach agreement on things and jointly develop action plans. Given that a large proportion of many workforces have mental health issues, it would appear logical and obvious to consult with employees on mental health, whether or not it is a legal requirement in your country.

Principle 7: Reporting. Luca Pacioli introduced financial performance measurement to the world in the fifteenth century. With a 500-year back-story, no wonder key performance indicators (KPIs) have become a way of life for most organisations. The need to measure performance has literally spawned an industry – the industry of reporting – which has been turbocharged by the digital revolution. Big data is now the big thing. Endless aspects of performance can now be monitored, measured and managed. But what should be measured when it comes to mental health? Answering this question is a vital starting point. If an employee said they had an idea to boost organisational productivity by up to 12% or even 25%, as we saw might be possible in chapter 6, leaders would listen. They would give the employee time to explain, they would develop a deep understanding of the idea, consider how it could work and deliberate on the feasibility of its implementation. A 12% or even 25% increase in productivity could be a game-changer, for customers and shareholders alike. There's no doubt about it – such an initiative would be high priority when considering what to measure. And this is exactly what the management of mental health and wellbeing represents: the opportunity to improve productivity by up to 12% or even 25%. Like any other significant initiative, mental health requires monitoring, measurement and management. In many organisations, some relevant measures will already be in place. These might include employee retention, average length of service and employee satisfaction. Other useful measures might be gender pay gap reporting, which is now a legal requirement in the UK. Measures such as this could provide a convenient first step by extending them to include employees with mental health issues. What is employee retention amongst employees with mental health issues? What is their average length of service? What is their average pay? What are the results of each of these questions, for each of the past five years? Is the trend positive or negative? In large employers, most human resources departments will be able to answers these questions; all leaders need to do is ask. Reporting provides leaders and managers with strategic and tactical measures for managing mental health. Through monitoring and reporting, leaders and managers can quantify the effect their approach to mental health is having on employees and upon the organisation. That said, leaders and managers should ask employees too. Some employees with mental health issues will really appreciate a senior manager taking a personal interest in how they feel.

Conclusion

A management system approach provides a set of protocols that set out how work should be undertaken. Protocols create a disciplined approach, providing clarity and certainty for managers and employees alike. As we saw earlier in this chapter when we spoke about the management of maternity wards and primary schools, management systems intend to make sure, through expert drafting, that the correct actions are taken and no mistakes are made. In the case of workplace mental health management, the use of a management system, along with related policies and procedures, provides clarity of instruction and increases the certainty of achieving the desired outcomes. Mental health is less tangible than physical health, so requires this structured approach. The structured approach proposed here brings mental health to life in the workplace in a way most leaders, managers and employees can relate to: through policies, plans and actions.

Some leaders and managers will have a concern that engaging more fully with mental health might be like opening Pandora's box. They might be uncertain about what might happen if they do it. However, leaders and managers should not be overly cautious about mental health. In reality, mental health is simply another management challenge. Employees with mental health issues require care, support and compassion. Leaders and managers can take a familiar management system approach to managing such employees, one that will provide clarity and certainty, as well as offering a good level of care and compassion. As we have identified, such a system may also provide many benefits, including increased productivity, increased employee retention and reduced sickness absence. If approached positively, mental health presents a real opportunity for all organisations, including potentially improving bottom line profitability.

In this chapter, we considered the utilising of a management system approach for mental health. We looked at examples of where such systems are already in use, including maternity wards, primary schools and when managing physical health and safety in everyday work life. The seven core elements, or principles, of physical health and safety management were introduced and their relevance to the management of mental health in the workplace was established. This management system approach offers greater protection to vulnerable groups because of the clarity and certainty it creates. A systemised approach need not be a dispassionate approach.

The main take-outs from this chapter are:

- Managing workplace mental health using a management system provides a strategic, structured and systematic approach.

- Some people might not see mental health as the type of subject that should be managed using a bureaucratic management system approach.

- However, when contemplating other places in society where high levels of care and compassion are required (eg. maternity units and primary schools), each was found to utilise a management systems approach to managing the people they care for.

- A management system approach is utilised to ensure policies and procedures prescribe the best course of action for the people being cared for and to minimise the chance of mistakes occurring.

- The workplace mental health management system proposed in this book comprises seven components: the management system itself, plus commitment, policy, risk assessments, the hierarchy of controls, consultation and reporting.

- Leaders and managers may hold fears about mental health and how best to manage it, with concerns relating to how to ensure they do the right thing and how to avoid potential mistakes and liabilities.

- These fears can be allayed through effectively planning and controlling how workplace mental health is managed – through a management system approach.

References

Health and Safety Executive (2013) *Managing for Health and Safety (HSG65)*. Available at: https://www.hse.gov.uk/pubns/books/hsg65.htm (accessed 2 January 2020).

Health and Safety Executive (online) *Expectant Mothers – FAQs*. Available at: *https://www.hse.gov.uk/mothers/faqs.htm* (accessed 25 February 2020).

UK Government (1999) *The Management of Health and Safety at Work Regulations 1999*. Available at: *http://www.legislation.gov.uk/uksi/1999/3242/contents/made* (accessed 5 January 2020).

US Occupational Safety and Health Administration (online a) *Recommended Practices for Safety and Health Programs – Hazard Identification and Assessment*. Available at: https://www.osha.gov/shpguidelines/hazard-identification.html (accessed 25 February 2020).

US Occupational Safety and Health Administration (online b) *Recommended Practices for Safety and Health Programs – Hazard Prevention and Control*. Available at: *https://www.osha.gov/shpguidelines/hazard-prevention.html* (accessed 25 February 2020).

PRINCIPLE 1: THE MANAGEMENT SYSTEM

In chapter 8, I outlined the rationale for a management system and gave a brief intro-duction to its seven principles. In this chapter, I focus on the proposed mental health management system itself. I start by reflecting on the management system used in physical health and safety in the workplace. I then draw out from this the core elements presented in this book, which comprise the proposed mental health management system. I then revisit the Plan-Do-Check-Act (PDCA) model and review it for the purposes of mental health management. I go on to suggest the use of a risk register approach to check mental health legal compliance, and a project management approach to implement the mental health plan. Finally, I explore the role of the leader and identify several essential leadership tasks that will ensure the success of a workplace mental health programme.

In chapter 3, I set out the core elements of the physical health and safety management system, and this is repeated here for ease (Figure 3.1).

Figure 3.1 *Core elements of managing health and safety*
Source: HSE, online

The mental health management system proposed in this book considers several of the core elements in Figure 3.1 to produce the '7 Principles' of workplace mental health management:

- **Principle 1: The management system.** The management system is covered in this chap-ter, which addresses the core element of 'managing for health and safety', as well as the elements of 'leadership' and 'management' in Figure 3.1.

- **Principle 2: Commitment.** This is covered in chapter 10. Commitment partly covers the elements of 'leadership' and 'management' in Figure 3.1, including how to gain the whole of the organisation's commitment to mental health.

- **Principle 3: Policy.** This is addressed in chapter 11. Policy also partly covers 'leadership' and 'management', but also relates to 'legal compliance' and managing 'business risks', or 'organisational risks' in the public and not-for-profit space (Figure 3.1). It is a legal requirement for employers to have a health and safety policy, which will be a core element of any mental health management system. Here, the notion of 'competence' is also introduced, as policies typically include details of the relevant organisation and management structure, and such a structure must include a competent person. In law, the notion of a 'competent person' exists. When managing mental health, policy will include details of the management structure and where the mental health competent person sits within it.

- **Principle 4: Risk assessments.** 'Risk profiling' (Figure 3.1) and risk assessments are presented in chapter 12. Risk management covers the standardised five-step approach to managing risks: identify hazards; identify who can be harmed and how; assess the risks and determine control measures; write up the risk assessment and implement it; and review the risk assessment.

- **Principle 5: Hierarchy of controls.** Chapter 13 covers 'managing for mental health and safety'. It does so by applying the hierarchy of controls to mental health, based on: elimination; substitution; isolation; engineering controls; administrative controls; and personal protective equipment, building on the 'risk profiling' element of Figure 3.1.

- **Principle 6: Consultation.** Employee involvement is achieved through 'consultation', the subject of chapter 14. Consultation addresses the 'worker involvement' aspect of Figure 3.1. Consultation is a two-way process that allows for exchanges between managers and employees, with the aim of improving the effectiveness with which mental health is managed.

- **Principle 7: Reporting.** This is addressed in chapter 15. It relates to the 'management' and 'managing business risks' components of the management framework used for managing health and safety (Figure 3.1).

My proposed system for the management of workplace mental health adopts and adapts the core elements of the HSE's management system and is presented in Figure 9.1.

Three of the proposed core components of this system address UK legal compliance issues: Principle 1, which relates to having a written mental health policy; Principle 4, which relates to undertaking mental health risk assessments; and Principle 6, which relates to consulting with the workforce in respect of health and safety, which includes consultation about mental health.

The mental health management system proposed here aims to mirror best practice from the HSE's (physical) health and safety management system, whilst seeking to ensure legal compliance in respect of mental health. It is designed to be robust and fit for purpose, providing organisations with a ready-made, easy-to-implement approach for managing workplace mental health.

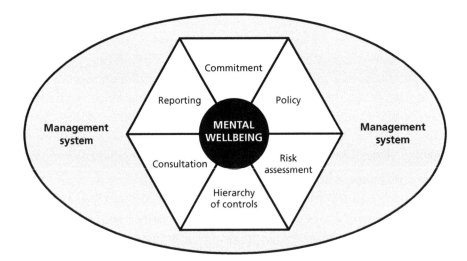

Figure 9.1 *Mental health management system*

Plan-Do-Check-Act

The Plan-Do-Check-Act (PDCA) model (Figure 3.2) provides us with a ready-made approach to mental health management.

The PDCA model can be developed to provide for the detailed actions required when managing workplace mental health. Some of the actions an employer might consider are presented in Table 9.1.

In reality, of course, the basic action plan in Table 9.1 would be developed to become far more comprehensive and would comprise many more actions, in the same way as an action plan for physical health and safety would be developed.

A project management approach might be advisable, certainly in the early stages of mental health programme design and implementation. In this case, the project manager may want to manage the project using methods such as:

- creating a risk register
- identifying project team members and coordinating them
- naming the person responsible for each task

- stating the 'due date' of each task

- monitoring the progress of effort (eg. the proportion of each task that has been completed)

- monitoring the progress of time (eg. amount of planned time per task that has elapsed and whether the 'due date' is likely to be achieved)

- identifying interdependent tasks and managing related risks

- establishing a colour coding system (say, traffic lights) to show the progress of each task.

Table 9.1   *The Plan-Do-Check-Act model as applied to a mental health action plan*

PDCA model steps	Actions
Plan	• Develop a mental health policy • Develop a mental health skills matrix* • Determine the mental health management structure • Appoint a mental health competent person • Gain senior leadership team approval for the mental health policy, plan and programme
Do	• Identify workplace mental health hazards and risks. Determine controls. Write up risk assessments • Implement the hierarchy of controls to manage mental health risks • Provide employees with mental health information, training, instruction and supervision • Implement mental health consultation groups
Check	• Develop mental health reporting tools and a report suite, and appoint people to produce reports • Measure the mental health of the workforce • Assess the impact of mental health initiatives • Investigate mental health incidents and improve control measures accordingly • Identify mental health best practice from external sources and incorporate learning into action plans
Act	• Review the mental health policy, action plans and programme • Identify lessons learned from incident investigation. Implement improvements • Identify issues from consultation groups. Implement improvement action plans • Identify issues from reports such as trends. Implement improvement action plans

* *Source: The Manager's Resource Handbook, 2016*

IThe mental health competent person or a project manager will almost certainly need to be appointed to oversee the management of the mental health programme's implementation.

The senior leadership team should take an active interest in the mental health programme, especially given that:

- it discharges similar responsibilities to those related to physical health and safety management, some of which are a legal requirement
- mental health creates employment dispute liabilities, which should be effectively managed and mitigated
- a significant productivity gain might be achieved if the programme is well-executed, driving the organisation's financial performance
- the programme may affect the organisation's ability to leverage commercial opportunities.

This book promotes the use of well-established management methods to manage mental health, not only in terms of the management system for doing so, but also in all other respects, including project management.

Managing Business/Organisational Risks

'Managing business risks' appears at the top of the HSE health and safety management model in Figure 3.1. This model shows that health and safety management is a subset of wider business risk management practice. These wider management practices, along with physical health and safety management practices, can be considered to determine the core elements of a typical risk management approach, which might include:

- risk register
- executive oversight
- internal and external audits
- external advisors
- avoiding complacency.

These aspects of risk management can then be applied to mental health management, as set out below.

Risk register: Each organisation must ensure it is operating in a legally compliant manner. Given the level of ambiguity that was identified in respect of the law as it applies to mental health (see chapter 5), it is prudent for organisations to check that their policies and practices adequately discharge their legal obligations. In many organisations, a legal compliance register approach is taken (Moses, 2017); suffice it to say that a similar approach is recommended for mental health. Typically, each entry on a risk register would include:

- the relevant Act or laws, along with the relevant section(s) of laws that apply
- the duties and obligations these laws impose upon the organisation
- how these duties are being discharged through specific actions
- the adequacy of these actions
- any vulnerabilities (eg. actions that do not fully discharge the legal obligation)
- the mitigation methods used to counter vulnerabilities
- the value and other impacts of any liabilities that might arise from obligations and vulnerabilities
- the source of funds and other measures that are available to meet these liabilities.

As the HSE is unlikely to award any sanctions for mental health non-compliance currently, most organisational risks are likely to relate to employment disputes arising under the Equality Act 2010, or through claims of negligence. Nevertheless, it would be prudent to manage risks, as a minimum, in accordance with HSE guidance so as to minimise the chances of a successful claim being brought against the organisation, especially as some of the legal cases presented in chapter 5 found against employers for failing to provide a safe place to work.

Executive oversight: Business risk is often concerned with potential disasters, commercial risks, information technology resilience risks, security risks, operational risks, pandemic risks and so on. In many organisations, a member of the Executive Leadership Team (ELT) oversees health and safety risks. This is especially the case in higher risk industries, such as construction, transport and manufacturing. Typically, the ELT member responsible will review health and safety performance at routine (eg. monthly, quarterly) meetings. Because of its scale and impact, and given legal compliance requirements, mental health should be given the same profile and attention as physical health, and should be overseen in the same way: through executive oversight.

Internal and external audits: Audits might be undertaken for a number of reasons, including checking compliance with the law, with ISO and other management standards and with the organisation's own policies. Having set out its mental health policy, leaders must ensure compliance with it. A variety of approaches can be taken, including: using internal auditors and/or external auditors (consultants); getting managers to check on each other; arranging for leaders to undertake inspections; and using employees to assess the compliance of their own and colleagues' activities. By checking that policies and procedures are being complied with, the likelihood of a risk becoming a liability is reduced.

External advisors: Risk management needs a continuous updating process to be in place. As circumstances change, risks may change, so new control measures will need to be developed as a result. Mental health, like physical health, represents a risk that needs managing. Mental health management is a relatively new discipline, as was established in chapter 4. It is also of strategic importance, since it affects much of the workforce and can have a profound effect on the organisation's activities and performance. Given these circumstances, it seems prudent to seek input from external experts. Experts are often amongst the vanguard, developing new and best practices they are in a position to share with leaders of employer organisations. By reaching out to advisors, organisations can help to increase the pace of implementation and the effectiveness of any mental health programme, so reducing related risks. External advisors can thus play an important role in managing workplace mental health.

Avoiding complacency: In the case of mental health, leaders themselves can sometimes represent a risk. They may think they know all about mental health and how to manage it. They may think their organisation is doing enough. Figure 7.1 showed how a perception gap can emerge, with leaders perceiving mental health management to be effective but employees feeling it to be far less so. As with any emerging management discipline, the early stage of development is often exponential. Leaders should ask two questions: What will our mental health policy and management practice need to be like in two or three years? And how will we get there? One thing is certain. Today's workplace mental health practices will be overtaken within a year. Leaders must identify how to keep up with, or even how to take a leading role in driving mental health market developments, thereby avoiding complacency. There are other methods of managing organisational risk. In addition to looking externally at best practice, leaders should read across from their other risk management methods and apply the most suitable techniques to the management of workplace mental health. Innovation also presents an additional way in which to drive the continual improvement of mental health management.

A rigorous management approach is required, given the scale of the issue, the strategic nature of the challenge, and the effect mental health can have on productivity and possibly profitability.

The Mental Health Management System and the Role of Leaders

Leadership and management are two core elements of the physical health and safety management model. Leaders have a crucial role to play in any mental health management programme.

Ultimately, leaders must find their own role regarding mental health. The more senior, the more committed and the more involved the leader is, the more effective their mental health management system is likely to be. The leader will also appear more authentic to employees, so will be more likely to gain their buy-in to the organisation's mental health management programme. Some examples of the sort of leadership activities required for good mental health at work are:

- establishing belief and purpose
- gaining senior leadership team support
- allocating resources
- establishing the strategic direction
- reviewing policies and procedures
- delegating authority
- leading by example
- reviewing progress.

Establishing belief and purpose: Leaders must believe in mental health. They must identify the risks and opportunities presented by mental health matters, just as they would with physical health and safety. Given the positive case for mental health (see chapter 6) and the opportunities it represents, leaders must develop belief amongst all the Executive Leadership Team (ELT) members, then garner support and commitment from across the organisation.

Senior leadership team support: All of the ELT must believe in mental health. Shaw Trust (2018) found although the majority were willing to work with someone with a mental health condition, 31% of senior managers would not be willing to do so. This stigma must be brought to an end. All ELT leaders must believe in mental health, and truly satisfy themselves that the mental health policy, plan and programme will achieve their goals for mental health. Having agreed the mental health approach, they must all get behind it. If this does not happen, it will undermine the optimisation of the mental health management system and any related hope of an improvement in productivity and financial performance.

Allocating resources: Having agreed their organisation's approach to mental health, leaders must authorise the allocation of resources to deliver the mental health plan and programme. Resources should be sufficient. The number of employees who suffer mental ill-health is ten times higher than the number who suffer physical injury at work; this shows the scale of commitment required. Given over half of the days lost through illness relate to mental health, and given that investment in wellbeing and mental health can potentially improve productivity by up to 12% or even 25% (see chapter 6), there seems to be clear justification for making such an investment.

Establishing the strategic direction: Leaders must develop their organisation's mental health goals and objectives, and have a strong hand in the design of any strategic management system through which mental health will be managed. They must shape the culture of the organisation and the place mental health has in that culture. And they must cascade policy and plans so as to bring mental health management alive within the organisation. It cannot be a tick-box exercise.

Delegating authority: Leaders often delegate authority. They do so, for example, to empower and motivate others, reduce their own workload and ensure decisions take account of relevant details. As with other examples of delegated authority, leaders must consider whether and how to delegate authority for mental health management. A consultation group may be given the authority to change working practices where such changes are likely to increase support for employees with mental health issues, reduce mental health harm or reduce legal liabilities. A consultation group or steering group may wish to determine the delegated powers it requires to operate effectively, and request that these powers be delegated by the leaders. This, of course, is an isolated example. One of the 12 workplace mental health risk factors (see chapter 12) relates to 'control' over work. Delegating can, in itself, help improve mental health.

Leading by example: Leaders must set the pace and tone for mental health. If leaders are not seen to be talking about their own (possibly poor) mental health, how can they expect their employees to do so? Leaders should share their own experience, whether that be lived experience, experience supporting a relative or friend, or experience supporting colleagues at work. Most leaders can find a story to tell – a story they must tell – as part of the process of establishing an open and proactive mental health culture.

Reviewing progress: Leaders must identify ways of reviewing progress. Project and programme implementation, policy reviews, consultation meetings, risk assessments and other tasks and events present opportunities for leaders to actively participate in the mental health programme. Their involvement brings a sense of importance to the subject and creates momentum. Leaders must review the progress of their mental health programme periodically, to sustain its focus and momentum.

The above list of leadership roles is not exhaustive. Leaders should determine their own role in the organisation's mental health programme, bringing it to life through their own energy, commitment, personality and style.

This chapter presented the mental health management system, which I have developed from the HSE's physical health and safety management system. The key elements of the HSE model I extrapolated for the purposes of mental health management were: the management system itself; commitment; policy; risk assessments; the hierarchy of controls; consultation; and reporting. I suggested organisations use a risk register approach to ensure they manage mental health risk in the same way they manage other aspects of compliance. I also suggested a project management approach should be used during the implementation phase of the mental health management programme. I considered the Plan-Do-Check-Act (PDCA) model and applied its use to a mental health programme of work. I also explored some of the key tasks faced by those in leadership roles.

This chapter set out some of the actions to be taken when designing and implementing a workplace mental health management system. The key take-outs for employers include recommendations to:

- establish the role leaders will play in the management of mental health. Leaders must create belief and purpose, set strategic direction and lead by example, and should exercise executive oversight of mental health.

- design and implement a mental health management system. The management system proposed in Part II of this book would be a suitable start. However, the system provided in this book is a straw-man framework, which organisations should develop for their own purposes.

- create a mental health management risk register and manage risks accordingly. Employers should use risk management methods that they already employ in other areas. They should also ensure that the management system discharges the organisation's key mental health management legal obligations. Leaders can read across from physical health and safety management to identify many of these, but should also refer to the Equality Act 2010 and the law as it relates to negligence.

- use the 'Plan-Do-Check-Act' model to create implementable action plans. Employers should then cascade the management system and action plan through the management structure.

- allocate sufficient resources to mental health. This might include investing in the skills of the mental health competent person and training for the workforce and management, but also – perhaps most importantly – investing in the control measures to reduce the adverse effects of mental health hazards.

- use skills matrices to determine what roles require what type of training. Based on the risk profile, employers should determine which training is mandatory and which is desirable. They should also establish routines to ensure renewal training is undertaken in a timely manner.

- appoint subject matter champions for each of the core elements of the mental health management system, and use these champions to design, monitor and report back on their element of the management system (this, in itself, is a way of gaining commitment).

- use a project management approach during the implementation phase of the mental health programme. The programme will have many stakeholders, will almost certainly comprise dozens if not hundreds of tasks and will take weeks or months to implement. Given its scale and complexity, along with its importance, a project management approach is recommended.

- keep up to date with emerging best practice. Mental health is a new management discipline and it is developing at a rapid rate. It is important to avoid complacency and arrogance; if need be, external consultants who can advise on best practice should be used.

- establish a mental health management system review process. This review process might dovetail with the policy review process explored in chapter 11.

References

Health and Safety Executive (online) *Delivering Effective Arrangements.* Available at: *https://www.hse.gov.uk/managing/delivering/index.htm* (accessed 5 January 2020).

The Manager's Resource Handbook (2016). *What is a Skills Matrix and How do I Create One?* Available at: *http://www.managersresourcehandbook.com/skills-matrix-template/* (accessed 6 December 2019).

Moses, P. (2017) It's a risky business without a risk register. *The Law Society* 6 June. Available at: *https://www.lawsociety.org.uk/news/blog/its-risky-business-without-a-risk-register/* (accessed 5 December 2019).

Shaw Trust (2018) *Mental Health at Work: Still the last taboo.* Available at: *https://www.shaw-trust.org.uk/ShawTrustMediaLibraries/ShawTrust/ShawTrust/Documents/Shaw-Trust-Mental-Health-at-Work-Report-2018-full_1.pdf* (accessed 29 November 2019).

10

PRINCIPLE 2: COMMITMENT

In this chapter, I consider commitment. I start by asking why and how commitment to physical health and safety is achieved, then explore why gaining commitment is important. I then introduce the commitment cycle, which comprises six steps relating to:

1   Leadership
2   Practice
3   Perception
4   Trust
5   Commitment
6   Recognition.

The commitment cycle model describes how to gain commitment and how commitment can help support the development of a positive mental health culture. I conclude the chapter by considering how to maintain the cycle of commitment and how to avoid breaking it.

What is Commitment?

Commitment can be defined as dedication to a cause; understanding it, believing in it and supporting it. We can say it exists when leaders, managers and employees all live by the values and behaviours called for by the policy that requires commitment, and they do so on a continuing basis.

The HSE (online) provides some useful information about commitment. In physical health and safety management terms, it states that:

> *If you can successfully secure senior management commitment you should be able to show that:*
>
> - *senior management are visibly demonstrating support and participating in communication activities;*
> - *resources are being allocated, e.g. extra funding or time; and*
> - *authority is being delegated to relevant groups, e.g. a steering group.*

In terms of mental health, commitment must see similar senior management visibility and participation, allocation of adequate resources and suitable cascading of authority.

Why Gaining Commitment is Important

For the leader, commitment is mostly about optimisation.

Leaders will want their employees to be as committed as possible to the most important aspects of work; those that drive organisational performance towards the greatest possible success.

For many organisations, health and safety is a priority. Given that mental health issues are ten times more prevalent than physical health issues (Figure 1.1), and given that mental health and wellbeing can affect productivity by up to 12% or even 25% (chapter 6), organisations should think about prioritising mental health as they do physical health. If they choose to do this, they may find they can employ the same methods to gain the workforce's commitment to mental health as they do for physical health and safety. The methods for gaining commitment presented in this chapter can be applied to any aspect of organisational management where commitment is required, although there is one big difference which I will address shortly. Here, the methods referred to are applied to workplace mental health management.

Gaining Commitment to Mental Health

Given the scale and potential impact of the management of mental health at work, the wise organisation may well choose to commit to it fully, giving it the same priority as physical health and safety but with its own distinct goals and objectives.

Leaders of such organisations will want to demonstrate their own whole-hearted commitment to mental health, and will want the management team and entire workforce to follow suit.

Organisational commitment to mental health can be achieved through similar methods to those used to gain commitment to physical health and safety. For mental health management, these might include:

- the most senior executive involved in the day-to-day running of the organisation (often the managing director) taking a leading role in mental health
- the organisation's commitment to mental health being expressed through a mental health policy
- making sure the mental health policy is communicated throughout the organisation (say, by issuing the statement of intent section of the policy to everyone)
- leaders checking on how effective the mental health policy is being implemented by participating in related meetings, reviewing related reports and talking to employees
- reviewing the mental health policy periodically or as necessary (eg. when a significant change occurs), and keeping it up to date.

In essence, leaders must determine priorities, set policy, communicate that policy, gain buy-in, check implementation and undertake reviews. Doing so should help create a positive mental health culture.

There is a difference, however, between gaining commitment to mental health and gaining commitment to other aspects of work. Most initiatives that require commitment will be presented, discussed, planned and developed, with most employees willing to engage in discussions about them. The same cannot be said for mental health and this is where a difference arises. As we discovered in Part I, only about half of employers want to employ people with mental health issues and only about half of employees feel comfortable talking openly about their mental health. Fear of reprisal was identified as one of the barriers to openness. In light of this, leaders clearly need to take a more nuanced and considered approach if they are to get their employees' commitment.

Many leaders aim to develop a particular culture, perhaps by developing a set of values that inspire employees to behave in a way that brings that culture to life. Culture and values are about how leaders want their workforce (and others) to think, feel and behave. In the context of mental health, leaders will want their employees to think, feel and behave in a positive way. They will want all employees to feel they work for a mental-health-friendly employer, for employees with mental health issues to feel understood and well supported, and for other employees to treat them well, with understanding and compassion.

Leaders set about gaining commitment in order to get employees to think, feel and act in a certain way. This approach can be thought of as the 'commitment cycle'.

The Commitment Cycle

Commitment plays a major part in achieving success. Each team member will only put in the maximum amount of effort if they are fully committed to the cause. Maximum effort, combined with a high level of skill and a little luck, will usually equate to maximum performance. So, how does the leader gain their employees' maximum commitment to mental health?

Commitment, including towards mental health, can be gained through a six-step commitment cycle (Figure 10.1).

Before I explore each of the six steps, I should say that this process need not be linear. Sometimes, employees may be prepared to make a *commitment* simply after hearing a motivational speech or learning of an inspiring plan. For more cautious members of staff – including many with mental health issues, especially those who are wary of disclosing their condition – all of the six steps may need to be followed.

Having said that, leaders must follow all six steps – in order – if they are to demonstrate and gain commitment. They must start the process, setting the tone, strategic direction, policies and so on, to make all employees aware that a change is coming. They must then make sure that practice is developed to bring about the desired change, that new ways of working are introduced and that new perceptions are cultivated and nurtured. Employees must see for themselves that the change is real and the leaders mean what they say. If there is a sustained period of consistent practice, employees will develop trust in the leaders' intentions. They will see that the leaders mean what they say and, perhaps more importantly, do as they say.

Having seen *leadership* and *practice* in action, and having built *trust* based on *perception*, employees should now feel comfortable about making a *commitment* to the leaders and the cause. The last thing employees want is to commit early to a cause only to discover that their colleagues and the organisation's leaders are not committed to it. If that happens, those employees who have made the commitment could become isolated, humiliated and exposed. Leaders must start the process, then see it through. So, let us look first at leadership.

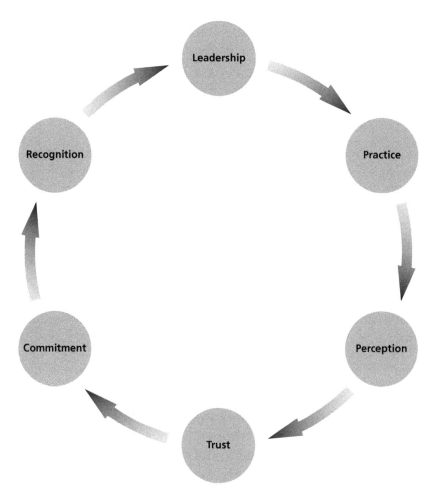

Figure 10.1 *The commitment cycle*

Step 1: Leadership

In chapter 9, I presented a number of leadership actions that can be taken, so at this point a summary of these should be enough for the reader to understand how leaders can make their own personal commitment towards mental health and start the process of gaining the commitment of others. At the *leadership* step of the six-step commitment cycle, leaders must:

- believe in the mental health cause
- garner the support of other leaders
- set the strategic direction for mental health
- put in place the mental health management structure
- approve the mental health policy, plan and programme
- allocate resources
- delegate authority
- participate, by being active in visibly checking on progress
- share personal mental health stories
- treat others fairly
- review performance.

Leaders can, of course, do far more than this. There are myriad ways to engage a workforce to gain buy-in and commitment. Leaders are encouraged to do all they can to do so.

However, a word of caution. Not getting involved, not showing commitment and not being visible will have the opposite effect. Failing to lead and participate will make employees feel that the mental health programme is simply something to pay lip-service to mental health, which will then seem little more than a current fad. Nobody, especially employees with mental health issues, will take it seriously. If there were issues around productivity, employee retention and sickness absence before the programme, they will continue. Leaders will only gain commitment from others, and turn negative issues into positive ones, when they demonstrate an authentic, whole-hearted commitment to mental health and have a high-visibility role in its administration.

Step 2: Practice

Practice relates to what actually happens. In most organisations, there are policies and procedures that set out what is to be done and how it is to be done. However, in many organisations, things happen that should not happen. Employees do things they are not supposed to. Take, as an example, an organisation that has a health and safety policy that details numerous arrangements, including the use of personal protective equipment (PPE). An employee performs an activity without wearing the PPE provided. Co-workers see the employee not wearing their PPE. They too decide not to wear it. A supervisor sees this happening. The supervisor turns a blind eye. Leaders are unaware of this non-compliance, and it goes on for many months. There is no enforcement. A lax health and safety culture emerges and employees perceive the organisation as one that does not care about their health and safety. In this case, despite the existence of good policies and procedures, health and safety *practice* is poor. This illustrates that leaders and managers must ensure that mental health policies and procedures are appropriate, that what happens in practice is in accordance with those policies and procedures, and that desired *practices* operate effectively throughout the entire organisation so that *practice* complies with policy. Only through rigorous and robust control of *practice* can leaders be sure their aims and intentions, set out in the mental health policies and procedures, will be properly implemented and the desired outcomes achieved.

Step 3: Perception

In the example of health and safety non-conformity in step 2, the perception of employees was that leaders did not care about their health and safety. This perception arose as leaders made numerous errors. They failed to check that their policies and procedures were being properly implemented. They failed to ensure the supervisor was doing their job properly. They let a non-compliant practice continue for many months. Ultimately, the leaders were responsible for the emergence of a poor health and safety culture, as well as for employees developing the *perception* that leaders did not care about their health and safety. Leaders and managers must manage the *perception* of employees, by ensuring mental health practice complies with policy. But managing perception, especially as it relates to mental health, must go further than this. Additional actions leaders may take include:

- taking a leading communication role in mental health (eg. actively promoting mental health as a priority)
- taking a participative role in how mental health is managed (eg. getting involved by checking effective practice and participating in feedback sessions)
- treating employees with mental health issues in a caring and compassionate manner
- doing good in a social setting that resonates (eg. supporting mental health charities).

Employees will believe things, and believe in things, that happen to them. If they are visited by a leader who asks about their mental health and that of their colleagues, employees will believe the leaders are genuinely interested in it. If an employee is invited to a consultation group about mental health, they will think the organisation takes it seriously. If employees hear toolbox talks about mental health, they will think the organisation is attempting to improve it. Employees' *perception* will be shaped by what happens in *practice*. Leaders must ensure the perceptions employees develop about mental health are in line with their own aspirations for mental health.

Step 4: Trust

Trust is built by consistently repeating a set of behaviours. The behaviours become predictable. Predictability creates reliability. Reliability creates trust. In terms of mental health, trust must be built if employees with mental health issues are to feel liberated and free from stigma and reprisals, so they can truly be the individuals they want to be and can perform as well as they can. (Of course, some may still choose not to disclose their mental health issues, even in a truly inclusive culture.) As we established in Part I, it does nothing for individual productivity if employees are carrying around secrets, wrestling with a condition alone and lying about the causes of sickness absence, rather than receiving support from their employer. Trust must be built if individual performance is to be optimised. And trust can be built through the perfect alignment of policy, practice and perception. This alignment requires leaders to explain their intentions about mental health, implementing related policies and procedures, checking on practice and, where necessary, enforcing compliance. This will create a positive cycle that creates a positive perception. A positive perception of mental health, and trust based on this positive perception, will only emerge when behaviours are consistently in accord with the workforce's definition of a fair and just mental health culture. A lax mental health culture must not be allowed to develop, and unfair treatment of people with mental health issues must not occur. Effective policies and procedures, combined with stringent enforcement, along with a huge amount of compassion, will lead to the workforce coming to trust their employer to support their mental health effectively.

Step 5: Commitment

As policy, practice and perception become aligned, trust is built. This is the point at which employees should feel able to share their mental health condition with their employer and possibly with colleagues, although understandably some may do so gradually, one step at a time. Once the employee has entrusted their mental health condition to their employer, there are two important things the employer must do immediately:

- The employer should ensure the management structure supporting the employee with mental health issues becomes 'tuned-in' to the employee. This might have to be achieved whilst keeping the employee's condition confidential. A degree of close management supervision by those 'in the know' may be required for a period, until supportive practices have been embedded, bearing in mind that local managers and supervisors may have no knowledge of the employee's condition.

- If the employee is experiencing stress and anxiety, the employer should ensure this improves as a result of their disclosure and does not deteriorate. Under no circumstances should an employee with mental health issues be made to feel regretful about their decision to disclose.[1] The employer must put in place the means to ensure employees who

---

[1]   This point is crucial. Employers may not realise how close they are to making the situation worse. They must keep in mind the *one small thing* principle (see chapter 1). Even after disclosure, there are two things the employer may still not know: 1) just how complex the employee's backstory is – many causes of symptoms such as PTSD may remain unknown to their employer; and 2) just how close to becoming distressed the employee may be. Handling disclosure poorly might push the employee from coping to distressed, and we cannot know what sort of a reaction might result. Suicide is all too common and is on the increase.

have disclosed their condition are protected – mainly from the known workplace risks to mental health (see chapter 12).

It is at the point of disclosure that care and compassion must be at their strongest, so that social good and employee welfare become the employer's priorities. This is where the employer may need to make the maximum investment in the employee with mental health issues. Get it right, and the employee is likely to show more loyalty and commitment to their employer than other employees.

Of late, there has been much talk of psychological safety. The aim of gaining commitment, as defined within this chapter, extends beyond the following four attributes of psychological safety as identified by the Institute of Healthcare Improvement Multimedia Team (2017):

1   Anyone can ask questions without looking stupid.

2   Anyone can ask for feedback without looking incompetent.

3   Anyone can be respectfully critical without appearing negative.

4   Anyone can suggest innovative ideas without being perceived as disruptive.

These four attributes focus on verbal comments, whether these are questioning, critical or innovative, and do not address non-verbal behaviours. Within the context of the 'the commitment cycle', for there to be psychological safety we should all accept unusual behaviours (verbal or non-verbal) caused by mental health conditions, without thought or comment. People who have mental health conditions that lead to them demonstrating 'odd' behaviours should be included, cared for, respected, trusted and valued, just like any other employee. A behavioural oddity isn't something to be mocked or looked down upon. So long as the behaviours are not actually unsafe, the ideal is for odd behaviours not to be perceived in a negative way, just as age, race, religion and gender should not be seen in a negative way. *That* would be discriminatory.

The cycle of commitment must achieve psychological safety for *all* people, whatever their background and however odd their behaviour.

Step 6: Recognition

Once the employer has created a positive perception of mental health and built trust, employees with mental health issues will feel more inclined to disclose their mental health condition to them. The support structure around the employee, and the employee themselves, must be well-managed. With the employer and the employee having come such a long way together, there remains one final action to complete the commitment cycle: *recognising the employee's decision to disclose* their condition and applauding their determination to see the journey of disclosure through to a place where the grass is greener – because the employer has made it so. Recognition gives the employee positive affirmation that they did the right thing in disclosing, that their fears of stigma and reprisal were misguided and unnecessary, and that they can truly trust their employer with knowledge of their mental health condition. Those employees who are willing to 'go public' about their mental health condition create the opportunity to speak about the support they have received from their employer, adding to the folklore of the organisation's positive mental health culture. With mental health, like in so many things, success breeds success. Good news stories will only encourage more employees to speak out and, as they do, the more likely it is that a positive cycle of encouragement and support for employees with mental health issues will develop.

The six-step commitment cycle provides a ready-made understanding for employers. It sets out the phases of commitment they must pursue to manage perceptions, build trust and gain commitment.

Avoiding Breaking the Commitment Cycle

We have seen how following the commitment cycle can lead to a wealth of positive consequences. The cycle must be perpetuated if it is to develop into a culture, however. Breaking the commitment cycle will have the opposite effect; simply, it cannot be allowed to be broken. The numerous risks that can arise that might break the cycle include:

- poor leadership commitment
- poor leadership involvement
- poor enforcement
- poor treatment of employees with mental health issues.

Breaking the commitment cycle can only undermine the objective of performance optimisation through the development of an effective mental health culture.

Poor leadership commitment: Leaders must *commit to mental health*. This is true for all of them – not just the managing director (or equivalent), but all members of the executive leadership team (ELT). As with any team, if just one member is off-message it can lead to the whole team failing. The first step is for the managing director to gain the commitment of all ELT members to the mental health agenda. Mental health will only become truly embedded in the organisation's culture if everyone presents as a united leadership team with a common purpose and shared vision.

Poor leadership involvement: Leaders must commit to mental health and *be seen to be committed* to it. All members of the leadership team must be seen to be open about mental health, actively interested in it, and firmly behind the organisation's mental health policy and plans. If they are not seen in this way it creates a void, which employees will fill with their own speculation about the leaders' attitudes. If there is no involvement, it will suggest there is no support. If there is no support, it will suggest there is no belief. If there is no belief, employees will believe that the policies and plans are just lip-service, and poor productivity, poor employee retention and poor sickness absence will be perpetuated.

Poor enforcement: Once leaders have made their commitment to mental health and are seen to be making that commitment, they must take an active role in checking progress and enforcing the mental health policy. This requires them to take a step beyond being seen to be involved. It requires them to *uphold* the policy. Every time a member of the ELT is involved in checking mental health policy implementation and finds that practice is not as intended, they must act to correct matters. Leaders must not allow poor practice to occur. If it does, it will spread, just as one bad apple rots the other apples in the barrel. Leaders must not turn a blind eye but must enforce, through appropriate means, the intent behind the policy. It was identified in chapter 1 that bullying, in particular, directly contributes to poor mental health. Leaders must never be bullies, and they must never tolerate or turn a blind eye to bullying. Policies (eg. anti-bullying) and procedures (eg. disciplinary) that exist to prevent undesirable behaviours must be enforced in order to stamp out negative behaviours, so that a positive mental health culture develops.

Poor treatment: Once they have gained the ELT's commitment, been seen to be involved, and enforced the policy, leaders must not let one mistake undermine their good efforts to develop a positive mental health culture. Leaders must ensure they treat employees who have mental health issues fairly so they are seen to be caring, compassionate and truly supportive of them. As we saw in Part I, around 20% of employees with mental health issues are demoted, disciplined, dismissed or forced to resign after disclosing a mental health issue at work (BITC, 2019). Employers who subject employees to this kind of treatment probably deserve the fruits of such activities: a poor reputation as an employer, poor productivity, poor employee retention and high sickness rates. By treating employees with mental health issues well, the narrative will change to one in which the friendly giant employer rescues the struggling employee. What sort of stories do you want people to tell about your organisation?

This chapter considered why commitment is required. It established that without commitment, it may be almost impossible to optimise organisational performance. The commitment cycle was introduced and explained, and its six steps (leadership, practice, perception, trust, commitment and recognition) were explored. The chapter concluded by asserting that leaders must not break the commitment cycle or allow it to be broken.

The main take-outs from this chapter are:

- Commitment is required throughout the organisation if performance is to be optimised.
- Commitment starts with the executive leadership team (ELT) – every single ELT member must be committed to mental health.

- Leaders must establish the commitment cycle, which has six steps: leadership, practice, perception, trust, commitment and recognition.

- Leaders must not only be committed to mental health; they must also be seen to be supportive of it.

- Leaders must enforce mental health policy. They must address non-compliance and improper behaviours (eg. bullying).

- Leaders must not allow the commitment cycle to be broken. Leaders must perpetuate it.

References

Business in the Community (2019) *Mental Health at Work 2019: Time to take ownership.* Available at: *https://www.bitc.org.uk/report/mental-health-at-work-2019-time-to-take-ownership/* (accessed 22 November 2019).

Health and Safety Executive (online). *Securing Commitment.* Available at: *https://www.hse.gov.uk/stress/standards/securing.htm* (accessed 25 February 2020).

Institute for Healthcare Improvement Multimedia Team (2017) How can leaders create psychological safety? *Institute for Healthcare Improvement* 14 February. Available at: *http://www.ihi.org/communities/blogs/how-can-leaders-create-psychological-safety* (accessed 29 March 2020).

11

PRINCIPLE 3:
POLICY

In this chapter I consider the role of *policy* in terms of physical health and safety management. I explore the key components of a good mental health policy, which are: statement of intent; organisation and management structure; and the arrangements (eg. procedures) that need to be put in place to implement the policy. The statement of intent considers how leaders can set out their aspirations for mental health management. I go on to discuss the organisation and management structure for managing mental health, along with the role of the competent person (CP). I make suggestions for arrangements for managing mental health in the workplace. I end the chapter by considering how and when to review the effectiveness of the mental health policy.

Before going any further, let us first give some thought to the policy itself. Is it best to review an existing health and safety policy and amend it to incorporate mental health? Or do you need to create a separate mental health policy from scratch? Should any new policy focus on wellbeing as well as mental health? Here, each organisation must consider its own particular circumstances and make the decision that best suits it. The organisation should consider things like the perception of mental health it wishes to create, where its focus lies and the scale of the mental health issue.

Perceptions of mental health: If the organisation's leaders are satisfied with mental health being seen as a subset of its existing health and safety policy, then it might be sufficient to adapt its existing health and safety policy. Will this send the correct message and create the correct response, however? The employer should consider what perceptions they want people to have of their company, including employees, and develop its policies and messaging to suit the goals of the organisation.

Focus of the issue: If mental health is not a key issue for the organisation, it might be more appropriate to develop a more wide-reaching wellbeing policy. Here, the emphasis will be on lifestyle factors rather than tackling particular mental health issues such as genetic conditions or past trauma which might lead to PTSD. A wellbeing or mental health risk assessment should reveal the type of focus the organisation should adopt. Mental health and wellbeing are different things, although they are clearly linked. However, a wellbeing-led approach might not necessarily improve mental health. Employers should identify the focus needed in their own organisation, and not simply jump on a bandwagon or follow personal beliefs about the best approach to take. A risk-based approach is recommended.

The scale of the mental health issue: The focus on mental health may be diluted if you incorporate it into a wider health and safety policy or take a broader wellbeing approach. So, if mental health is a key issue in your organisation, giving the issue its own focus – say, through a separate policy – might have a more significant effect. Given that ten times the number of people experience mental ill-health than physical injury at work, organisations should weigh this up before making a decision. With finite resources, any dilution of the mental health focus potentially diminishes the impact of mental health-related actions. Many employers believe they are being more strategic by taking a wellbeing approach as opposed to a mental health approach, but this is not necessarily the case. Leaders must therefore develop an understanding of both mental health issues and wellbeing issues as they present in their organisation. From this position, leaders will be in a better place to judge which approach is most relevant.

Once the considerations that precede the development of any policy have been explored, the policy itself can be developed.

The Role of a Health and Safety Policy

Health and safety laws will state any obligation to produce a policy. In the UK, the Health and Safety at Work etc Act 1974 (HASAWA) requires all employers, other than the very smallest, to produce and update a written health and safety policy statement that outlines the arrangements they have put in place to implement the policy.

Typically, an organisation's occupational health and safety policy, as applied to physical health and safety management, is a written statement that provides a commitment to manage health and safety effectively. It establishes the organisation's commitment and sets its direction in respect of health and safety management. An effective health and safety policy:

- makes a 'top down' commitment, usually by the managing director (although a whole organisation commitment is required, as explored in chapter 10)
- establishes an organisation-wide and proactive culture of health and safety management
- sets out the health and safety values and principles the organisation is committed to
- sets out the management structure for the control of health and safety at work, with roles and responsibilities clearly assigned (including, in some cases, the name of the competent person)
- details the arrangements that have been put in place to manage health and safety
- is communicated to every employee through a variety of methods (online, email, toolbox talks, notice boards, etc).

Most policies incorporate three elements: the statement of intent; the organisation and management structure through which health and safety will be managed; and the arrangements (or procedures) that the policy requires to be put in place.

Writing a Mental Health Policy

Mental ill-health is far more prevalent than physical ill-health. In the UK, health and safety legislation does not distinguish between physical health and safety management and mental health management. In some other countries, such as Australia, health and safety laws expressly apply to mental health. However, in the UK, regulator enforcement focuses almost exclusively on physical health and safety, as does the vast majority of in-house and external training. Little thought is given to mental health management in most health and safety policies. This lack of alignment between the law, regulation, advice and practice creates ambiguity, as was established in chapter 4.

The policy is therefore the starting point in most organisations for managing physical health and safety. This should therefore be the starting point for mental health management. A policy for mental health management should follow a similar structure to that of most health and safety policies, containing the key elements of statement of intent, organisation and management structure, and arrangements.

Statement of Intent

A statement of intent should set out the goals and objectives of the organisation, along with the level of commitment the organisation expects from its employees.

In policies that address physical health and safety, goals are typically conveyed through statements such as 'zero harm' or 'zero incidents'. They might include statements like 'everyone going home safe and well every day'. These statements set out goals and demonstrate commitment.

As 'zero harm' is often a goal for physical health, so it should be for mental health. 'Zero harm' is emphatic; and goals for mental health should be as emphatic as they are for physical health. For example, employers could have the following goal:

Zero distress to be caused by work-related activities.

Or...

To eliminate undue work-related stress.

Employers should set out to minimise any mental health issues being caused or exacerbated by work or work-related activities. This would be a powerful statement of intent.

The management of physical health and safety incorporates objectives as well as goals. Typical wellbeing objectives might include raising awareness (say, through campaigns) and improving the lifestyle of employees (say, through diet and exercise). Objectives are often based on inputs, such as the number of people who have been trained (eg. in mental health first aid). They might also measure outputs of the mental health programme (see chapter 15).

There is no need to look far to identify the objectives for mental health. As is true of many of the suggestions in this book, reading across from physical health and safety often offers some ready-made answers. Performance measures related to physical health typically focus on 'lost-time injury rate' and 'all-injury rate', and the input measures include 'number of people trained'. In most organisations, the human resources team will be able to provide statistics related to sickness absence caused by, say, work-related stress. This is an example of a mental health 'lost-time injury' that provides a possible starting point when setting mental health objectives. An objective might be, for example, to reduce the previous year's stress-related sickness absence rate by 20%.

Organisations may want to consider the following objectives and measures regarding mental health:

- Percentage of new recruits who have declared a mental health condition
- Number of mental health training days per annum
- Percentage of all employees who disclose a mental health condition
- Mental health injury rate
- Mental health injury frequency rate[2]
- Percentage of 'leavers' who have a declared mental health condition (measured by dismissals and by resignations).

The formula for calculating the frequency rate of lost time due to mental health injury is:

$$\frac{\text{Number of lost time injuries in accounting period}}{\text{Total hours worked in accounting period}} \times 1{,}000{,}000$$

Source: Safe Work Australia, online

This method of calculation is standardised across most developed countries, so provides a common understanding and allows for benchmarking. To apply the equation to mental health, simply use the number of injuries and hours related to absence arising from poor mental health (eg. work-related stress). Employers may wish to measure mental health absence by work and non-work causes. Both should be measured and addressed.

The list of measures that might relate to the objectives above is not exhaustive, and they will vary from organisation to organisation. Employers should develop measures that best suit their organisation, sector or industry.

As with most measures of performance, the employer should determine a target level of performance and undertake actions to drive an improvement to reach the target within a

---

[2]   See HSE (online a)

particular timeframe. For example, this approach should be used to achieve a year-on-year fall in the measure of the rate of mental health lost-time incidence.

The next step is to consider commitment (considered in its wider sense in chapter 10). In terms of the policy, all that is needed is for it to express the organisation's commitment to mental health – it's a great opportunity to refine this and put it into words.

The most convenient time to introduce mental health into an organisation's health and safety policy is when the health and safety policy has its formal review, unless the organisation has decided to introduce a separate policy specifically for mental health. When the policy is introduced or reviewed, the managing director or other organisation leader can ask for the policy to be updated to:

> **make an express commitment to treat mental health and safety like physical health and safety.**

It is important that a commitment such as this is made, and stated in the policy, in order to put mental health on a par with physical health throughout the organisation. By making a specific commitment to mental health, the organisation sends a message to all employees that they are expected to show tolerance, be supportive and act in an inclusive manner. The message the organisation sends to employees with mental health issues is one of care, compassion and support. This commitment gives employees permission to talk about their condition and signposts that the organisation is strategically placed to listen and respond appropriately.

This message to employees must be enforced by the most senior people within the organisation if a positive and proactive mental health culture is to emerge and be sustained (see chapter 10).

Organisation and Management Structure

The organisation, including the management structure as it relates to mental health, should be set out in the policy. The organisation should extend from the most senior leader in the structure through the middle managers to the more junior managers at the front line of the organisation. It should include details of the competent person (CP) who will be responsible for the implementation of the mental health policy. The policy document should therefore:

> **identify the competent person responsible for mental health.**

The CP may be a health and safety professional who understands the management methods used in managing physical health. They may be someone with responsibility for compliance with employment law, such as a human resources (HR) professional. Or they might have an occupational health background. However, it is not enough simply for the CP to understand physical health and safety management or HR management. The HSE (online b) states:

a competent person is someone who has sufficient training and experience or knowledge and other qualities that allow them to assist you properly. The level of competence required will depend on the complexity of the situation.

Given the technical ambiguity that can arise, as identified in chapter 4, having knowledge, experience and training of health and safety, or HR or occupational health may not be enough to constitute sufficient mental health management competence as is required in law. Additionally, given the current immaturity of the discipline of workplace mental health management, few organisational managers are likely to have sufficient experience. A deep understanding of mental health management is required. The CP will be a figurehead for mental health within the organisation, acting as an expert on the subject, co-ordinator of activities and controller. There is therefore an issue that will probably need to be addressed.

Organisational leaders who appoint a CP will need to:

invest in developing the expertise of the mental health competent person.

The CP will need to develop wide-ranging expertise that includes:

- a sound knowledge of physical health and safety management, so that best practice from this area can be introduced into mental health management

- a sound knowledge of employment law, to ensure compliance and best practice – knowledge of the law must include but should not be limited to the Equality Act 2010, where considerations around 'mental disability' and protected characteristics arise (the CP should refer to expert advisors as necessary)

- an understanding of risk management as relates to mental health negligence

- an ability to empathise with employees with mental health issues

- a deep understanding of mental health hazards – at work and outside it – and the control measures that can reduce their effects

- a sound understanding of mental health management and related arrangements; the CP will need to design and manage the mental health management system and programme

- a solid understanding of external support arrangements, such as occupational health

- an enquiring and creative mind; as mental health management at work is an emerging field, CPs will need to develop new ways of working that their organisation has not utilised before and that might not be widely utilised outside of the organisation.

The CP does not need to have a qualification or interest in psychology. As is clear from the myriad of books and websites about mental health, most mental health practitioners do not have an understanding of physical health and safety management so, as far as employers are concerned, most practitioners would not be in a position to set out guidance on how to treat mental health in a similar way to physical health in the workplace, in line with the '7 Principles' set out in this book.

The new mental health policy – whether it is a health and safety policy updated to incorporate mental health or a new, dedicated mental health policy – should be communicated to all organisational employees and, where necessary, subcontractors and other stakeholders. There are many ways to do this, including:

- replacing previous versions of the policy on display in all offices, buildings and sites the organisation operates from, so it can be seen by all members of staff
- by email and other forms of electronic information communication (eg. apps, internal communication and social media tools)
- inclusion in training course material, especially at induction, so that, from the outset of their employment, all staff are aware of the policy and the standards of behaviour they are required to demonstrate
- at team meetings, through cascade communications
- at toolbox talks and other worker briefings
- through formal consultations, such as worker consultations, perhaps involving unions.

Once it has been introduced into the organisation, the policy should be used as the basis for managing mental health, just as the physical health and safety policy forms the basis for health and safety actions and behaviours.

Arrangements

The arrangements section of the health and safety policy should be used to:

detail the specific actions, procedures and resources that will operate to ensure mental health is managed effectively.

An organisation's health and safety policy provides an established way of working that is simple, quick and convenient to adopt and adapt, and through which the organisation's commitment to mental health is conveyed.

Arrangements should be put in place that follow the principles of a physical health and safety management system (see chapter 3). The information in this section will depend on the type of activities being undertaken. Common items in the arrangements section of a typical mental health policy include:

- mental health support procedures
- mental health incident reporting and investigation procedures

- mental health emergency procedures

- mental health first aid procedures

- mental health risk assessment procedures

- site safety inspection procedures for mental health

- control of exposure to specific mental health hazards (eg. witnessing distressing scenes, experiencing significant performance pressures, dealing with difficult customers, anti-bullying measures)

- mental health training procedures

- procedures for dealing with the mental health of contractors and visitors (eg. through exposure controls)

- mental health welfare provisions

- arrangements for consulting with employees about mental health.

Each of these arrangements is now briefly explored.

Mental health support procedures: Mental health procedures would typically apply to either a commonly occurring or a singularly significant stressful event or situation. They may also be developed for the purposes of supporting employees with known conditions, such as genetic conditions. These procedures should provide a step-by-step guide to what employees should do to protect themselves mentally, given a certain set of circumstances. Mental health procedures should be made available to people at risk and to people supporting or managing those at risk. Organisations may be able to source such procedures from charities (Mind, online), although they may choose to write their own. Some examples of mental health procedures are:

- Coping with stress

- Guidance for those with PTSD, depression, anxiety etc

- Stress respite procedures (eg. to reduce exposure time to known stressful conditions)

- Mental health absence procedures (eg. permitted time off to have routine appointments with a therapist or psychiatrist.).

Mental health incident reporting and investigation procedures: As with physical injuries, the more serious mental health incidents require investigation. Generally, mental health issues should be investigated based on the severity of the incident or the frequency of its occurrence, and possibly the duration of the related absence (eg. all mental health absences lasting more than 30 consecutive days). An appropriate independent manager should investigate the incident, with a suitably senior person reviewing the case. An identical procedure to physical health and safety investigations can be used. This procedure should already be established in most organisations, as part of their health and safety arrangements.

Mental health emergency procedures: Mental health emergencies relate to those incidents from which known mental trauma is likely to arise. As in the case of death or serious injury at work, emergency procedures must be in place. There are various types of trigger that might cause a mental health emergency, such as:

- a sudden, severe psychological injury or illness (eg. an employee suddenly becomes particularly distressed – perhaps emotions related to a past traumatic experience are triggered)
- experiencing trauma (eg. experiencing bodily harm that causes significant distress)
- witnessing trauma (eg. witnessing particularly distressing scenes).

Whilst the trigger itself may not stem from a severe or significant single event, *one small thing* (see chapter 1) may happen that has a sudden, severe adverse effect on somebody with latent mental health issues. *One small thing* could lead to an employee who has no apparent mental health issues suddenly becoming distressed.

Whatever the cause, should such an emergency arise, written procedures should guide supervising staff through the actions that need to be taken. These procedures will probably be written by somebody with suitable knowledge of mental health.

Mental health first aid procedures: A structured approach to mental health first aid should be taken. As with physical health, mental health first aiders should be designated and trained, and their role should be communicated to all employees. Information on mental health first aid is widely available, so should be easy to access, for example, through St John's Ambulance *(https://www.sja.org.uk/courses/workplace-mental-health-first-aid/)*.

Mental health risk assessment procedures: In the UK and some other countries, mental health risk assessments are a legal requirement. Mental health risk assessments require organisations to identify the potential and actual causes of mental health harm in their organisation. 12 standard mental health risks have been determined, along with 12 work-place mental health risk factors, enabling a specific approach to risk management to be taken. These are examined in chapter 12, which covers risk assessment more fully. Once an employer has identified the potential and actual mental health risks their organisation faces, they can go about managing those risks.

Site safety inspection procedures for mental health: Procedures should be drafted setting out the frequency and scope of site mental health inspections. The aim of a site mental health inspection is to check that risk assessments and control measures have been properly implemented and are proving effective. Unlike physical health and safety, the mental health site inspection will contemplate intangible aspects of mental health, safety and welfare, for example the effect of environmental factors on mental health (eg. noise, light, heat). It will also consider the effects activities may have (eg, highly complex, highly mundane). But it might also consider aspects such as working relationships, workload, and deadlines and targets. Mental health site inspection procedures should allow the assessor to undertake inspections and make recommendations to protect and continually improve workplace mental health.

Control of exposure to specific mental health hazards: Control procedures should be written to minimise the adverse impact of events and circumstances that are known to cause distress. For example, witnessing distressing scenes (eg. medical emergencies, child abuse, warzone conflict), excessive working hours (Afonso, Fonseca and Pires, 2017) and exposure to psychoactive substances may all represent circumstances that can have an adverse effect on an employee's mental health. Clearly, that list is not exhaustive; employers must research and determine those circumstances within their organisation that have been established to have an adverse mental health effect, so that appropriate control measures and related procedures can be drawn up and implemented. There are exposure time limits for the use of certain equipment known to cause physical harm (eg. pneumatic drill); it may make sense to develop time limits for exposure to certain known mental health hazards where they cannot be eliminated.

Mental health training procedures: Employers should develop suitable mental health training procedures. They should determine what mandatory training is necessary, based on the circumstances of each role within the organisation, in the same way as training matrices (CITBNI, online) are used to control the provision of physical health and safety training. It should be mandatory for employees who are likely to face highly stressful or distressing circumstances to participate in suitable training in subjects such as mindfulness, resilience and the use of control measures. By following the principles of physical health and safety training, a comprehensive set of procedures for mental health training can be created and implemented.

Procedures for dealing with the mental health of contractors and visitors: Arrangements must be put in place to minimise any mental health risks to contractors, visitors and others whose mental health might be affected by the activities of the organisation. Examples might include cleaning teams at accident scenes or people disposing of body parts in hospitals. Each organisation must assess its activities to determine which might cause mental health harm. Procedures might include developing a log book of the mental health risks that contractors and visitors could be exposed to, providing site induction training before any risk of exposure arises, and supervising access to areas where exposure may be most severe. Post-visit interviews could also be conducted to assess any adverse after-effects. Relevant staff should be trained in how to ensure contractors, visitors and others follow the required procedure and are properly cared for.

Mental health welfare provision: In physical health and safety terms, welfare relates to basic necessities, such as toilet facilities, fresh running water and so on. In mental health terms, necessities might include rest breaks, exposure to natural daylight, access to counselling, and mental health checks and examinations for those experiencing regular exposure. At a basic level, mental health welfare should provide several elements including: knowledge of mental health hazards; information about control measures; a level of respite; health check-ups to ensure no harm is being experienced; resilience-building support (eg. training). Welfare provision should be risk-based. Employers should use foresight (see chapter 5) to determine and plan welfare arrangements.

Arrangements for consulting with employees about mental health: It is a legal requirement that organisations consult their employees in respect of health and safety. UK law does not distinguish between physical and mental health. It is therefore a legal requirement that organisations consult with their workforce regarding mental health. Consultation arrangements are comprehensively addressed in chapter 14.

The above list of arrangements is not exhaustive; an organisation may include 20 or 30 arrangements in its organisation's mental health policy. Employers should use their own initiative, look externally and seek expert opinion regarding additional arrangements that might suit their organisation.

A useful example of a stress policy is available from the HSE (online, c), which provides a good starting point for employers. This example is limited to stress, of course, so does not relate to practices to support other mental health issues. The HSE's stress management standards (HSE online, d) are similarly useful but limited in scope, presenting six stressors compared to the 24 mental health hazards I identify in chapter 12.

As with all policies, the mental health policy must be brought to life within the organisation. This can be achieved through a variety of methods. In addition to those suggested in chapter 10, organisations could consider appointing a champion with responsibility for one of the arrangements. The champion would ensure the arrangement is properly designed, communicate it throughout the organisation, deliver any related training and review the policy at appropriate times. The CP could hold regular review meetings with champions to ensure they are discharging their responsibility properly. Employers should develop their own methods for bringing their mental health policy 'alive' within their organisation.

In this chapter, I explored the structure of the mental health policy and presented three key sections of the policy: the statement of intent; the organisation and management structure as it relates to mental health; and the arrangements that will be put in place to implement the policy. I discussed the role of the competent person (CP) and the need for them to possess the right knowledge, experience and training to be able to perform the role. I presented some of the arrangements employers should consider adopting, and stressed how important it is for them to ensure their mental health policy is brought to life through a variety of methods.

The main take-outs from this chapter are:

- Leaders must determine whether to have a policy that is focused exclusively on mental health or whether to include mental health in an existing health and safety policy.

- This judgement will probably need to take into account the perceptions the employer wishes to create, the scale of the mental health issue within the organisation and whether adopting a broader approach (eg. wellbeing) might dilute the focus and resources that could otherwise be used on mental health.

- The following sections should be included in the mental health policy as a minimum: a statement of intent; the organisation and management structure as it relates to mental health; and arrangements that will be put in place to implement the policy.

- The statement of intent will express the leader's commitment to mental health, it may set out some goals and objectives and it will state how employees are expected to behave under the policy.

- The management structure for mental health should be hierarchical, with the leader in the ultimate position of authority with reportability for the policy's implementation, flowing down through management layers to the front line. The competent person should be identified (possibly by name) as the expert on the subject of mental health.

- The arrangements section sets out the procedures through which the policy is to be implemented. These procedures will be numerous (20 or 30) and will set out what employees are expected to do under certain circumstances.

- Leaders are encouraged to ensure the mental health policy is brought to life in their organisation, helping to support the development of a proactive mental health culture.

References

Afonso, P., Fonseca, M., and Pires, J. F. (2017) Impact of working hours on sleep and mental health, *Occupational Medicine*, Volume 67, Issue 5, July 2017, Pages 377–382. Available at: *https://academic.oup.com/occmed/article/67/5/377/3859790* (accessed 28 March 2020).

Construction Industry Training Board of Northern Ireland (online) *Training Needs Analysis*. Available at: *https://www.citbni.org.uk/Training/Training-Plan.aspx* (accessed 19 March 2020).

Health and Safety Executive (online a) *Injury Frequency Rates*. Available at: *https://www.hse.gov.uk/statistics/adhoc-analysis/injury-frequency-rates.pdf* (accessed 26 February 2020).

Health and Safety Executive (online b) *A Competent Person*. Available at: *https://www.hse.gov.uk/involvement/competentperson.htm* (accessed 26 February 2020).

Health and Safety Executive (online c) *An Example of a Stress Policy*. Available at: *https://www.hse.gov.uk/stress/assets/docs/examplepolicy.pdf* (accessed 20 March 2020).

Health and Safety Executive (online d) *What are the Stress Management Standards?* Available at: *https://www.hse.gov.uk/stress/standards/* (accessed 20 March 2020).

Mind (online) *How to support staff who are experiencing a mental health problem*. Available at: *https://www.mind.org.uk/media/550657/resource4.pdf* (accessed 27 March 2020).

Safe Work Australia (online) *Lost Time Injury Frequency Rates (LTIFR)*. Available at: *https://www.safeworkaustralia.gov.au/statistics-and-research/lost-time-injury-frequency-rates-ltifr* (accessed 26 February 2020).

12

PRINCIPLE 4:
RISK ASSESSMENTS

We reflected on the process of risk assessment as it applies to physical health and safety in chapter 3. The same risk assessment process can be applied to mental health. The usual five-step risk assessment process, as outlined in chapter 3, is:

1   Identify what can cause mental health harm

2   Identify whose mental health can be harmed, and how

3   Evaluate the mental health risks and determine control measures

4   Write up and implement the mental health risk assessment

5   Review the mental health risk assessment.

Please bear in mind that mental health risk assessments are very different to physical health and safety risk assessments. Although we are applying the same risk assessment approach, hazards to mental health are different, mental health control measures are different and psychological effects are different; psychological effects may be masked or even deliberately concealed. Inevitably, then, different thinking is required, albeit within the same risk assessment framework.

This chapter should not be regarded as definitive, but used as a guide. When contemplating mental health risk assessments, you should consult your organisation's mental health competent person (CP) or other suitably qualified expert. This chapter aims to stimulate thinking and present some of the key issues to consider, as opposed to representing a comprehensive user manual or set of instructions.

I will now explore each of the five elements of risk assessments as they relate to mental health. I should stress that the risk assessment should be undertaken by somebody competent to perform it. They should have knowledge of the activities and hazards involved and how they affect mental health; and if you engage an advisor or consultant to help undertake the risk assessments, managers and employees should still be involved, just as they are with physical health and safety.

Step 1: Identify What Can Cause Mental Health Harm

Most physical hazards are observable. Potential causes of harm are often obvious, such as injury from tools, machinery, equipment, heat, falls from height or vehicle accidents. When it comes to mental health, however, the hazards and potential harm are not necessarily apparent. Employers must therefore *enquire* about and *foresee* mental health risks (see chapter 5). The competent person or other person undertaking the risk assessment must use their experience, knowledge and training to identify hazards, establishing and foreseeing what might cause harm.

So, what are the mental health hazards that should be assessed, and how can the likelihood and severity of harm be assessed?

Part I of this book included information related to mental health and identified three principle causes of mental ill-health: the *person*, their *circumstances* and their *relationships*. Based on these three causes, and my research and assessment of studies, I identified the most common categories of mental health risk, which I have developed into a framework of 12 general mental health risk factors (Figure 12.1). This framework answers the question: 'What types of risk need to be considered when undertaking mental health risk assessments?' and informs an approach that employers might take when undertaking such assessments.

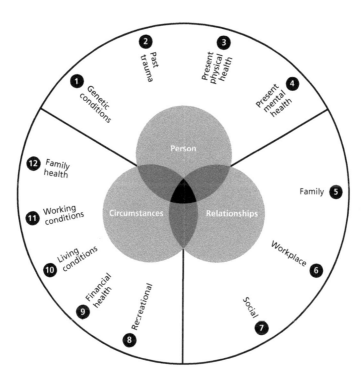

Figure 12.1 *The 12 general mental health risk factors*

The model in Figure 12.1 identifies the most commonly occurring mental health risk factors but may not include them all. Employers should identify the risks that occur in their own organisation and change the framework accordingly; they may identify fewer or more than 12 risks, for example, or they may identify risk categories that are quite different to the ones in Figure 12.1. As with all risk assessments, they must be bespoke and adapted to suit the circumstances.

The 12 general mental health risk factors model provides organisations with the first step in identifying mental health hazards. Some of the 12 risk factors are too broad to be meaningful, however, so they each require further examination and a more focused approach.

Further research revealed the 12 most common work and work-related causes of poor mental health. These are shown in Figure 12.2.

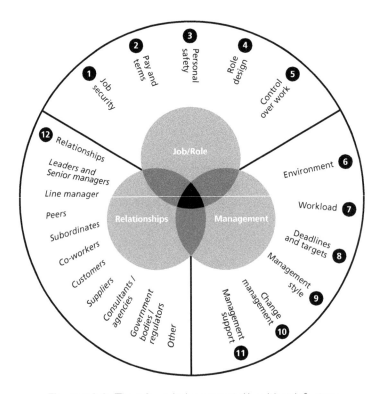

Figure 12.2 *The 12 workplace mental health risk factors*

Together, Figures 12.1 and 12.2 set out the '12 x 12 mental health risk factors'.

Risk assessments must suit the circumstances, so employers may well identify additional or alternative workplace risks to those listed in Figure 12.2. Risk assessments must also be dynamic, so employers should adapt the approach to accommodate changing situations.

It is of the utmost importance that leaders identify the extent to which the risk factors affect their employees. The approach to workplace mental health management should be risk-based. Only by identifying the extent to which each risk factor is affecting employees can risk-based controls be determined and implemented.

Chapter 1 presented survey findings that showed the proportion of employees affected by specific causes of poor mental health. *Workload* was consistently shown to be a top cause of stress, and it is known that long working hours correlate with poor mental health (Afonso et al., 2017). It is clear that there are many employers who need to do more to measure workload, its reasonableness, what undue level of stress (if any) it is causing and what to do about it. Workload may vary, say, through changes in seasonal demand, so when that workload increases it could well increase stress. In physical health and safety terms, when an activity becomes more hazardous, the employer has a legal duty to increase control measures to take account of any increase in risk. The same should be the case with mental health. How do you, as a leader, currently increase your mental health control measures during times of higher than usual workload? The 'dots' must be joined in this way: greater risk = greater controls.

This illustrates the need for leaders to put in place ways to regularly measure each of the mental health risk factors across the organisation, so they can respond in a way that is proportionate and reasonably practicable. It is inadequate to do nothing when high mental health risks are present and when they increase. I return to this subject later in this chapter, in Step 3, which contemplates the *likelihood* and *severity* of mental health hazards.

Using Figures 12.1 and 12.2 as a starting point, it is possible for organisations to determine what can cause harm. This is the first step in the five-step risk assessment process. Next, we consider the second step: who can be harmed, and how?

Step 2: Identify Whose Mental Health Can be Harmed, and How

Physical health and safety risk assessments can be undertaken for particular individuals when their work is unique, or for particular groups in which a number of people all face identical circumstances. This latter example can lead to the creation of a generic risk assessment.

For mental health, the same approach may be applied to groups and individuals, but its effectiveness cannot always be assured. There are several key reasons for this:

- When employees embark on a role or task, each of them may have a very different state of mental health, despite doing exactly the same work as each other.

- The law, as it relates to physical health and safety, requires employers to undertake suitable and sufficient risk assessments based on full knowledge of conditions, with ignorance being no defence. With mental health, the employee is not legally required to tell their employer of any particular mental health condition or issues they might have, so the employer may not have full knowledge. The employer cannot reasonably be expected to manage mental health risks they are not aware of (unless, of course, they were patently foreseeable).

- Employers must attempt to foresee the potential impact of a mental health hazard but they may not be able to do so accurately in every case, as they may not be able to determine each employee's susceptibility to mental harm.

Mental health risk assessments must, therefore, be tackled differently to those undertaken to protect physical health.

Having determined what can cause harm, employers then have a duty to foresee mental harm. Based on knowledge gained during hazard identification, employers are then required to foresee who can be harmed and how, taking a proactive and preventative approach.

In considering who can be harmed and how, we have seen that work circumstances and work relationships can cause harm. Now that we are aware of the 12 general (Figure 12.1) and 12 workplace (Figure 12.2) mental health risk factors, two risk-based approaches should be taken:

1   An approach that is applicable in high risk situations (including situations that have the potential to cause significant mental harm)

2   An approach that is applicable to vulnerable employees (and others, who must be protected as far as is reasonably practicable), as they may have a high susceptibility to mental harm.

It is common when contemplating physical health and safety risk assessments to pay particular attention to anyone who might be exposed to highly hazardous situations and who may be considered vulnerable. The same considerations should be given to employees and others when undertaking mental health risk assessments.

'No job in itself is intrinsically dangerous to mental health.' This was the opinion of the Court of Appeal in the case of *Sutherland v Hatton, 2002* (chapter 5). However, in considering high risk situations, Robinson (2018) poses some interesting questions and shows that the workplace itself, in addition to the work, may be causing or contributing to mental harm. Based on Ogle et al.'s (2013) and Forbes et al.'s (2019) research discussed in chapter 1, it is clear that some occupations can involve witnessing trauma, which can lead to PTSD or similar conditions. Such jobs include nursing, military service and child protection. Roles like these must surely be considered intrinsically dangerous to mental health. It was established in chapter 1 that PTSD is prevalent in 4.4% of the population (Mind, 2017). The Advisory Board (2019) reports that one in four nurses suffers from PTSD because of witnessing trauma first-hand; nurses appear to be five times more likely to suffer PTSD than the general population. Nurses see people die, they resuscitate people, they stem bleeding and they have end-of-life discussions. I would argue that their job (and other jobs involving similarly traumatic circumstances) can be intrinsically dangerous to mental health. Far more consideration must be given to the potential for mental harm at work when conducting mental health risk assessments than the Court of Appeal in the *Sutherland v Hatton* case suggests is necessary.

People can be considered to be particularly vulnerable when they:

▪   are undertaking high risk tasks or involved in high risk situations (see above)

▪   have disclosed a mental health issue

▪   have indicated they have a high susceptibility to mental harm.

Given the duties and obligations of employers established in chapter 5 – to foresee risks to mental health – it is evident that employers must make some effort to determine what can cause harm, who can be harmed and how.

I now turn to the matter of understanding how mental health hazards might affect employees. At this point I would like to revisit Principle 2, commitment (chapter 10). Mental health risks can only be assessed effectively if two aspects of mental health are identified:

1   any mental health issues the employee has

2   the effects of work and work-related factors on the employee's mental health.

For these two points to be discussed as part of the risk assessment process, commitment must have been established. Only when commitment (including trust) has been established will employees feel sufficiently comfortable about disclosing the above two points: what mental health issues they have and how work is affecting their mental health. Given that only half of employees disclose their mental health issues, this may represent a challenge for employers.

Not only must employees feel comfortable, but employers must too. In chapter 1, it was established that employers may feel less comfortable talking to employees about mental health today than they felt ten years ago (Shaw Trust, 2018). The person undertaking the risk assessment must feel willing and able to enquire about the employee's mental health, if mental health hazards and their effects are to be accurately determined and controlled.

This collaborative approach of enquiry and disclosure is required if effective mental health risk assessments are to be undertaken effectively (Figure 12.3).

Figure 12.3   *Disclosure and enquiry – a collaborative approach*

Employers must reasonably foresee how hazards might cause harm to mental health. Making enquiries will assist employers in undertaking this task. In reality, the employer is doing little more than they would when asking about employee mental health under the Equality Act

2010. The employer is asking the employee if they have any mental health issues, how any such issues affect them and what steps the employer can take to support them. This is the same 'cause-effect-control' approach as applies to physical health and safety risk assessments. If the employer has made enquiries and used foresight, they will have gone a long way towards fulfilling their legal obligations.

Here, a word of caution is needed. With physical health and safety, employees cannot choose which risks they take and which they do not. The employer must assess the risks and put in place control measures to protect the health, safety and welfare of employees and others affected by their activities. With mental health, the employer's duty may only extend to enquiring about the employee's mental health and putting in place suitable controls based on the outcome of that enquiry. If the employee chooses to withhold information about their mental health, the employer cannot reasonably be expected to know about it. In effect, the employee can choose which mental health risks they take. The employer only has a duty to reasonably foresee risks, which they can only do based on the knowledge provided by employees and which they otherwise possess (eg. data sheets, manufacturers' warnings, historic records). The *Rorrison v West Lothian College and Lothian Regional Council* case (Scottish Courts and Tribunals, 1999) case in chapter 5 provides an example of where an employee did, in fact, suffer psychological harm, but the harm suffered was not foreseeable, so the employee's case against their employer failed.

One consideration in law, here, is that in the UK, under health and safety law (UK Government, online), employees have a duty to take care of their own mental health and that of others, and to cooperate with their employer on matters of health and safety. Clearly withholding knowledge that prevents the employer undertaking an effective mental health risk assessment could be deemed to be uncooperative. Yet under the General Data Protection Regulation 2016 (GDPR), employees have rights related to privacy and confidentiality, so have no duty to disclose the state of their mental health. This is yet another contradiction in the current legal system.

Given the legal complexities of the above points, suffice it to say you should take relevant legal advice, as opposed to using this book as a definitive guide.

We can now move forward to Step 3, in which risks are assessed and control measures determined.

Step 3: Evaluate the Mental Health Risks and Determine Control Measures

In Step 3, the competent risk assessor assesses the hazards, to determine the risk each represents.

In evaluating the risks, the risk assessor must gather information about mental health hazards, weigh that information and assign a risk score to each hazard. I present three tools for doing so:

1 Mental health risk assessment matrix

2 Individual mental health risk assessment

3 Group mental health risk assessment

Mental Health Risk Assessment Matrix

The risk assessment matrix from chapter 3 is reproduced here (Figure 12.4). The risk assessment matrix considers *likelihood* and *severity*.

Potential severity of harm

		Slightly harmful 1	Harmful 2	Extremely harmful 3
Likelihood of harm occurring	Highly unlikely 1	Trivial 1	Tolerable 2	Moderate 3
	Unlikely 2	Tolerable 2	Moderate 4	Substantial 6
	Likely 3	Moderate 3	Substantial 6	Intolerable 9

Figure 12.4 *Risk assessment matrix*
Source: HSE, 2020

This matrix approach to risk assessments is well known in many countries. It provides an easy-to-use and readily understood scale of risk, although some have adapted the matrix to create a 25-point scale instead of a 9-point scale. Either will suffice.

In considering *likelihood*, the assessor will think of how often a hazardous situation occurs. If mental harm is occurring frequently, or lasts for a long time, a high rating should be applied.

With *severity*, the assessor should consider the effect the hazard is having. Is it leading to mental harm and, if so, how severe is that harm? It may be appropriate to use a notion from chapter 1 (Figure 1.2): whether the employee is *content*, runs the risk of becoming *distressed* or is somewhere in between. Each employee's susceptibility may vary, so, although a number of employees may be exposed to the same situation and stressors, the mental harm each of them suffers may vary. Some form of individual employee assessment is therefore essential.

The risk assessment matrix approach can be applied to individual employees and to groups of employees (eg. the whole organisation, or a particular site, department or team). A mixed risk assessment will almost certainly be required, where both individual and group risk assessments are undertaken.

Each of the 12 *general* mental health risk factors (Figure 12.1) and the 12 *workplace* mental health risk factors (Figure 12.2) can be considered, along with the likelihood and severity with which each occurs. The scoring matrix can be applied and hazards ranked to determine priorities. Combined, this '12 x 12' approach provides employers with a starting point when determining which risks to assess. Given that each individual employee may have a different mental response to similar circumstances, some level of individual risk assessment is required. What one employee finds mentally hazardous, another might not. Given that employees may not all perceive mental health risks in the same way, group discussions about risks may be helpful. As was identified earlier, some employees may not be open about their mental health and some may even lie about it. I referred to GDPR and the employee's right to privacy earlier, so I will not raise it again here.

Risk assessments can be undertaken face-to-face or remotely (eg. by questionnaire on paper, online or via an app). Each approach has its benefits and drawbacks, but an anonymous approach may be preferable until the confidence of employees has been gained and they feel they can be more open.

Individual Mental Health Risk Assessment

Individuals must be given the opportunity to participate in individual mental health risk assessments. They should be given the opportunity to document their own mental health and assess the risks they foresee, in the same way they might document their use of equipment during a display screen equipment (DSE) risk assessment. This approach need not be complex or onerous. The risk assessments can be self-administered by each employee, may only take a few minutes to complete and can be done on a pro forma document (electronic or manual). This approach can also be confidential and/or anonymous. Explanations of each question and how to use the response scale should be provided.

The individual risk assessment may pay particular attention to the individual's past (eg. historic trauma), present and future mental state, along with their likely ability to cope. It might therefore focus on past traumatic events, current pressures inside and outside work, and how effective the employee feels their *resilience buffer* is (Figures 1.9 to 1.11) in coping with past, current and future pressures. It might include an attempt to determine the individual susceptibility to mental harm, although the involvement of a suitably qualified expert may be advisable.

At the individual level, a more targeted approach should be taken. The fictional case study of Brad below, demonstrates how an individual mental health risk assessment might be conducted.

Case Study 2 – Brad – Construction Manager

Brad (aged 52) heads up a team of six supervisors, each of whom oversees a team of twelve construction workers. Brad's team has been working long hours on a building project for three years, in all seasons and weathers, to get the job done. Despite his severe stress, Brad is totally reliable. He is ex-military; a veteran of the first Gulf War in Iraq, where he saw combat and witnessed trauma repeatedly. He has PTSD. He has been overweight for a long time, which he is highly self-conscious about, having been so fit in the military. As a result, he doesn't socialise. His mother has cancer; at one point she was close to death but now appears to be doing well. Brad doesn't have time to exercise as he's working as much as he can to earn money: his overtime goes some way to meeting bills, but he has a large mortgage and is broke. His boss is really understanding. She is aware of Brad's PTSD and stress, and lets Brad have time off every Friday morning to take his mother to hospital for chemotherapy. Brad works extra hard at the weekend to pay his boss back for her kindness. Despite his weight and the fact that he doesn't exercise, Brad is never sick. He has a happy family life and a nice home.

Brad and his boss have a candid relationship; Brad has never minded sharing, and she knows all about his situation. His openness has helped his boss complete the risk assessment, the result of which is shown in Table 12.1.

Table 12.1 *Individual mental health risk assessment – completed example (9-point scale)*

Cause	Subset	Brad
Person	Genetic conditions	2
	Past trauma	6
	Current physical health	6
	Current mental health	4
Relationships	Family	2
	Workplace	4
	Social	6
Circumstances	Recreational	6
	Financial health	4
	Living conditions	2
	Working conditions	2
	Family health	9
Total		53

Brad scores a total of 53, which is at the lower end of a high score. Action is required. Brad is good at his job, and loyal. Is his employer going to give him the help he needs, or stand by and wait for him to become *distressed*?

Brad's case is not uncommon. As we established in chapter 1, exposure to traumatic events has a cumulative effect over time and those who experience this are likely to suffer from multiple causes of poor mental health (Ogle et al., 2013).

Employers should determine rules for individual mental health risk assessments, which might include things like:

- Any individual whose mental health risk assessment includes four or more scores of nine requires a detailed recovery plan to be produced.
- Any total score of 50 or above requires a detailed recovery plan to be produced.
- All risk assessments that fall into one or both of the above two categories must be escalated to the mental health competent person (CP), who must monitor the development of recovery plans, along with the individual's recovery.

Having evaluated the risks, the risk assessor must next draw up a plan that determines the appropriate control measures. Brad's plan might have several components:

- Utilise the employer's Employee Assistance programme and/or occupational health department to help Brad lose weight through exercise and diet.
- Access medical interventions that can be used to help Brad with his weight.
- Allow Brad to leave work early on Tuesdays and Thursdays to go to the gym for an hour on the way home from work.
- Give Brad resilience training that has two aspects to it: coming to terms with past trauma (PTSD); and building resilience to cope with future stressors.
- Bring forward Brad's pay review as he currently needs every penny he can get.
- Invite Brad out more, especially to work social events.
- Hold regular meetings with Brad to see how his mother's chemotherapy is going, to monitor how her illness is affecting him.

Brad's employer knows about his PTSD and stress. She has also had a 'trigger' (chapter 5), in that he has verbally told her about his mental health issues; in the UK, this means that as Brad's employer, she has a duty to support him in managing his mental health.

Moving away from the case study, open and confidential (as opposed to anonymous) individual risk assessments allow the causes of poor mental health to be identified and highly specific recovery plans to be developed that offer the most effective form of support.

Group Mental Health Risk Assessment

Group mental health risk assessments can be undertaken at organisational, site, department or team level. They should be undertaken by somebody suitably trained to do so, and with sufficient knowledge and experience. The risk assessor should consider work-related risks, including work-related *circumstances* and work-related *relationships*, and should consider workplace mental health hazards objectively. Consultation with employees should also be undertaken, as is required in law, possibly using a team approach where several people participate in a discussion about mental health hazards and controls. This group risk assessment will inform the general control measures that will subsequently be developed to protect employees.

When looking at the group approach to risk assessments, there are a couple of factors to take into account:

- Group risk assessments can be anonymous or they can be open. Private group meetings from which managers are excluded and anonymous surveys can reveal group mental health risks on an anonymised basis. Some employees may want to remain anonymous as they may not wish to share sensitive personal information, known as special category data (ICO, online). In this case, control measures may not be able to be tailored to an individual's specific needs. Open approaches amongst co-workers can be beneficial as they stimulate debate about hazards, their frequency and severity, and the priority they should be given, and a consensus is usually reached.

- A word of warning about open group risk assessments in which teams hold group discussions about risks. Some hazards, such as workplace relationships, can involve intangible hazards (eg. bullying). Team members may be reluctant to talk openly in a group about someone who has been bullying, about being bullied or about the effects of bullying, so the issue may pass without being addressed. This means the adverse mental health effects of bullying will continue, even after the risk assessment. The mental health risk assessor will need to consider their risk assessment approach to ensure they gain a full understanding of all prevailing hazards and the effect of each.

Responses to group risk assessments should be recorded. Your organisation's health and safety manager will be able to provide risk assessment forms. An example is provided in Figure 12.5, in the shape of the HSE's template risk assessment form (HSE, online). The health and safety manager may be able to help adapt this HSE form, or the form already in use in your organisation, to make it suitable for assessing mental health risks.

HSE
Health and Safety Executive

Risk assessment template

Company name: **Assessment carried out by:**

Date of next review: **Date assessment was carried out:**

What are the hazards?	Who might be harmed and how?	What are you already doing to control the risks?	What further action do you need to take to control the risks?	Who needs to carry out the action?	When is the action needed by?	Done

More information on managing risk: www.hse.gov.uk/simple-health-safety/risk/

Published by the Health and Safety Executive   10/19

Figure 12.5 *HSE risk assessment template*

Source: HSE online

Group risk assessments provide for one type of approach. Each employee within the group might be individually assessed, with the scores aggregated to arrive at a group score (as illustrated in Table 12.2). Unlike physical risks, which are identical across numerous employees, mental health risks are individual to each employee. Hazards may be common but their effects may not be.

Table 12.1   *Group mental health risk assessment scoring table (9-point scale)*

Cause	Subset	Employee 1	Employee 2	Employee 3	Employee 4	Total
Person	Genetic conditions	2	2	6	2	12
	Past trauma	9	2	2	4	17
	Current physical health	2	4	2	2	10
	Current mental health	4	2	6	2	14
Relationships	Family	2	2	6	2	12
	Work	6	6	2	2	16
	Social	4	2	2	6	14
Circumstances	Recreational	2	2	2	2	8
	Financial health	4	4	9	2	19
	Living conditions	2	2	6	2	12
	Working conditions	2	2	2	2	8
	Family health	9	2	2	2	15
Total		**48**	**32**	**47**	**30**	**157**

An approach such as the one in Table 12.2 allows data to be analysed and aggregated, so mental health causes and subsets can be assessed to determine which are having the most profound adverse effect upon a group of employees. Immediately, it becomes apparent that in the example in Table 12.2:

▨ Two employees may be struggling with their mental health.

▨ Financial health, past trauma and workplace relationships are the top three causes of poor mental health.

▨ Several employees have either moderate or poor financial health.

▨ Two employees may require urgent assistance in respect of coming to terms with past trauma (employee 1) and in respect of their financial health (employee 3). These employees appear at immediate risk of becoming *distressed*.

Again, you may wish to develop rules about how your organisation responds to and manages groups whose risk assessment score is high.

It is evident from this example why both individual and group risk assessments are required. Individual risk assessments allow for control measures to be tailored to individuals. Group risk assessments identify those issues more broadly affecting a number of employees, allowing for a broader approach to be taken. Even when anonymised, this data is of great benefit. In the example in Table 12.2, if the risk assessment was anonymous, the line manager would not know which specific employees faced significant issues; however, they would understand what the issues were, so would be able to take action across the team, providing at least some level of support.

The aggregation of data allows for 'hotspots' of risk to be identified, which:

- allows you to undertake causal analysis, which may identify which team, site or department is causing or experiencing the 'hotspot' and may therefore be most at risk

- allows for areas of greatest risk to be more closely monitored to ensure control measures and related procedures are operating effectively

- allows for control measures and related practice to be emphasised, so providing more effective control (eg. in high-risk groups, supervision and monitoring activities may be undertaken more frequently, such as consultations with workers, toolbox talks and inspection visits).

Individual and aggregated group responses can be cross-referenced to ensure they correlate with each other. If they do correlate, the risk assessment may well be considered accurate. If they do not, care should be taken when determining control measures.

Other Considerations

At a strategic level, action plans may be drawn up to help improve mental health across the organisation. Plans should be based upon risk assessment data, to ensure there is a focus on priority areas. Strategic plans are likely to focus especially on 'working conditions' (such as culture, management style, change management and control over work activities) and workplace relationships. However, non-work-related causes of poor mental health should not be forgotten. The mental health of the individual employee as it is affected by factors outside of work should also be considered, and related control measures should be developed if reasonably practicable. These might include personal and professional development, supporting the employee's financial health, socialising and therapies such as ecotherapy.

Some hotspots of risk may be intangible. When focusing on 'workplace relationships', for instance, it may not be obvious to the person undertaking the risk assessment that there are poor working relationships. A nuanced approach may therefore be required. For example, some employees may not be wholly truthful in scoring 'working relationships' during the risk assessment exercise, for fear of reprisals. Methods of identifying more intangible causes of poor mental health may need to be determined. For example, when contemplating workplace relationships, 360-degree assessment may be undertaken. This may involve asking people outside the team being assessed for their perception of working relationships within the team being assessed. Inputs may be sought from the manager of the team being assessed, other team leaders who work alongside the team, and employee representatives such as union officials. By seeking multiple opinions a more accurate picture can be formed, improving the accuracy of the risk assessment. If 'working relationships' is identified as a cause of poor mental health at work, steps can be taken to improve relationships.

Through a risk assessment matrix approach, individual and group risk assessments can thus be undertaken to determine 'hotspots' of poor mental health, allowing for the development of specific control measures that are most relevant (and perhaps most necessary) in an organisation.

Step 4: Write Up and Implement the Mental Health Risk Assessment

An example of a risk assessment form has been provided in Figure 12.5.

Writing up the risk assessment can be a straightforward exercise. Your organisation will almost certainly have its preferred method for doing this, and you should refer to your health and safety manager or other competent person for details.

As mental health risk assessments are undertaken at individual and group level, it may be appropriate to write up the risk assessment as it applies to both levels. It is therefore possible that a number of risk assessment documents will be created.

In larger organisations, as identified in Step 3, at a group level, mental health risk assessment data can be aggregated to form a more strategic view of risks across a team, department, site, country and/or the entire organisation. Risk assessment forms might be created at these more strategic levels.

When implementing mental health control measures, you might find the Plan-Do-Check-Act (PDCA) model (chapter 3) useful. The planning of the control measures should be risk-based, with risk assessments informing the planned control measures. The risks and control measures should be discussed with individuals and groups as necessary and appropriate (eg. respecting any need for confidentiality). Following such discussions, the control methods should be implemented. This is likely to involve internal and/or external resources and arrangements. For example, training may be required or the working environment adapted, say, to increase natural light.

It will then be necessary to check with individuals and groups that the planned control measures are having the desired effect, and that causes of poor mental health are being mitigated by the controls. Where control measures are not proving sufficiently effective, action must be taken to remedy the situation, starting again from the 'Plan' part of the PDCA cycle.

Implementation may need the involvement of many people. Given the complexity of mental health and its treatment, it is not surprising to find multiple parties involved in a recovery plan. Four elements of support play a part in any recovery plan (Figure 12.6): the employee themselves; their employer; their therapist doctor or other clinician; and perhaps members of the employee's social community, such as their church, fitness club, sports or other social association.

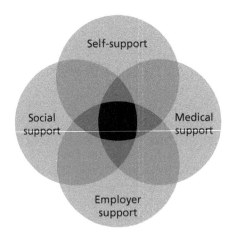

Figure 12.6   *The four supports of mental health*

Everyone involved in the plan (as shown in Figure 12.6) has a role to play. Rarely does recovery fall to one party alone. And, like physical health, the employer can be vital in achieving an effective and speedy recovery.

When writing up and implementing risk assessments, some thought should be given to vulnerabilities. Vulnerabilities arise where control measures do not fully address the risk, meaning that residual risks remain. It may be that leaders, in consultation with the competent person, agree to accept this risk, understanding that it cannot be controlled. This is not necessarily wrong, so long as these vulnerabilities are understood, the risks are understood, considered acceptable and accepted, and the people affected by the risks have agreed to accept them. Some element of risk may remain even after a risk assessment has been implemented, such as the risk of accident faced by drivers. No matter how safe the vehicle and how well trained the driver, the risk of an accident remains. Clearly, greater levels of monitoring may be required to ensure those affected are able to bear the risks envisaged. An example might be nursing, which inevitably requires nurses to witness trauma. This is unavoidable: the role requires nurses to accept this risk. However, greater emphasis might be put on recruitment and selection to identify each nursing applicant's resilience buffer and susceptibility, and more emphasis may be placed upon health checks, to check each nurse's state of mental health once they are in post. Again, a risk-based approach may be taken, with accident and emergency (A&E) nurses perhaps more likely to witness death and trauma than nurses working in a phlebotomy unit.

Implementation may call for a project approach, or even a programme approach. In reality, as with physical health and safety, generic methods and resources for controlling risk will be determined by the department or person leading on mental health, and mental health control measures will be tailored to suit the local risk profile. In physical health and safety terms, an organisation's head office selects PPE and makes it available, with local managers determining the PPE that is required in their area. The same should be true for mental health. The department leading on mental health must make a wide array of mental health support measures available, with local managers selecting and implementing the necessary mental health control measures and support, based on local risk assessments.

Given that many mental health hazards relate to management practice (eg. management style, managing change), training is likely to form a key part of the implementation of any mental health programme. Training must be aligned with the mental health aspirations of the organisation, and its effectiveness must be assessed to ensure it is proving effective.

Step 5: Review the Mental Health Risk Assessment

As part of the process of checking that the mental health policy has been effectively implemented, leaders may arrange for risk assessments to be reviewed or audited. Such reviews or audits should be undertaken to ensure the risk assessments:

- have been properly undertaken
- have been properly implemented
- are proving effective.

Risk assessments should be reviewed on a periodical basis, usually annually, or when a significant change occurs. The competent person must ensure procedures are in place to make sure this is done.

Periodic reviews: Generally, most policies are reviewed every year. This would typically be the longest period between reviews. This should also be the case with mental health risk assessments, unless there has been a significant change that necessitates an earlier review. The aim of the periodic risk assessment review is to ensure the risk assessment is still suitable and sufficient, to update it (eg. to incorporate best practice developments in the market) and to check the details in it are still correct (eg. management structure).

Change in workplace conditions: Changes that might affect the mental health policy include those identified in Figures 12.1 and 12.2. Working conditions might change, for example, through a change in role, an increase in workload, a period of significant restructuring, or a change in leadership and culture. In many instances, changes to leadership, work patterns, workloads and team leaders will have little effect upon mental health. But in some cases, especially those where activities carry a higher risk and where particular groups are more vulnerable, changes of this nature can have a more profound impact. In such cases, these changes might provide a significant 'shock to the system' for some employees or they may represent the *one small thing* that tips an employee's mental state from *coping* to *distressed*. Workplace relationships might change too; for example, a new boss might be appointed or an employee with very long service might retire, losing the team's maternal or paternal figure as a result. In some cases a trusted confidant can be lost. Changing relationships can change culture, mood, understanding and cooperation. Changes that might have a significant effect upon workers might necessitate a review of the mental health risk assessment.

Change in employee vulnerability: It is also worth contemplating the workforce and their vulnerability. Group and individual vulnerability can change. Individuals may experience traumatic changes in their lives, such as pregnancy, birth-related issues or the menopause, perhaps a severe traffic accident or the development of a chronic health condition. All of these experiences can have an adverse effect on mental health. Although it is less common, groups of employees can also find themselves facing challenging circumstances; for example, a group might experience the sudden and unexpected bereavement of a beloved colleague, which can lead to PTSD or similar issues (see chapter 1). In such a case, the group's resilience buffer may be reduced and their mental state may deteriorate, with some members of the group running the risk of becoming *distressed*. As the whole group is affected, the mental health risk assessment should be reviewed as previous control measures may not now prove adequate.

Note that this chapter has focused on employees, but the reader should also contemplate other groups affected by the organisation's activities, such as the public, visitors, contractors and maintenance staff, who might also be at risk from mental health risk factors.

In this chapter, I set out the five-step risk assessment process. I considered each of these five steps as they relate to mental health: 1) Identify what can cause harm; 2) Identify who can be harmed and how; 3) Evaluate the risks and determine controls measures; 4) Write up and implement the risk assessment; and 5) Review the risk assessment. I presented 12 general mental health risk factors, along with 12 workplace mental health risk factors, providing a 12 x 12 approach to risk assessments. I recommended that risks should be evaluated using a risk assessment matrix, using a 9-point or 25-point scale, which provides a means of assessing the likelihood and severity of potential risks. I explored individual and group risk assessments; individual risk assessments consider an employee's past, present and future, whereas group risk assessments contemplate those control measures most relevant to a number of employees. I showed how aggregating risk assessment data allows for 'hotspots' to be identified, which indicate localised causes and teams most at risk. I explained that risk assessments should be written up using the risk assessment forms currently in use in the organisation, and included an alternative in the form of the HSE's template. I ended by stressing that risk assessments

should be reviewed periodically (eg. annually), when significant changes to workplace circumstances arise and when groups of employees become more vulnerable.

The main take-outs from this chapter are:

- Mental health risk assessments should be undertaken using the same risk assessment process that is applied to physical health and safety.

- The five-step risk assessment process should: identify what can cause harm; identify who can be harmed and how; determine what control measures are required; write up the risk assessment and implement it; and review the risk assessment.

- There are 12 general mental health risks.

- There are 12 workplace mental health risks.

- When assessing mental health risks, employers should use all the information in their possession, whether this is provided by the employee or gleaned through other means.

- Unlike physical health and safety, where ignorance is no defence, ignorance (eg. having no knowledge) in respect of mental health (eg. where an employee does not disclose a mental health issue) may provide the employer with a defence in law.

- Employers must foresee mental health risks, using all the information in their possession. They must enquire about employee mental health.

- A 9-point or 25-point scale can be used when applying the risk assessment matrix, which considers the likelihood of the risk arising and the severity of its impact.

- Risks with high scores must be managed as a priority.

- Reviews and audits of risk assessments should be carried out to ensure they have been properly undertaken, properly implemented and are proving effective.

References

Advisory Board (2019) *Why 1 in 4 Nurses Suffers from PTSD (and How to Help Them).* Available at: *https://www.advisory.com/daily-briefing/2019/05/15/nurse-trauma* (accessed 3 March 2020).

Afonso, P., Fonseca, M. and Pires, J. F. (2017) Impact of working hours on sleep and mental health. *Occupational Medicine* 67:5, 377–382. Available at: *https://doi.org/10.1093/occmed/kqx054* (accessed 30 March 2020).

Forbes, D., Pedlar, D., Adler, A. B., Bennett, C., Bryant, R., Busuttil, W., Cooper, J., Creamer, M. C., Fear, N. T., Greenberg, N., Heber, A., Hinton, M., Hopwood, M., Jetly, R., Lawrence-Wood, E., McFarlane, A., Metcalf, O., O'Donnell, M., Phelps, A., Richardson, J. D., Sadler, N., Schnurr, P. P., Sharp, M-L., Thompson, J. M., Ursano, R. J., Van Hooff, M., Wade D. and Wessely, S. (2019) Treatment of military-related post-traumatic stress disorder: challenges, innovations, and the way forward. *International Review of Psychiatry*, DOI: 10.1080/09540261.2019.1595545. Available at: https://www.kcl.ac.uk/kcmhr/publications/assetfiles/2019/forbes2019.pdf (accessed 21 March 2020).

Health and Safety Executive (online) *Managing Risks and Risk Assessment at Work.* Available at: *https://www.hse.gov.uk/simple-health-safety/risk/risk-assessment-template-and-examples.htm* (accessed 2 March 2020).

ICO (online) *Special Category Data.* Available at: *https://ico.org.uk/for-organisations/guide-to-data-protection/guide-to-the-general-data-protection-regulation-gdpr/lawful-basis-for-processing/special-category-data/* (accessed 27 March 2020).

Mind (2017) *How common are mental health problems?* Available at: *https://www.mind.org.uk/information-support/types-of-mental-health-problems/statistics-and-facts-about-mental-health/how-common-are-mental-health-problems/#.XbmhHUagLIU* (accessed 30 January 2020).

Ogle, C.M., Rubin, D.C. and Siegler, I.C. (2013) Cumulative exposure to traumatic events in older adults. *Aging & Mental Health* 18:3, 316–325. Available at: *https://www.ncbi.nlm.nih.gov/pmc/articles/PMC3944195/* (accessed 5 January 2020).

Robinson, B.E. (2018) Is your job hazardous to your mental health? *Psychology Today* 20 May. Available at: *https://www.psychologytoday.com/us/blog/the-right-mindset/201805/is-your-job-hazardous-your-mental-health-0* (accessed 1 March 2020).

Shaw Trust (2018) *Mental Health at Work: Still the last taboo.* Available at: *https://www.shaw-trust.org.uk/ShawTrustMediaLibraries/ShawTrust/ShawTrust/Documents/Shaw-Trust-Mental-Health-at-Work-Report-2018-full_1.pdf* (accessed 29 November 2019).

UK Government (online) *Health and Safety at Work etc. Act 1974.* Available at: *http://www.legislation.gov.uk/ukpga/1974/37/section/7* (accessed 30 March 2020).

13

PRINCIPLE 5:
HIERARCHY OF
CONTROLS

In this chapter, I present an approach to managing mental health hazards that uses the well-known hierarchy of controls (HoC), which comprises six levels: elimination, substitution, isolation (which is included in some HoC models), engineering controls, administrative controls and personal protective equipment (PPE). I describe the hierarchy and how each of its levels can be applied to mental health management. I briefly revisit the 12 general mental health risk factors and 12 workplace mental health risk factors (introduced in chapter 12), and work through examples of how the hierarchy of controls can be used to address several of the 12 x 12 mental health risk factors. I conclude the chapter by calling for leaders to optimise mental health, rather than simply trying to minimise harmful effects upon it.

The hierarchy of controls is a systematic way of controlling health and safety risks (Figure 13.1). Once the risks have been assessed (chapter 12), the hierarchy of controls can be used to determine the most suitable control measures for each risk factor.

Hierarchy of Controls

The onus is on the employer to take responsibility for hazard control; in other words, the employer must take proactive and preventative steps to manage mental health hazards and put suitable controls in place, as far as is reasonably practicable. In the UK, this is a legal requirement that extends to managing mental health hazards at work.

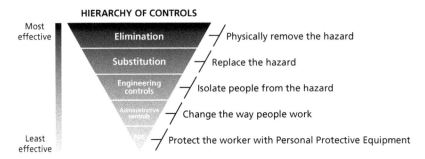

Figure 13.1 *Hierarchy of controls*

Source: CDC/NIOSH, online

I would like to start by considering the 12 general health hazards framework (Figure 13.2) and the 12 workplace mental health risk factors (Figure 13.3) I introduced in chapter 12.

Together, Figures 13.2 and 13.3 represent the 12 x 12 mental health risk factors.

At this stage it is vital to refer to the *group* and *individual* risk assessments explored in chapter 12. Along with any relevant senior managers in the health and safety management structure set out in the organisation's mental health policy, the competent person (CP) is required to oversee the control measures to be implemented to mitigate mental health risks or to make them acceptable.

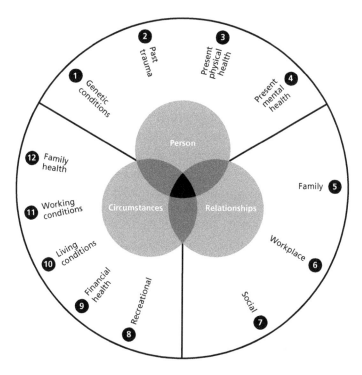

Figure 13.2 *The 12 general mental health risk factors*

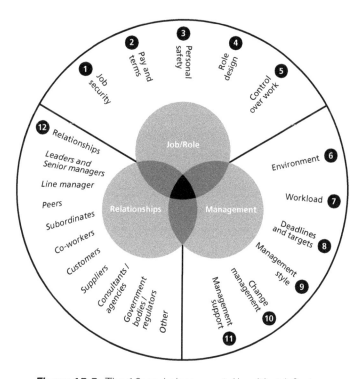

Figure 13.3 *The 12 workplace mental health risk factors*

When determining how to apply the hierarchy of controls and what actions to take, the management team should link the cause, the effect and the control measures, at both *group* and *individual* levels. For example, at the *group* level, a team may be suffering from stress as a result of a high workload. The cause of stress is the workload. The effect of the high workload is stress. The control measures need to address the cause and reduce the effect. One control measure may be to add more employees to the team, which may spread the workload across more team members, reducing the group's stress level. At the *individual* level, an employee may have told their employer in confidence that they have stress caused by seemingly (to the employee) impossible monthly targets. Here, the employer might check the appropriateness of targets and review their frequency, making adjustments where reasonably possible.

Control methods need not be a significant burden to the employer. Minor adjustments can have an incredibly beneficial effect on the employee's overall mental health.

The mental health management team should take this 'cause-effect-control' approach. It involves working through the hierarchy of controls, identifying the preferred methods of hazard control that are reasonably practicable and implementing these first. The least preferred control methods should be identified, and only implemented after the most preferred methods have been exhausted.

I will now explore the six levels of the hierarchy of controls (elimination, substitution, isolation, engineering controls, administrative controls and personal protective equipment (PPE)), starting with the first consideration for managers: *eliminating* mental health hazards.

Eliminate: In terms of physical health and safety, the risk of harm from a fall, for example, is eliminated by lowering an item from the roof and repairing it on the ground. A similar approach is needed for mental health hazards. Elimination is by far the most preferred method of all hazard controls, whether we are talking about physical health and safety or mental health, and elimination should be the first thing to consider when addressing the 12 x 12 mental health risk factors. If any employees are unduly stressed, the goal should be to eliminate undue stress, as opposed to beneficial stress (Mental Health Foundation, online). Actions that might eliminate workplace mental health hazards should focus on eliminating the causes of mental harm. The aim is not to eliminate all of the work, activity or circumstances that have been identified as the cause, but simply to address the undue element. Bullying is an obvious example. Most employers have an anti-bullying policy. All leaders need do is enforce it. The bully may not even realise their behaviour amounts to bullying, and somebody who does not think they are a bully will not think they need to pay special attention to an anti-bullying policy. Leaders must therefore define bullying, measure it, lead by example, train employees in the correct behaviours, develop and implement action plans, and review performance, in order to eliminate it. Targets, too, are known to cause undue stress. Are targets really needed each month, every month? What would happen if targets were eliminated for one month? Readers may wish to consider McGregor's Theory Y (Wikipedia, online), in which managers assume employees are motivated to work for their own fulfilment rather than external rewards. If employees understand the organisation's vision, mission, goal and objectives, perhaps they do not need such frequent targets to bring about success. Perhaps the undue stress caused by targets can be eliminated without any reduction in performance, by establishing targets less frequently. Management style is another known stressor. Leaders and managers should reflect on the consequences of their own management style and adapt it to ensure it has a more positive effect. Paying wages monthly is known to stress some employees, whereas paying weekly may not. Wage systems are usually designed to benefit the employer, with little thought given to how the system might affect employee mental health. Paying wages more frequently may eliminate stress. As is evident, creativity may be required. The key point here is that by far the preferred method of mental health risk reduction is for the employer to *eliminate* mental health hazards. This means eliminating sources of stress and other causes of mental harm (excessive workload, how change is managed, toxic relationships, bullying and so on). Employers should also consider risk factors outside of work, such as financial health (which levels of pay may have a bearing on), lifestyle, socialisation, family health and so on. Elimination places the onus on the employer, who must act to reduce the causes of mental harm before expecting the employee to act and before moving on to other control measures in the hierarchy.

Substitute: Physical health and safety considers substituting dangerous circumstances for less dangerous ones. Replacing lead-based paint with water-based paint is an obvious example. Substitutions can also be found in the case of mental health. Let us take as an example a customer service department that takes calls from customers who are often angry. The employees taking the calls may be subjected to abuse, causing stress, anxiety and possibly other mental health issues. In a situation like this, alternative customer response systems might be employed, such as online information and online complaints forms, an interactive voice response (IVR) telephone system, or a 'bot'. Here, an automated process might substitute for phone calls, eliminating any opportunity for the customer to be abusive towards employees, reducing adverse mental health effects. If the organisation needs the service to be personal, role rotation can be used, in which employees rotate between more stressful and less stressful roles. Employers should explore possible substitutions within the context of their own workplace.

Isolate: In terms of physical health and safety, isolation can be where a hazardous item is moved to a remote area where the likelihood of wide-scale harm is minimised. It is also possible to use isolation to control psychological risks. We found earlier that it is mentally harmful to witness trauma. The number of people witnessing traumatic scenes might be minimised by using screens to visually isolate the incident and protect employees, passers-by and others. The length of time employees spend in roles where they are exposed to traumatic scenes might be cut from, say, months to weeks at a time, with role rotation happening more frequently and with longer periods of 'respite' between periods of 'exposure' to traumatic scenes.

Engineering controls: In physical health terms, engineering controls typically relate to ways of controlling employees coming into contact with sources of harm, such as fitting covers over moving parts, such as a guard on a grinder wheel. With mental health, similar considerations can be made. It has been established that natural daylight is preferable to artificial light (Agarwal, 2018) as it staves off seasonal mood changes and can help to aid sleep and boost vitamin D. If no more light can be channelled into the workplace, letting employees take short breaks out in the daylight might help. Noise reduction methods might be appropriate in some environments (Webber, 2019). Sound insulation and absorption, say, through wall coverings and screening might prove useful. Display screen equipment assessments should be undertaken, as monitors and screens can strain sight and cause glare, which might cause headaches and have other adverse effects. Leaders and managers should assess the physical elements of the workplace that can be *engineered* to support good mental health.

Administrative controls: These controls generally relate to administrative arrangements that provide the employee with information, training, instruction and supervision (ITIS). Organisational leaders and managers should provide employees with a variety of ITIS supports that help create the culture that is most conducive to good mental health. This might include the provision of events and procedures that focus on:

- diversity and inclusion (with a focus on mental health and anti-bullying)
- managing change
- personal and professional development
- managing workplace relationships
- consultation, with a focus on mental health
- workshops on healthy lifestyles.

Supervision may be undertaken in which, for example, employees have a one-to-one meeting with their line manager to discuss the employee's life inside and outside of work. The line manager would steer the discussion to identify whether the employee is experiencing issues in areas that are likely to cause mental harm (financial health, family health, living conditions and so on). The manager may wish to pay particular attention to those aspects of mental harm that arise outside of work, as they may be less obvious. Other administrative controls might relate to the 'management style' cause of harm. In this case it might not just be a manager's behaviour that is examined, but also the policies and procedures the manager puts in place. Empowerment can reduce stress associated with inadequate control over a role and work. For example, when dealing with difficult customers, if the employee is given increased financial authority, it may lead to customers having more belief in the employee's authority to resolve their concerns, reducing customer anger and aggression and thus reducing the employee's stress. Organisations are steeped in administration. Understanding the mental health impacts of the administrative structure and procedures may well identify opportunities to improve mental health, especially where the current administration seems burdensome, controlling and even punitive.

Personal protective equipment (PPE): In physical health and safety terms, PPE is the protection (eg. gloves, masks) clothing and other items worn or used by people to protect them from harm. When it has been accepted that there is a hazard that presents a chance of harm and the most preferred control measures have been applied, any remaining risk is controlled by the use of PPE, such as puncture resistant gloves to protect cleaners when handling discarded syringes. In terms of mental health, PPE relates to things like: mindfulness; resilience training (eg. coping techniques); breathing techniques; sleep and relaxation techniques; assertiveness training; and therapies (eg. ecotherapy, coming to terms with past traumatic events). The employer should have done everything possible to reduce the effects of mental health hazards using the most preferred and effective controls, *before* putting in place the mental health 'PPE' measures. They should have undertaken a mental health risk assessment, put in place all reasonably practicable control measures and communicated the mental health risks to the employees. As Croner (online) explains: 'Some critics of mindfulness have pointed out that it does not address legitimate issues within the workplace. In some cases, mindfulness is used as a tool to help employees cope with needlessly stressful or negative situations. Mindfulness should not be a substitute for an actual solution.'

As is evident when contemplating the hierarchy of controls in the context of mental health, there is plenty of overlap between the various elements, approaches and methods. This does not matter. The onus is on the employer to act first, before the employee is expected to act. Mental harm reduction must be approached in the order of the hierarchy of control's six levels, with elimination as the starting point, followed by substitution, isolation, engineering controls, administrative controls and finally PPE.

Need for New Thinking

Leaders and managers must be creative when determining initiatives to improve mental wellbeing. Barriers to mental health innovation may include:

- attitudes (conscious and subconscious, such as prejudices)
- policies and procedures (these usually impose controls. Are they really necessary?)
- custom and practice ('We've always done it this way.' Why?)
- lack of innovation (apply innovation management techniques; Hamel, 2006)
- gut feeling ('It doesn't feel right.').

Let's take for example 'job security', the first workplace mental health risk factor in Figure 13.3. If the organisation doubled the notice periods, employees' fear of losing their job at short notice would be reduced and this would be good for the workforce's mental health. Would that work? Could that be done? The above barriers might prevent this sort of thinking. But what is the issue? Cost? Okay, let's model the idea. What are the considerations? 'Notice period' only creates a cost liability when the organisation wishes to terminate someone's employment. How often does this happen? Is it likely? When might it occur? How many people might be involved? What actual cost liability would arise in a given year? Costs would need to be offset by the benefits that arise from the initiative. How would improving mental health by extending notice periods improve productivity, employee retention and sickness absence? Are there other benefits to be taken into account? Now, do the benefits justify the cost? Is this an investable business case? Let's work through an example. There are approximately 400,000 redundancies in the UK each year (Statista, online). This amounts to around 1.25% of the UK's national workforce of 32 million (BBC, 2019). If this percentage is applied to an employer of 1,000 people, it means the employer would make 12.5 people redundant each year. If we assume the one-month notice period is doubled through the extended notice period initiative to two months, at an average salary of £25,000 per annum, the total notice period cost liability for 12.5 employees increases from £26,000 to £52,000 per annum; an increase of £26,000. With 1,000 employees, this represents an increase in the total workforce's 'cost to employ' of £26 per employee per annum. The entire workforce's 'cost to employ' must be considered, because the benefit of improved mental health resulting from the initiative will be experienced by the entire workforce. So, the question arises: is the value of greater productivity, retention, sickness absence and other financial benefits (there may be non-financial benefits) arising across all 1,000 employees greater than the cost of the initiative? Would you, the organisational leader, pay £26 per employee per annum to improve mental health, if the return on investment (ROI) justified doing so? Some leaders might do so, even if the ROI were weak, on the basis that improving mental health is the right thing to do. 'What about compromise agreements?', I hear you ask. My response is: 1) you should take into account whatever costs you feel should be included (eg. length of service, age); 2) perhaps just apply the 'extended notice period' to front line staff, who are less likely to be the subject of a compromise agreement; and 3) you can always find reasons not to do something, so apply fresh thinking to look for reasons to actually *do* things differently. As for the cost of £26 per employee per annum – well, mental health awareness training courses cost much more than that, and their results are uncertain (chapter 1). Simple, low-cost initiatives aimed at actually improving mental health, as opposed to talking about improving it, may prove more worthwhile. New thinking is required.

Workplace mental health management is a new and rapidly developing discipline. If it has the potential to unlock a productivity increase of up to 12% or even 25% (chapter 6), new ways of thinking may be necessary to determine how to do it. The fact that such a productivity increase may be available implies that previous management practices have in some cases not been as effective as they might have been.

The 'notice period' initiative above is just one simple example of how and why current thinking needs to be challenged. When were notice periods for all workers last reviewed in your organisation? Never? Are they just a 'thing' that nobody thinks about? What other aspects of your organisation might there be that are given little thought but are having a profound effect on mental health? Take targets and deadlines, for example. We live by them. Some are mandatory, such as statutory reporting requirements. But how many do you really need? When did you last test the necessity or effectiveness of your deadlines and targets? If targets were removed, would employees continue to hit high standards? If McGregor's Theory Y applies and people are highly self-motivated, do they need so many deadlines and targets? If you were to cut the number of targets you have by half, what would happen to performance? And what would the effect be on employee mental health, given that deadlines and targets can be harmful to it? Would an increase in productivity arising from improved mental health offset any loss in productivity caused by having fewer targets? It has been shown removing road markings can, in some circumstances, lead to improvements in road safety. Counter-intuitive, but effective. Perhaps the same thinking can be applied to targets.

Convention must be challenged. Leaders must step up and take a leading role in challenging the status quo if workplace mental health innovation is to prove an effective way of optimising productivity and organisational performance.

Leaders need to give thought to the issues in Table 13.1, to determine how to unlock the potential 12% to 25% increase in productivity some have found to be available.'

Table 13.1 *How to manage workplace mental health risk factors*

Hazard/risk factor	Possible approach to control measures
Job security	<ul><li>Increase perceived and actual job security</li><li>Reduce the threat of job loss</li></ul>
Role	<ul><li>Design roles to maximise mental health</li><li>Minimise stress and other forms of mental harm arising through role design</li></ul>
Environment	<ul><li>Design and implement a working environment conducive to good mental health</li><li>Minimise those environmental factors that adversely affect mental health</li></ul>
Personal safety	<ul><li>Maximise the feeling of personal safety and security</li><li>Minimise negative feelings of being at physical and mental risk</li></ul>
Pay and terms	<ul><li>Maximise financial wellbeing</li><li>Minimise adverse mental health effects related to finances</li></ul>

Hazard/risk factor	Possible approach to control measures
Workload	<ul><li>Maximise employees' positive feelings created by workload (eg. motivated by the mission, stimulated by the challenge, positive stress)</li><li>Monitor and manage workloads to minimise the amount of time during which the employee's workload is causing undue levels of stress</li></ul>
Deadlines and targets	<ul><li>Ensure deadlines and targets are necessary and relevant</li><li>Minimise the use of deadlines and targets where possible</li></ul>
Management style	<ul><li>Utilise management style to maximise mental health</li><li>Minimise the adverse effects of management style</li></ul>
Change management	<ul><li>Manage change so as to have a positive impact upon mental health</li><li>Minimise stress and other adverse effects arising from change</li></ul>
Control over work	<ul><li>Maximise employee control over work</li><li>Minimise the adverse mental health effects of work control impotence</li></ul>
Management support	<ul><li>Design management support to maximise employee mental health</li><li>Eliminate negative and ineffective aspects of management support</li></ul>
Workplace relationships	<ul><li>Create psychological safety; develop a culture of caring, compassion and kindness</li><li>Eliminate the stimuli and behaviours that have a negative impact on workplace relationships</li></ul>

The list in Table 13.1 is not exhaustive. Each of the 12 workplace risk factors needs to be considered, with specific actions taken to address each one. For example, I have suggested increasing notice periods, and cutting the number of targets. If you simply ask employees how they would design their role differently or whether their role conflicts with that of others, it can have a powerful effect when the question has genuine intent and you listen to and, where possible, implement the responses. This type of approach may reduce stress as it may make employees feel they have greater control over work.

Employers should develop their own approach to mental health improvement by maximising related opportunities more effectively and through more effective mental health hazard control.

Mental health management is far more than stress reduction. Turning this notion on its head, the aim should first be a positive one – to maximise organisational performance through maximising mental health. Employers should determine the sort of good mental health they aspire to for their workforce, then set out related goals and objectives, perhaps within their mental health policy (chapter 11). Having set these goals and objectives, employers can develop plans to bring about the changes required to optimise employee mental health.

At this point it should be noted that first aid, including mental health first aid, does not feature in the hierarchy of controls. First aid is a post-injury intervention. The hierarchy of controls is concerned with proactive prevention, which starts with the elimination of hazards. Any employer who believes it is adequate to simply put in place mental health first aid to address mental health is kidding themselves. Remember, in the UK, employers have a legal duty to undertake suitable and sufficient mental health risk assessments and to act on them.

Some leaders may balk at the mental health 'elimination-first' approach set out in the hierarchy of controls, given the financial cost of some of the related initiatives. However, this investment may well prove worthwhile, given the financial returns that can result from improving mental health and wellbeing, through increased productivity, increased staff retention and reduced sickness absence. Before dismissing potential mental health control measures as fanciful, leaders and managers are encouraged to undertake a cost-benefit analysis, run pilot schemes and otherwise tests these and other ideas. In addition to the cost-benefit analysis, employers should also consider the other arguments for supporting employees' mental health, including the legal case, the moral case and the technical case, as well as the commercial case (chapter 6). Perhaps doing more to support mental health, and employees with poor mental health, will fit with your organisation's corporate social responsibility and social wellbeing policies.

Books on mental health, such as this one, must become a staple of any manager's reading list. Only by deepening their understanding of the subject can leaders and managers expect to get right the various judgement calls they may have to make that relate to mental health. Given the increasing suicide rates, and given that *one small thing* at work can make the difference between an employee *coping* and becoming *distressed*, leaders and managers have a responsibility to develop their skills in mental health management.

In this chapter, I set out the hierarchy of controls, along with the suggested management approach based upon the 'cause, effect and control' method. I considered the six levels of the hierarchy of controls, in respect to how each of them might apply to mental health, placing significant emphasis on the *elimination* of mental health hazards before implementing the equivalent of mental health PPE – the least preferred approach. I went on to present the notion that employers should seek not only to minimise mental health harm through the hierarchy of controls but also to optimise mental health through the use of goals and objectives, and through the development and implementation of related plans.

The main take-outs from this chapter are:

- The hierarchy of controls provides a proactive and systematic approach to mental health hazard control and risk management.

- The hierarchy of controls approach is known throughout the world. It will be included in any assessment of adequacy faced by an employer when their health and safety management practices are scrutinised (eg. to assess compliance with the OHSAS 18001 standard, when facing legal claims of health and safety negligence).

- The hierarchy of controls approach requires employers to be proactive and to take a preventative approach.

- The hierarchy requires employers to consider six stages of risk control: 1) elimination; 2) substitution; 3) isolation (where possible); 4) engineering controls; 5) administrative controls; and 6) personal protective equipment (PPE).

- Employers should develop hazard control methods that address work-related and non-work-related causes of mental harm.

- The hierarchy of controls can be applied following risk assessments, through which work-place mental health hazards should have been identified.

- Each control method has a varying degree of effectiveness. Elimination is considered the most effective, with PPE the least effective. Employers should prioritise the most effective methods of mental health risk control.

- Mental health hazards can be managed by applying a systematic approach of 'cause, effect and control'. Employers should focus on reducing causes as far as is reasonably practicable, with controls effectively addressing any residual effects.

References

Agarwal, P. (2018) How does natural lighting affect mental health in the workplace? *Forbes* 31 December. Available at: *https://www.forbes.com/sites/pragyaagarwaleurope/2018/12/31/how-does-lighting-affect-mental-health-in-the-workplace/#17bcf4554ccd* (accessed 3 March 2020).

BBC (2019) UK employment total hits record high. *BBC* 22 January. Available at: *https://www.bbc.co.uk/news/business-46958560* (accessed 3 March 2020).

Centers for Disease Control and Prevention / The National Institute for Occupational Safety and Health (online) *Hierarchy of Controls*. Available at: *https://www.cdc.gov/niosh/topics/hierarchy/default.html* (accessed 20 February 2020).

Croner (online) *Should Companies Offer Mindfulness Training?* Available at: *https://croner.co.uk/resources/pay-benefits/companies-offering-mindfulness-training/* (accessed 19 March 2020).

Hamel, G. (2006) The why, what, and how of management innovation. *Harvard Business Review* February. Available at: *https://hbr.org/2006/02/the-why-what-and-how-of-management-innovation* (accessed 3 February 2020).

Mental Health Foundation (online) *Stress*. Available at: *https://www.mentalhealth.org.uk/a-to-z/s/stress* (accessed 3 March 2020).

Statista (online) *Number of People made Redundant in the United Kingdom (UK) from 1st Quarter 2014 to 1st Quarter 2018*. Available at: *https://www.statista.com/statistics/284145/redundancy-level-in-the-united-kingdom-uk/* (accessed 3 March 2020).

Webber, A. (2019) Noisy offices affect wellbeing for four in ten staff. *Personnel Today* 13 March. Available at: *https://www.personneltoday.com/hr/noisy-offices-impact-on-wellbeing/* (accessed 3 March 2020).

Wikipedia (online) *Theory X and Theory Y*. Available at: *https://en.wikipedia.org/wiki/Theory_X_and_Theory_Y* (accessed 3 March 2020).

14

PRINCIPLE 6:
CONSULTATION

In this chapter I explore the sixth principle of the management system: consultation. I open by revisiting the legal requirement for employers to consult employees, then present other justifications for engaging in employee consultations, before moving on to explore the purpose of consultations and how they might be governed to ensure legal compliance. I end by examining group and individual consultations, including the justification for each and some of the methods that might be employed.

Legal Requirement to Consult Employees on Mental Health

The legal requirement to consult employees was covered in chapter 3. However, it is worth taking time to explore consultations as they relate to mental health.

In the UK, Australia and some other countries, employers have a legal duty to consult their employees in respect of health and safety. In the UK, there are two regulations that require employers to consult their workforce about health and safety:

- the Safety Representatives and Safety Committees Regulations 1977 (as amended)
- the Health and Safety (Consultation with Employees) Regulations 1996 (as amended).

In workplaces where trade unions are recognised for collective bargaining purposes, the Safety Representatives and Safety Committees Regulations 1977 will apply.

In workplaces where employees are not in a trade union, the employer does not recognise the trade union and/or the trade union does not represent those employees who are not in the trade union, the Health and Safety (Consultation with Employees) Regulations 1996 will apply (HSE, 2013).

The Justification for Mental Health Consultation

Beyond the legal requirement to consult, the UK's health and safety regulator, the HSE (2013), states that consultations provided several benefits to organisations including:

- *increased productivity – businesses with good workforce involvement in health and safety tend to have a better productivity rate;*
- *improvements in overall efficiency and quality; and*
- *higher levels of workforce motivation.*

The management of mental health in the workplace is not just about supporting people with genetic conditions. It is also about supporting people who have stress, phobias, anxiety, depression, eating disorders and other conditions caused by the numerous factors identified earlier in this book, many of which can be directly caused or exacerbated by work, or be caused outside of work but with symptoms manifesting at work.

Mental health consultations are, perhaps, even more important than those undertaken for physical health and safety purposes, for a number of reasons. These include things such as the scale of the issue, the need to gain buy-in, the invisibility of some of the issues, and the possibility of there being a perception gap.

Scale: The proportion of the workforce that will suffer with mental health issues is far greater than will suffer physical injury. More 'lost time' may arise through mental health than physical health. The scale of the issue alone should justify the need to consult on mental health.

Gaining buy-in: It may be more challenging to gain buy-in to mental health policies, procedures and practices than is the case with physical health. I presented evidence in chapter 1 that suggests a level of discrimination exists, meaning that there are some leaders and managers who do not believe their employer should employ and support people with mental health issues. Far fewer people object to measures relating to physical health and safety. Consultation may help gain buy-in, as it represents a chance to share thinking, ideas and information. It also places a responsibility on workforce representatives to talk to both management and the workforce about mental health, which will almost certainly reveal the need for action.

Invisibility of issues: Mental health issues are mostly invisible (unlike most physical health and safety issues), so consultation performs an important role in revealing them to management. Workforce input is essential in determining causes of mental health issues, hazards and suitable control measures, and in establishing the effectiveness of these controls.

Perception gap: It may be the case that the leaders of an organisation believe they have highly effective mental health policies, procedures and practices in place, while at the same time the workforce feels these measures are anything but effective. Figure 14.1 shows the potential for a perception gap to occur. Consultation helps to ensure no such gap arises and that management and the workforce share the same perspective about mental health-related matters.

Figure 14.1 shows responses to questions about organisational mental health culture. The nature of the questions can be identified from the statements at the bottom. For example, 'Employee input into mental health programmes' will have been posted as a statement for respondents to respond to in the affirmative or negative, creating the score represented by the bar. The statements at the foot of the bars may be useful to you when you are determining the questions to include in your engagement surveys.

Mental health management, including consultations, plays an important role in establishing a culture in which employees and their wellbeing are valued as much as their productivity and performance.

Given the justification for mental health consultations, employers should invest time and resources into ensuring that they establish an effective consultation process.

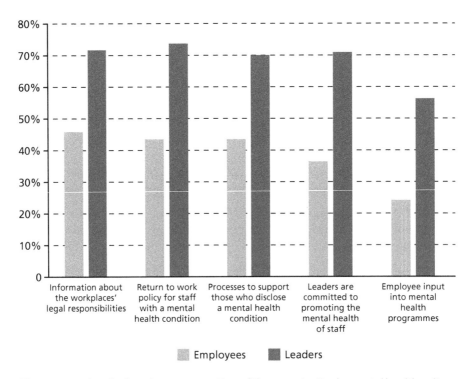

Figure 14.1 *Leader/employee perception of the organisation's mental health culture*
Source: Consult Australia/BeyondBlue, 2014

Purpose of Consultations

In several countries, health and safety laws require consultation with employees to be undertaken. There are clear guidelines about what the workforce should be consulted about. Reading across from health and safety consultation guidance provided by the HSE (2013), when they are planning mental health consultations, employers should consult with employees or their representatives about:

- the introduction of any measure that may substantially affect the mental health of the workforce. Here, the 12 workplace mental health risk factors should be considered (eg. significant increases in workload or targets, tightened deadlines; see chapter 12), along with any significant change in working practice (eg. new working patterns or the introduction of mandatory, significant and prolonged overtime working)

- making arrangements for competent people to help the workforce comply with workplace mental health laws (a competent person is someone who has the necessary knowledge, skills and experience to help an employer meet the requirements of workplace mental health law)

- the information employers must give employees about the mental health risks and harm arising from their work, measures to reduce or get rid of these risks, and what employees should do to mitigate the risks
- the planning and organisation of mental health training.

These are the four areas of consultation recommended by the HSE. By consulting as set out above, employers will be fulfilling their obligations in law as well as providing their employees with what amounts to a best-practice level of mental health support.

Governance of Consultations

As I have established, holding consultations with employees is a legal requirement; but leaders should want to conduct the consultation process properly and effectively in any case. It is important to establish a method of making sure your organisation's consultation process is operating as it needs to operate and as you mean it to operate.

The organisation and process of consultation has many elements. These include:

- the governance and compliance arrangements
- the make-up of the consultation group
- roles and responsibilities
- the consultation group's remit or mandate
- the consultation process itself
- the process for gathering information
- the effectiveness of consultations.

Governance and compliance: The aim of governance is to ensure the consultation process is legally compliant (where applicable), effective and fair. An independent means of evaluating the consultation process should be established. A suitable leader should be put in place as sponsor, to establish the mental health consultation group and process; this should be somebody with powers of oversight, so they will probably be an experienced and independent consultant, a senior manager or possibly a non-executive director. The mental health consultation process may stand alone or it may form part of a wider process (for example, it might be a subgroup of a general health and safety consultation). A stand-alone process provides a singular focus and has its own momentum. On the other hand, when consultation is part of a wider process (eg. part of the health and safety consultation process), it provides for the sharing of best practice and the adoption of established routines. Given that consultation is a legal requirement in the UK, it should follow a structured approach. An independent audit process should be established to ensure mental health consultations are operated in line with the prescribed processes and that these processes comply with the law. A legal compliance 'register' approach may be appropriate (see chapter 9).

The make-up of the consultation group: Employees with poor mental health can have chronic or acute symptoms, with severe or mild effects. They may have disclosed their condition or they may not. Given that half of employees with a mental health issue do not disclose it, and given the wide range of conditions and symptoms that can arise, employers should encourage wide participation in consultations. Of course, other employees who do not have mental health issues should also be involved as they may have good ideas about how to support employees with mental health issues. The same is true of management (who may themselves have poor mental health). Everyone, in all parts of the organisation, should be represented, especially managers who are more likely to experience poor mental health than employees (chapter 2).

Roles and responsibilities: ACAS (2014) recommends that senior managers, line managers, supervisors and trade unions should be involved in the consultation process. Trade union representation may not always be available; if this is the case, workers' representatives should be appointed. A chair will probably be appointed. If the group has access to resources, especially a budget, a process for accounting for expenditure and measuring benefits arising from investment will need to be established, Goals and objectives will probably be set. The creation of a standard agenda may help establish a routine for meetings, especially around the process of determining and implementing new ideas and measuring results. The activities to be undertaken by the consultation group should be assigned to members, and objectives and timescales should be set.

The consultation group's remit or mandate: Like most consultation groups, the mental health consultation group will be established at the behest of the senior sponsor, who will appoint the chair. Together, the sponsor and chair will agree the terms of reference for the group, including its remit or mandate, which should be focused on improving the mental health of all employees. The mental health of management team members may also fall within the group's reach. The remit or mandate will almost certainly include: the determination of current levels of mental health of employees; the identification of actions to improve employee mental health; and the ongoing monitoring of the mental health of employees. Suitable methods for doing this might include engagement surveys, site mental health inspections, routine health checks (as they relate to mental health), and team and individual employee consultations. Once the current mental health of the workforce has been determined and properly analysed, a risk-based approach can be developed. The analysis and the related action plan will probably be reviewed and approved by the consultation group. The consultation group will then lead or advise the mental health improvement project team or manager and scrutinise their actions.

The consultation process: The consultation process can operate at two levels: the organisational level and the individual level. Organisation-wide consultations consider strategic issues – issues that affect the whole workforce. Key methods for consulting with the whole workforce might include: committees or consultation groups; conferences and events; inspections and observations; and engagement surveys. Each of these consultation methods is briefly explored later in this chapter.

The process for gathering information: Different types of information will be gathered by the consultation group, using a number of methods that might include:

- *determining employees' mental health* – engagement surveys and other methods should be utilised to determine the mental health of the workforce

- *determining the effectiveness of control measures* – interviews with employees (team and individual), inspections and surveys should be utilised to determine the effectiveness of mental health control measures

- *determining best practice* – external information may be gathered that relates to workplace mental health management best practice. This information may take the form of books, journals, academic studies, the practices of other organisations and input from consultants

- *determining mental health performance* – reports and statistics, such as those held by the human resources department, should be analysed to determine performance and trends, along with the effectiveness of new control measures put in place to improve mental health.

- *Innovation* – ideas from the workforce (and management) should be captured, assessed and where viable, implemented.

The required information, sources of information, how to obtain it and how to present it must all be determined. Mental health is a newly emerging management discipline, so information may be in short supply. Bear in mind too, that some of the information that is available may lack credibility.

The effectiveness of consultations: Leaders will want to make sure the consultations are proving effective. In large organisations, it is likely that consultation groups are already in operation, and mental health consultation groups will probably operate in a similar way. Those employers who have already established ways of checking the effectiveness of their consultations can easily extend these checks to mental health, but the most obvious way of checking employee consultation effectiveness is to ask the employees! Do they think the process is adequately representing them? Do they feel they have a voice? Do they feel they are being listened to? Has their input led to action? The more strategic effects of any mental health programme, including consultation, are discussed in chapter 15, which covers reporting.

Consultations can be loosely divided into *group* consultations (involving the whole organisation, sites, departments or teams) and *individual* consultations in cases where singular case studies provide valuable insight or there are special circumstances that need to be better understood. Individual consultations can provide for confidentiality, perhaps where an employee wishes to keep a mental health condition private or wants to discuss colleagues, say where bullying is occurring. Group and individual consultations are now explored.

Group Consultations

Consultation groups operate in many organisations, especially large ones; the practice is well-established and widespread. There are many forms of consultation but it typically plays a role in health and safety management, when discussing pay and terms of employment, and in product development. Employers should establish an organisation-wide consultation group for mental health with the same role as groups for physical health and safety. The group might also:

- analyse and assess information supplied by management related to mental health (eg. risk assessments, lost time incident rates)
- consider suggestions from the workforce about how mental health can be more effectively managed
- consider information from third parties about mental health management practice, research and other information that may help the organisation achieve and maintain a best-practice standard of mental health management
- develop action plans, based on various inputs and their own ideas, about how mental health can be more effectively managed
- audit existing practices to ensure mental health is being managed as it should be
- listen and respond to the employer's proposals on changes to mental health management practice
- raise specific mental health incidents that the employee representatives on the consultation group would like to be formally investigated.

Consultation can provide a valuable role in helping to design, implement and manage a mental health programme. Consultations can be held in a wide variety of settings, including in meetings, at engagement events (eg. conferences, exhibitions) and through engagement surveys.

Meetings: Consultation meetings can be held with groups of employees and/or their representatives. These meetings typically explore causes of mental harm, control measures and their effectiveness, and proposed new solutions (suggested by employees or management). Changes to the working environment that might have a substantial effect on employee mental health should be discussed well in advance of such changes being introduced. This allows time for employees to work with management and the competent person to develop and implement new control measures in a timely and effective manner. As consultation is a legal requirement, it requires a structured approach. Meeting notes should be taken, with actions documented and a follow-up process implemented, in line with the requirements of whatever consultation governance methods are in place.

Engagement events: Engagement events such as conferences, exhibitions, trade fairs and training events present the perfect opportunity to promote good workplace mental health. They give leaders a chance to communicate the organisation's mental health policy and explain how it will operate, the responsibilities of employees, information about self-care, welfare arrangements and much more. It allows them to bring in external presenters such as experts and people with lived experience. These events also provide an opportunity to establish 'break-out' groups that might be appropriate to establish a two-way dialogue for problem solving and other discussions. Exhibitions, as part of a conference or in reception or restaurant areas, give employees access to information, training and other materials that might help them better understand mental health and how to take care of their own.

Engagement surveys: Engagement surveys are common nowadays. They generally focus on how committed employees are to their organisation and role. Some less progressive surveys focus on activities such as whether training has been provided and whether a performance review has been held. In theory, the more 'engaged' an employee, the more effective (eg. more productive) they will be in their role. Engagement surveys provide an ideal opportunity to explore mental health issues. However, all-out mental health questions such as "How is your mental health?" are not advised. Even the dreaded "How are you?" will often be greeted with an evasive "fine" or "okay". It has been established in this book that only half of employees feel comfortable talking about their mental health at work; there would be no point in making these employees feel uncomfortable and perhaps compelled to lie. The organisation must therefore be careful about the questions it asks, and judge whether to use direct or indirect questions about mental health. Where a pro-mental health culture has become well-established, and where employees and managers are comfortable talking about mental health openly, direct questions about mental health might be appropriate, such as, "To what extent does your job and workplace affect your mental health?" Where a pro-mental health culture has not yet become well-established or where many employees and managers are still uncomfortable talking about mental health openly, indirect questions might be more appropriate. There is little point using surveys to gather information from employees if a significant number of them lie in their responses. However, if questions are designed with care and presented in an appropriate manner, there is no reason why mental health-related questions cannot be asked in an engagement survey and be answered openly and honestly. Posing such questions may prove fruitful for leaders trying to develop a proactive and preventative mental health culture. Rather than ask directly about mental health, certainly in the early stages of any mental health programme, it may therefore be more appropriate to focus on causes rather than effects. By asking indirect questions linked to known causes of poor mental health (see Figures 12.1 and 12.2 for these), the results can be used to infer the state of mental health of employees. Some examples of indirect questions that might be posed in an engagement survey are presented in Table 14.1.

Table 14.1   *Examples of engagement survey mental health questions*

Known workplace mental health hazard	Suggested engagement survey questions
Workload	In the last 12 months, has your workload increased?
Management style	To what extent does the management style of the organisation/your line manager help you do your job?
Change management	Is the organisation effective at managing change?
Deadlines and targets	Are your targets for this year more or less achievable than last year?
Workplace relationships	Generally speaking, do you get on well with most of the people in your team?

Known workplace mental health risk factors (eg. workload, management style, change management) can be made the subject of survey questions. If a high proportion of employees respond negatively to these questions, the employer might infer that known risk factors are having a detrimental effect upon employee mental health. Similarly, questions asking how things have changed over time may indicate if employee mental health is likely to have improved or deteriorated. Some people may not like applying an approach to engagement questions based upon inference and causality. However, more bias may arise from not doing so, given that such a high proportion of employees are not willing to talk about their mental health and some even lie about it. The alternative is not to ask questions about mental health at all. However, as I have already established, this would lead to control measure approaches being applied generally, whereas mental health is highly individualised, so needs some form of tailoring. It is also necessary to enquire about mental health if risk assessments are to be undertaken effectively.

Engagement surveys often raise controversies. Are there too many questions in the survey? Should certain topics even be raised? Could the wording of questions skew responses? Is the response scale appropriate? Organisations will have to determine their own approach to such surveys. The point of Table 14.1 is to show how questions can be linked to known causes of poor workplace mental health which were established earlier (Figures 12.1 and 12.2). Table 14.1 suggests a few types and wording of questions that might be used, especially in organisations where the mental health culture is not mature. It explains a conceptual approach, rather than a definitive one. By linking questions to known causes of poor workplace mental health, the questions can be designed to appear general and not specifically related to mental health, encouraging respondents to answer questions accurately and truthfully. The answers, when aggregated, may indicate the state of mental health of employees. By tracking their responses in repeated surveys over time (eg. every six months or every year), it can be assessed whether workforce mental health is likely to have improved or deteriorated. The aim of organisation-wide engagement surveys is to enable a picture to be built up across the entire organisation. Classification of survey participants allows for results to be segmented by country, division, site, team and so on, allowing 'hotspots' to be identified. However, bear in mind disaggregation can undermine survey statistical validity because low sample numbers may affect results.

Individual Consultations

Individual consultations allow granular detail to be captured about the causes of mental harm an individual might face, as well as the types of controls in place and their effectiveness. This can provide deeper insight than group consultations and thus may be of use to management in planning mental health improvement initiatives.

Individual consultations can be held with employees where an individual has a known mental health condition and where an employee does not.

Consulting with employees who have no known mental health condition is vital because:

- it normalises individual consultations, minimising any stigma that people may experience when their mental health condition is public

- it acts as a proactive, preventative step, minimising the chance of *one small thing* (chapter 1) tipping an employee from a state of positive mental health to a state of distress.

Consultations with employees who have a known mental health condition (whether it is a protected characteristic or not) are also vitally important. Key reasons are that:

- it leads to a better understanding of their mental health condition and how to support them

- it is an opportunity to agree with the employee what reasonable adjustments they require

- it enables the effectiveness of measures to support employees with poor mental health to be determined (note that necessary adjustments may need to change over time if the employee's symptoms change).

- Employees must be given the choice of whether to participate openly (when their condition is public) or on an anonymous or confidential basis. There is a subtle difference between 'confidential' and 'anonymous':

- 'Confidential' might mean the employee has disclosed their mental health condition to a manager but does not want anyone else to know about it.

- 'Anonymous' might mean the employee does not want *anyone* in the organisation knowing of their mental health, be it good or poor. However, in this case, for example, an employee may disclose their mental health condition in an anonymous survey.

If reasonable adjustments are required, presumably the individual will have disclosed their condition to their employer, although they may wish it to be kept confidential beyond those managers who have been informed.

Whilst an open approach is likely to be preferable to the employer, each employee's right to confidentiality must be respected. If an anonymous approach is taken, it is still better for the employer to know what conditions employees have, even if they do not know exactly who has them.

Individual consultations can be held face-to-face if the process is open and transparent, or through an anonymous administration process, such as a paper-based, online survey or via an app. Alternatively, an employee representative can be engaged, in which case the representative might know of an employee's condition but hold that knowledge in confidence. Online surveys are commonplace nowadays and are typically used, for example, by delegates attending a resilience training day. Self-administered surveys are undertaken by the employee and may only take a few minutes to complete. Self-assessment surveys allow for anonymity, and responses provide the employee (and possibly the employer, depending on how the information is used) with insight. Ultimately, online systems can be tailored to control and restrict who has access to certain information. With any form of survey, online or otherwise, a great deal of thought should be given to the questions, the response fields, the scale, and the instructions. Reliable survey results will only be achieved if effective research methods are employed.

In this chapter I explored consultations. I opened by considering the legal requirement to consult, then presented further justification for holding consultations. I explored the purpose of consultations and how they might be governed to ensure legal compliance. I then considered the questions to be used in engagement surveys, and how questions can be linked to causes of poor mental health in organisations where the mental health culture is not that mature. I concluded by explaining how group and individual consultations might be undertaken, along with some of the methods that might be used.

The main take-outs from this chapter are:

- In some countries, including the UK, it is a legal requirement to hold mental health consultations with employees.

- Consulting with employees is also required because of the scale of the mental health issues, to help gain buy-in to any mental health programme of activity, to help reveal the otherwise intangible nature of mental health issues and to align the perceptions of leaders and employees.

- As mental health consultations are a legal requirement, consideration must be given to the governance and compliance of these consultations. A form of independent audit of the consultation group and its processes is advisable.

- Group and individual consultations should be held, both with employees who have no known mental health conditions and with those who are known to have mental health issues.

- Group consultations can be held through meetings, engagement events and engagement surveys.

- Engagement survey questions need not refer to mental health. The 12 workplace mental health risks could be used as the basis of questions, with mental health effects inferred from the answers.

- When consulting with employees, employee desire for confidentiality and anonymity must be respected.

References

ACAS (2014) *Employee Communications and Consultation*. Available at: https://archive.acas.org.uk/index.aspx?articleid=663 (accessed 5 December 2019).

Consult Australia (2018) *Striving for Mentally Healthy Workplaces.* Sydney: Consult Australia. Available at: *http://www.consultaustralia.com.au/docs/default-source/skills/striving-for-mentally-healthy-workplaces---web.pdf?sfvrsn=2* (accessed 1 April 2020).

Health and Safety Executive (2013) *Consulting Employees on Health and Safety.* Available at: https://www.hse.gov.uk/pubns/indg232.pdf (accessed 19 March 2020).

15

In this chapter I examine the seventh and final principle of the management system: reporting. I look at the aims of reporting, the legal reporting requirements around mental health, the type of reports that might monitor mental health practice and performance, and the potential for errors and bias in reporting. I also present some of the mental health performance measures employers might consider when determining how best to monitor mental health management performance in their organisation.

Reporting is a control tool. Generally, reports are used to achieve two aims:

- to monitor practice
- to monitor performance.

Monitoring allows knowledge and understanding to be built. This informs decision-making, which in turn provides management control.

Reports that monitor practice typically take the form of inspection and investigation reports. Inspection reports can be used to identify how something is happening. An inspection report might be produced as part of a routine checking procedure, to check how activities are being performed, perhaps to monitor the quality of work in progress, or monitor hygiene. An investigation report might be produced following an event such as an accident, in which case the aim might be to report on what happened, who was involved and why it happened, in order to avoid such an incident happening again.

Reports that monitor performance typically scrutinise the standard to which an event, activity or operation has been completed. Monitoring reports might relate to financial performance, health and safety performance, and aspects of human resource management such as employee engagement. In addition to identifying the standard of performance, performance reports might also use a trend analysis to investigate how performance has changed over time.

Reporting for physical health and safety (see chapter 3) considers:

- legal reporting obligations
- types of report
- measures of performance.

As with all seven of the workplace mental health management system aspects, practices in physical health and safety management can be applied to mental health management, including to reporting.

Aims of Mental Health Reporting

When contemplating workplace mental health management, leaders and managers will want to monitor practice and performance to understand how effectively mental health is being managed in their organisation by, for example:

- measuring mental health performance

- tracking trends in mental health performance

- examining specific cases of mental harm

- auditing activity and checking compliance (say, with mental health policies and procedures)

- introducing benchmarks for mental health performance.

As mental health issues affect a large proportion of any workforce, the responsible leader will want to ensure work and work-related factors are not having an unduly severe effect on the mental health of their employees.

Legal Reporting Requirements for Mental Health

In terms of physical health, in the UK it is a legal requirement for employers to report specified injuries or illnesses to the HSE, along with any injury that prevents an employee from undertaking their normal range of duties for seven consecutive days or more (HSE, online a). Other jurisdictions will have similar reporting requirements.

By comparison, the HSE (online b) does not require organisations to report incidents relating to mental health (with one exception, which I will return to), no matter how the incident was caused or how severe its effect. An employee can be absent with work-related stress or because of harassment for months and may be suicidal because of work or work-related factors – and may even actually commit suicide – yet the law does not require the employer to report the incident. Suicide is not reportable to the HSE (HSE, online c).

The exception I referred to above relates to the reporting of group or mass stress. The HSE (online d) states:

> HSE will consider investigating concerns about work-related stress where:
>
> - There is evidence that a number of staff are currently experiencing work-related stress or stress-related ill health, (i.e. that it is not an individual case), but
>
> - HSE is not the appropriate body to investigate concerns solely related to individual cases of bullying or harassment, but may consider this if there is evidence of a wider organisational failing, and
>
> - HSE would expect concerns about work-related stress to have been raised already with the employer, and for the employer to have been given sufficient time to respond accordingly.

It goes on to say: "Cases of bullying and harassment would more commonly be dealt with as issues of discipline eg breaches of policies on expected behaviours, discrimination, victimisation or equality" (HSE, online d). In such cases, the HSE provides no regulation and offers employees no protection.

The HSE's own data indicates that violence, threats or bullying account for 13% of all reported stress (HSE, 2019). In addition, some courts are finding employers guilty under such circumstances for failing to provide a safe place to work. Yet the HSE refers employees to other legislation, seemingly attempting to absolve itself of any responsibility. It is my belief that the HSE is finding excuses not to be involved in mental health at a time when its involvement is most needed.

To be clear, the above circumstances in which the HSE may investigate group stress do *not* impose a duty upon employers to report this type of mental health incident. Such incidents simply present an opportunity for employees to ask the HSE to investigate. The HSE makes no particular commitment to do so.

At the time of writing, I am awaiting a response from the HSE to a Freedom of Information request in which I seek to identify information related to group or mass stress incidents (referred to above) that have occurred since the introduction of the related reporting process in October 2019. In particular, I am seeking to identify:

- how many such incidents have been reported to the HSE
- how many reported incidents have been investigated
- the most significant sanction issued against an employer following an investigation.

My belief is that the HSE has introduced a change in reporting policy that, to date, has had zero effect, and that offers employees no greater protection than before it was introduced. I hope I am proved wrong.

Despite the numerous recommendations made by Stevenson and Farmer (2017) that specifically relate to the HSE, along with the findings from the many other reports cited in this book and elsewhere, and despite a seemingly exponential increase in public awareness of mental health, it appears that the HSE still is not stepping up and providing mental health leadership. Instead, it seems to be moving forward at a snail's pace and against its will, suffering the same lack of understanding and the same uncertainty as some employers (Figure 1.7).

Types of Mental Health Report

As with physical health and safety, mental health reports might seek to monitor practice and measure performance.

Inspection/audit reports: Mental health inspection and audit reports should aim to assess whether policies and procedures are being employed effectively in practice. A wide variety of control measures may be employed to reduce mental health risks. These might include aspects of the working environment, working patterns, workload and rest periods. Organisations should consider whether the practices assessed during an inspection or audit are being implemented in accordance with their mental health policy, plans and procedures. Evidence should be noted, compliance assessed and remedial actions recommended. Inspections should be undertaken on a regular and routine basis to ensure mental health is being effectively managed over time. These inspections should be undertaken by somebody in an independent position, to ensure there is no bias in the inspection process. Given that the potential for discrimination and a lack of buy-in is very real, this independence is even more important than it is for physical health and safety inspections, especially as the line manager of any given team may, through their management style, be associated with the causes of workplace stress. Inspections are usually undertaken using a pro forma report (electronic, hard copy, or via an app), a template for which should be developed with input from the mental health competent person or other suitably qualified manager or adviser. Inspections will almost certainly require employees to be interviewed to identify if they are experiencing mental health issues and whether control measures are proving effective. Confidentiality will almost certainly be required. This inspection process will play a vital role in independently verifying that mental health management practices have been properly implemented and are proving effective in controlling mental health-related risks.

Incident reports: Mental health incidents will be defined by the organisation itself. An incident might relate to somebody experiencing severe mental distress, or employees being absent because of work-related stress. As with physical health and safety incident reports, mental health incident reports should identify who was harmed, how they were harmed, the extent of harm caused and why the incident happened, along with any mental health first aid provided, plus recommended actions to prevent a recurrence. Employers should investigate and report on mental health incidents, just as they would physical health and safety incidents – the investigation and reporting procedure should be almost identical. The only differences will relate to the causes and consequences of harm and the support required by those affected by the incident. It should be noted that unlike physical injuries, where the employee usually recovers in a matter of days or weeks, mental health issues can last much longer. Mental health incidents that do not actually cause harm but which have the potential to cause harm (eg. a near miss (HSE, online e)) may also be made the subject of an incident report.

Statistical reports: Organisational leaders will find management reports that present data, statistics and trends particularly useful. Leaders will wish to ensure that any mental health programme is having a positive effect and that, generally speaking, the mental health of their workforce is improving. Later in this chapter, I will cover those aspects of mental health performance that leaders and managers might be interested in monitoring.

Benchmarking reports: Benchmarking typically involves comparing an organisation's mental health practices and performance with that of other similar organisations. Unlike physical health and safety, mental health does not place a legal duty upon employers to report, so the HSE and other organisations are not in a position to provide benchmarking information against which employer organisations can compare themselves. However, several mental health charities and other bodies do undertake research in the field of workplace mental health, so employers may find that this research can provide them with a route to undertake mental health performance benchmarking. Many of the sources cited in this book provide examples of such information, such as Business in the Community (2019) and Shaw Trust (2018).

Other types of report leaders should consider when contemplating mental health management include:

- risk assessment reports, which will identify those workers most at risk, amongst other things
- engagement survey reports, which may reveal the state of workforce mental health and mental health programme performance
- data captured by the human resources department about recruitment and employment, such as the proportion of employees who have disclosed a mental health condition (obviously respecting confidentiality).

Some types of report can be employed to monitor and measure mental health performance.

Measures of Mental Health Performance

Diversity and inclusion (D&I) will be high on the agenda for most organisations, with a significant focus on aspects such as gender, race, religion and disability.

In many organisations the reporting of D&I performance has been in place for some years, for example to monitor gender and ethnic mix within the workforce. The basis for measuring mental health should already be in place as a result, so it should be straightforward for most organisations to determine the measures of performance for mental health.

Most leaders will understand the need for reliable data, statistics and reporting. Measures are required to make sure that:

- the results produced can be considered reliable. One set of results may be corroborated (or not) by another (eg. increased inputs should, in theory, lead to an improvement in outputs)
- root causes can be identified and corrective actions can be focused on specific problem areas
- the benefits of any actions (eg. the return on investment (ROI) of mental health initiatives) can be established.

Reading across from these other aspects of organisational management and applying them to mental health, four aspects of mental health reporting can be identified: input, indirect, direct and output (Figure 15.1). I will now briefly explore each of these.

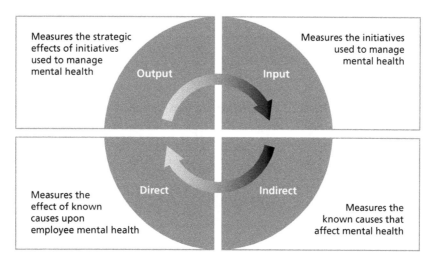

Figure 15.1 *The four aspects of mental health reporting*

INPUT (measuring the initiatives used to manage mental health): Organisations will undertake a variety of activities to manage mental health such as, for example, communications to build awareness and training to develop skills. These initiatives can be considered mental health inputs. Measures should be put in place to determine the volume or number of activities undertaken (eg. training courses, awareness sessions). If each activity has merit, it is likely that the more the activity is undertaken, the greater its beneficial impact. Measuring the number of times each mental health activity is undertaken may therefore, to some extent, determine the likely impact of it. When measuring inputs, results will mostly be identifiable and quantifiable because, for example, the exact number of training courses undertaken can be identified and quantified. The right inputs should, at least in theory, lead to favourable outputs.

INDIRECT (measuring the known factors that affect mental health): Using the known factors which affect mental health (Figures 12.1 and 12.2) as a way to infer the state of employees' mental health was explored in chapter 14. Here, it was suggested that these known factors could become the subject of engagement survey questions. For example, if the responses of employees in an engagement survey indicate that their workload has increased significantly since the previous year, it might be inferred that their stress levels are likely to have increased as well. An alternative approach based upon observation can also be used to assess the factors that affect mental health. For example, monitoring the volume of work may identify changes in workload, with high workload known to be a stressor. Should a significant process change occur (ie. a new IT system is implemented), observation can reveal how employees are adapting to the change (ie. how competent they are in using the new IT system). An assessment can then be made about the effectiveness of change management, change having been identified as another known stressor. As a final example, work outputs (eg. units produced, jobs completed, customers served) can be correlated with hours worked, providing a measure of productivity. Leaders should, of course, aim at higher productivity, but be mindful of any adverse effects on mental health. Work and activity can be monitored to infer if undue stress or other adverse mental health effects are occurring, providing a useful indirect means of monitoring workplace mental health.

DIRECT (measuring the effect of known factors upon employee mental health): Having used methods to monitor the indirect factors that affect mental health, establishing the direct effects of these factors on mental health must also be determined. One way to identify the effects is to ask employees. Employee involvement is probably the only realistic way to understand how employees feel and what has caused them to feel as they do. Clearly, bias can occur in the responses of employees, either because of understatement, where employees are reluctant to state how stressed they truly feel, or through exaggeration, where employees wish to make a point in the strongest possible terms. To help minimise bias, results from direct and indirect measures can be correlated. For example, if observation indicates that workload has decreased but employees say workload has increased, clearly only one of those positions can be right. Direct measures of the effect of known factors upon mental health will therefore probably rely on employee involvement, with there being a need to eliminate bias as far as is reasonably possible.

As an aside, new wearable technologies, such as stress monitoring devices, are being introduced that allow the stress levels of employees and other aspects of health to be monitored, and in some instances, this may allow employers to have access to individual or group data. Here, some thought needs to be given to the legal implications of such technologies, and not just to privacy, although the General Data Protection Regulation 2016 (GDPR) will be a concern. In chapter 5, it was established that an employer has a legal duty to address the causes of poor mental health should something 'trigger' the employer's knowledge and make them aware an employee is struggling psychologically. These new technologies may well do just that, potentially placing a legal duty upon the employer to do something about, say, prolonged undue stress. Even where the employer does not have access to the data, a manager simply enquiring about how an employee is getting on with the technology may unwittingly lead to the employer being provided with 'knowledge' or a 'trigger', as defined in law. If the employer then fails to reduce any prolonged undue stress, they may find themselves facing a legal claim for mental health negligence. Health monitoring can clearly provide significant benefits; however, the new technologies may create a legal liability for employers, so they should investigate the related legal obligations and liabilities before committing to such methods.

OUTPUT (measuring the strategic effects of initiatives used to manage mental health): At a strategic level, mental health programmes and initiatives should realise four key benefits: improved attendance, engagement, productivity and retention (see Figure 15.2). Employees with good mental health will be more likely to *attend* work as often as can reasonably be expected, with mental health-related sickness absence being minimised. *Engagement* was found to relate to levels of commitment and motivation of employees. Employees can be expected to be more participative, for example, in their roles, in team-working scenarios and in going the extra mile. Levels of engagement can be established through engagement surveys. High levels of engagement are likely to manifest if good mental health exists. And if engagement is high, *productivity*, too, may be high; as was established in chapter 6, improved productivity may result from investment in wellbeing and mental health programmes. Finally, if the workforce has good mental health, resulting in high attendance, high engagement and high productivity, it stands to reason that the organisation will have the best chance of doing well and becoming successful, with employees feeling they have made a worthwhile contribution. This feeling of doing well and feeling valued (subject to the right recognition, as explored in chapter 10) is likely to lead to higher levels of *retention*, as employees are more likely to remain loyal to an employer for whom they enjoy working. These measures should be applied to the whole organisation, with the aim of driving improvements across all of it. As half of employees with mental health issues are unlikely to disclose their condition, it is vital that leaders take a strategic, whole-organisation approach, rather than simply trying to manage the attendance, engagement, productivity and retention of employees with mental health issues.

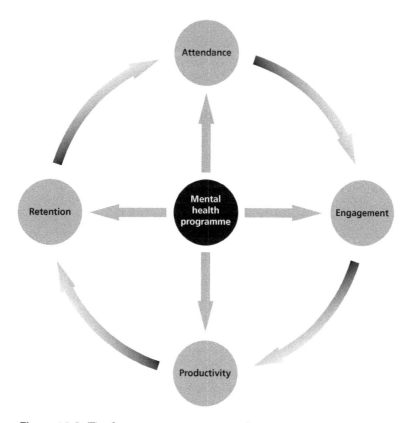

Figure 15.2 *The four strategic outcomes of mental health management*

Earlier in this chapter, I said I would return to measures of mental health management performance and I do so now. Beyond the strategic measures of attendance, engagement, productivity and retention, organisations can determine other relevant performance measures by reading across from existing measures that relate to similar aspects of management, such as gender, age, religion and so on. The organisation can consider an array of measures and select those that are most suitable. Measures of mental health management performance might include those shown in Table 15.1.

Table 15.1   *Measures of mental health performance*

Measure	Purpose
Percentage of top 10% of earners who have publicly disclosed a mental health issue	Demonstrates to workforce that leaders are willing to lead by example and that it has a positive mental health culture; might also indicate if a 'glass ceiling' exists
Percentage of job applicants presenting with mental health issues during recruitment	Indicates how attractive the organisation is to people with mental health issues
Comparison of the hiring rate between applicants disclosing a mental health issue and those not	Aims to identify any prejudice (and the potential for liability) in the recruitment and selection process
Percentage of total employees who have disclosed a mental health issue	Indicates how confident employees are in being open about their mental health issues
Percentage of employees who have disclosed a mental health issue and who have been promoted	Indicates how open leaders are to putting people with mental health issues into more senior roles
Mental health pay equality	Indicates whether those with mental health issues are paid fairly compared to those with no mental health issues
Employee retention rate amongst employees who have disclosed a mental health issue	Indicates how employees with mental ill-health feel about their employer and whether they believe the employer is mental-health-friendly
Percentage of employees who have been disciplined who have a disclosed mental health issue	Indicates how positive management attitudes are towards employees with mental health issues
Percentage of dismissed employees who have a disclosed mental health issue	Indicates how positive management attitudes are towards employees with mental health issues
Sickness absence rate amongst employees with mental health issues (NB – employees are known to lie about the cause of sickness absence)	Identifies whether employees with mental health issues are more likely to have time off sick; this may also indicate if greater support is required

Measure	Purpose
Sickness absence days lost to mental ill-health	Indicates the trend, along with the effectiveness of the organisation's mental health programme
Mental health training days	Indicates the level of investment an organisation is making in support of employee mental health
Return on mental health programme investment	Indicates the financial and other returns gained from investment in mental health improvement programmes and initiatives

The list of measures in Table 15.1 is not intended to be exhaustive. Organisations should develop their own measures of performance to assess the effectiveness of their mental health management programme.

Generally, the measures of mental health are ratios of measures already in use in many organisations, for example:

- the proportion of black and minority ethnic job applicants

- the proportion of women in the executive team

- the numbers of days the average employee is absent due to sickness.

Each of these measures can easily be extended and applied to the area of mental health. Organisations should monitor the performance of their mental health programme:

- to determine the current state of their employees' mental health

- to identify those members of the workforce who are most in need of mental health support

- to determine whether their mental health programmes and initiatives are proving effective

- to determine the return on investment of their mental health programmes

- to ensure compliance with legislation and to manage liabilities.

On this last point, most employers will be eager to ensure their organisation is free from discrimination, intended or not. By measuring mental health performance, potential risks can be identified and practices improved to ensure they are not only equitable, but also legally compliant.

Leaders will also be eager to support employees and leverage productivity and other advantages available through mental health management. Given the scale of the issue and its potential impact upon an organisation, most leaders will want to measure performance in order to ensure it is effectively managed.

Errors and Bias in Reporting

Leaders and managers should be wary of mental health reporting results that are based on employee input, as this offers potential for error and bias. As was identified in Part I, some employees feel uncomfortable:

▦ disclosing their mental health condition during the recruitment process

▦ disclosing their mental health condition once employed

▦ disclosing mental health issues as their reason for sickness absence.

Some employees will either not disclose their mental health issue or will lie to cover it up. This type of misreporting can skew statistics and mar reporting, potentially misleading leaders and managers. With approximately half of all employees with mental health issues not willing to talk about them, some form of bias is likely in certain report results.

If an organisation's culture is perceived by employees as being pro-mental health, less evasion and deception is likely, and greater reporting validity may be achieved.

Lying by employees does not necessarily invalidate a report. If lying affects report results consistently, say year on year, any change in a given trend may still be valid, as changes to other variables will be driving the trend direction, while lying will not cause any change in trend direction even if it does skew the results.

Planning and Undertaking Improvement Actions

The inevitable consequence of reporting is *action*.

Turning back to the Plan-Do-Check-Act model (chapter 3), reporting should be used in the 'check' phase of the cycle to ensure plans are being implemented and delivering benefits as intended.

In the checking phase, mental health performance reporting will demonstrate one of two outcomes:

▦ Mental health practices are being implemented and mental health performance is being realised as intended.

▦ Mental health practices are being implemented and mental health performance is not being realised as intended.

Once the results have been assessed through performance analysis, the 'act' phase of the cycle can be considered.

If practice and performance are being realised as intended, efforts should be made to maintain the current high performance and push on to even greater levels of attainment.

If practice and performance are not being realised as intended, an analysis of the root causes may be required. There may be the potential for severe mental harm, in which case an urgent and immediate investigation will be required to ensure employees are not exposed to mental health hazards that might have a severe adverse effect. If they are, it must be stopped. Risks should be brought under control and severe exposure limited. In reality, this is likely to relate to two at-risk groups of workers:

- employees who are likely to be putting their personal safety at risk by working in highly hazardous environments and those likely to experience or be exposed to trauma

- employees with high susceptibility, who may have a severe adverse reaction to even mild levels of stress (eg. vulnerable groups of people).

It should be noted that susceptibility is often overlooked. Physical health and safety management makes special provisions for vulnerable groups, such as pregnant women and young people. Mental health provisions may need to take account of the mentally vulnerable.

Returning to the identification of plans that are not delivering the expected results, it is more likely that there is not potential for severe mental harm and no urgent and immediate response is required. However, an investigation may still be merited to identify why the actions have not had the desired effects. The routine of checking and acting/correcting should be followed until solutions have been found and mental health management can be considered to be performing in a consistently satisfactory manner.

In this chapter I identified the key aims of mental health reporting: to monitor and measure mental health performance. I went on to explore different types of report and considered inspection/audit reports, incident reports, statistical reports and benchmarking reports. I presented some measures of mental health performance, hopefully providing readers with a good understanding of how they can measure mental health performance within their own organisation. I concluded by presenting the need to turn reports into action, in order to continually drive mental health performance improvements.

The key take-outs from this chapter are:

- Reporting should be used to monitor mental health practice and mental health performance.

- Mental health reports should include inspection/audit reports, incident reports, statistical reports and benchmarking reports.

- A wide variety of mental health performance measures are available. Many of these are similar to those used when considering the performance of other protected characteristics.

- Organisations should monitor mental health performance for a variety of reasons, including: to identify the current state of mental health in the organisation; to ensure mental health initiatives are proving effective; and to ensure compliance with the law.

- A degree of caution should be applied when reviewing report results because errors and bias may affect the results, given that employees can be reluctant to disclose mental health issues and may even lie about them.

- Inputs and outputs of the mental health programme, along with indirect and direct measures of the state of employee mental health, should be measured.

- Strategic measures of the mental health programme will include: attendance, engagement, productivity and retention.

- Organisations might use a wide range of measures, including those suggested in this chapter. Over and above these, leaders and managers may wish to determine their own measures, taking a lead from other aspects of management, such as those that relate to gender, age, race and religion.

- When applying the Plan-Do-Check-Act model, reporting is part of the 'check' phase. When checked, if the results are not in accordance with expectations, corrective action will be required. On occasion, urgent action may be required, especially when vulnerable groups are involved.

- Having assessed the results of the mental health programme and related initiatives, a process of continual improvement should be adopted.

References

Business in the Community (2019) *Mental Health at Work 2019: Time to take ownership.* Available at: *https://www.bitc.org.uk/report/mental-health-at-work-2019-time-to-take-ownership/* (accessed 22 November 2019).

Health and Safety Executive (online a) *Types of Reportable Incidents.* Available at: *https://www.hse.gov.uk/riddor/reportable-incidents.htm* (accessed 20 March 2020).

Health and Safety Executive (online b) Reporting Injuries, Diseases and Dangerous Occurrences in Health and Social Care: Guidance for employers. Available at: *https://www.hse.gov.uk/pubns/hsis1.pdf* (accessed 20 March 2020).

Health and Safety Executive (online c) *Examples of Reportable Incidents.* Available at: *https://www.hse.gov.uk/riddor/examples-reportable-incidents.htm* (accessed 20 March 2020).

Health and Safety Executive (online d) *Reporting a Concern.* Available at: *https://www.hse.gov.uk/stress/reporting-concern.htm* (accessed 20 March 2020).

Health and Safety Executive (online e) *Accidents and investigations.* Available at: *https://www.hse.gov.uk/toolbox/managing/accidents.htm* (accessed 5 April 2020).

Health and Safety Executive (2019) *Work-related Stress, Anxiety or Depression Statistics in Great Britain, 2019.* Available at: https://www.hse.gov.uk/statistics/causdis/stress.pdf (accessed 20 March 2020).

Shaw Trust (2018) *Mental Health at Work: Still the last taboo.* Available at: *https://www.shaw-trust.org.uk/ShawTrustMediaLibraries/ShawTrust/ShawTrust/Documents/Shaw-Trust-Mental-Health-at-Work-Report-2018-full_1.pdf* (accessed 29 November 2019).

Stevenson, D. and Farmer, P. (2017) *Thriving at Work: The Stevenson/Farmer review of mental health and employers.* Available at: *https://assets.publishing.service.gov.uk/government/uploads/system/uploads/attachment_data/file/658145/thriving-at-work-stevenson-farmer-review.pdf* (accessed 28 October 2019).

16

RECOMMENDATIONS:
A 10-POINT PLAN

In Part I of this book I introduced the mental health problem and explored some of the challenges it poses for employers. My aim was partly to encourage employers to develop empathy with employees with mental health issues. In Part II, I have presented a solution – a strategic management system approach through which employers can provide effective support for their employees.

In chapter 5, I identified some laws that relate to mental health. In the UK, employers must manage mental health in accordance with the requirements of various laws as they relate to:

- negligence
- discrimination (Equality Act 2010)
- health and safety (Health and Safety at Work etc Act 1974).

Each national jurisdiction has its equivalent laws.

Although this book transcends borders and the legal jurisdictions in different countries, this chapter relates specifically to the UK. Readers in other countries should still find points of interest in it, however.

In the UK, an individual employee can report a physical health and safety incident to the HSE, which may investigate and, if necessary, prosecute the employer. The same process is not available for employees who want to report an incident of mental harm. Following a failed attempt at internal resolution (eg. through a grievance process), the employee's only course of redress is through the courts; when it comes to mental health and safety, they are on their own. The balance of power in the employer-employee mental health relationship is skewed towards the employer because the UK government's enforcer, the HSE, does not hold employers to account. This relationship must be made more equitable.

Before presenting the actions required to improve mental health, I want to give a recap of the problems and limitations in managing mental health that I have identified in this book:

- The scale of the mental health crisis is vast. Yet there is no clear, committed leader spearheading transformational change amongst employers. When she was Prime Minister of the UK, Theresa May initiated the Stevenson/Farmer review of mental health and employers, *Thriving at Work* (2017). This led to very limited and painfully slow change, as the HSE's response to the report shows. Nadine Dorries MP, the current Parliamentary Under-Secretary of State for Mental Health, Suicide Prevention and Patient Safety, has a remit that is largely focused on public service provision; certainly thus far. A far greater focus is required on *workplace* mental health.

- The definition in law of 'mental disability' only protects people with long-term conditions that affect their ability to perform short-term activities. No protection is provided to people who have a long-term condition that affects their long-term activities, such as securing and keeping a job.

▓ Some of the legal precedents related to mental health are based on thinking that is 20 years old, despite the fact that our understanding of mental health and the scale of the mental health crisis have developed dramatically in recent years. It is time to review precedents where they fail to recognise new evidence and today's circumstances.

▓ Too many employees who disclose a mental health issue at work face demotion, disciplinary action, dismissal and being forced to resign, as well as stigma. Some employers seem to feel they can act towards these employees in this way with impunity. Employees with mental health issues deserve greater protection as they explore with their employer what reasonable adjustments can be made to accommodate them at work.

▓ The HSE (2013a) states that 'stress is not reportable as an occupational injury, even when accompanied by a medical certificate stating it is work-related, because it does not result from a single definable accident'. This statement is flawed and requires urgent change.

▓ Employers are not required to report any type of mental injury or illness. They also face no sanctions whatsoever (eg. no notices or fines), even if they were the cause of it and no matter how serious their mental health negligence. An employee can suffer unlimited mental harm because of work or work-related factors and can be absent because of the mental harm they have suffered for months, yet the employer has no obligation to report such incidents to the HSE. Employers are not required to report the suicide of a member of staff, even when it is suspected that work-related stress might have caused or contributed to this. In contrast, seven-day absences arising from physical harm must be reported to the HSE. Why is mental health treated so differently?

As a result of these areas of concern, I have developed a 10-point plan of action that calls for change, and I present this plan in this chapter. The plan aims to address the areas of weakness in current workplace mental health management, and calls for changes in leadership, changes to the law and changes to law enforcement.

The 10 points call for:

1   The appointment of a *Workplace* Mental Health Tsar

2   A change to the definition or interpretation of 'mental disability' to take account of people with long-term conditions that affect their *long-term* activities

3   A change to the 'Hatton Propositions' (see chapter 5) to recognise that some occupations are intrinsically more dangerous to mental health than others

4   A change to the 'Hatton Propositions' to create a general duty for employers to enquire about the mental health of employees

5   A change to the law relating to employment protection, so that employees can disclose a mental health issue without fear of reprisals as a result of greater protection.

6   Health and safety laws to expressly relate to mental health

7   A change to the HSE's position to recognise that causes of mental injury can be identified

8   A change to law enforcement through new reporting requirements, including introducing the reporting of '30-day' psychological injuries and illnesses

9   A change to law enforcement to introduce new sanctions that penalise offenders

10 Prominent figures in society to bring about the policy changes proposed in this chapter.

Each of these recommended actions is now explored in more detail.

1. Appointment of a Workplace Mental Health Tsar

As we identified in Part I, mental health is a twenty-first-century crisis, and it is estimated that tens of millions of people in the UK and USA suffer with mental health issues each year. Employers can play a significant role in addressing this crisis. However, their role is unclear, their actions limited and their effectiveness questionable. Given that two in five (see chapter 1) of people with mental health issues state that work has caused or contributed to their poor mental health, employers must do more to help improve the situation.

Recognising this issue, when she was Prime Minister, Theresa May commissioned the Stevenson/Farmer review, which led to the *Thriving at Work* report (Stevenson and Farmer, 2017). However, mental health outputs have deteriorated since the report was published. According to the Shaw Trust (2018):

■   employers are less likely to hire a person with poor mental health

■   employees are no more willing to talk about mental health at work

■   managers are less confident talking to an employee about their mental health.

With weak central government leadership on workplace mental health, weak laws and weak enforcement, the time for more significant action has come.

Recent efforts have been made by the UK Government to improve mental health (Woodcock, 2019). However, these efforts are largely reactive, expanding support services for people who already have issues. Additional preventative actions are required, especially in the workplace. Clear and decisive leadership is required if workplace mental health management is to play a significant role in bringing the current mental health crisis under control. Existing leadership and structures have proven inadequate. It is now time to bring about a transformational change in mental health management through the appointment by Government of a Workplace Mental Health Tsar, with the new role reporting to the Parliamentary Under-Secretary of State for Mental Health, Suicide Prevention and Patient Safety.

The appointed Tsar would focus on the following priorities:

- developing and implementing strategic plans that aim to improve workplace mental health
- bringing about an appropriate alignment of workplace physical health and safety management and workplace mental health management
- strengthening existing laws and introducing new laws to ensure the legal framework motivates employers to manage mental health more effectively
- strengthening the policies and powers of enforcers (eg. the HSE) to ensure it can take action to uphold the law as it relates to workplace mental health
- procuring the resources necessary to implement and administer the changes to the law and to law enforcement
- holding employers to account for their mental health performance.

The rest of my recommendations, the work they will create and the impact they will have should help to explain why a Workplace Mental Health Tsar is required.

2. Change to the Definition of 'Mental Disability' in Law

The current UK government definition of 'mental disability' is a mental illness that has a substantial effect, is long-term (more than 12 months) and affects a person's normal day-to-day activity (see chapter 5). There are two points to consider here.

Firstly, in normal day-to-day activity, a primary earner would be expected to secure a job, keep that job and remain in employment for the most part of their working life, with work being a day-to-day activity. Career changes and breaks in employment might occur, but for the bulk of their working life, a 'normal' primary earner would expect to remain in some form of employment for at least, say, 90% of their working life. Therefore, it could be argued that if a person cannot get a job and remain in employment for a similar proportion of time as a 'normal' primary earner (for example, someone with poor mental health who is in employment for only 50% of their working life), their condition can be said to be having a substantial effect on their day-to-day activities.

Secondly, insight can be gained from reading across from equality law. Equality laws exist to ensure that certain groups are not disadvantaged and that members of minority groups have the same opportunities in life as everybody else. Although it is the characteristic possessed by the minority group that is protected, the protection afforded protects a person's right to equal opportunities. In the case of mental health, certain conditions, like ADHD, often lead to people earning lower wages, having numerous jobs and experiencing longer periods of unemployment than would typically be expected. These circumstances can lead to people with mental health issues experiencing poor living conditions and poor physical health, not just for themselves, but for their families too. These circumstances can lead to people with poor mental health experiencing inequality of opportunity because of their condition.

The law should be applied in its current form, or it should be changed if its current form is found to be ineffective, so as to recognise a pattern of circumstances that demonstrate a person's mental health condition is having a long-term effect on their 'normal day-to-day activity'. Such a pattern of life circumstances might include:

- a high number of different jobs
- a significant cumulative period of unemployment
- a consistently low or significantly declining level of earnings
- a significantly declining standard of domestic accommodation.

Currently, a 'mental disability' exists where a person has a long-term condition that affects their day-to-day activities; however, the law fails to protect people who have a long-term disability but cannot easily undertake long-term activities, like getting and keeping a job.

The cycle of hunting for work, commencing employment, being fired, being unemployed and suffering financial hardship must be broken, or at least slowed. By affording people with mental ill-health some protection in employment, such as a slowing or breaking of the cycle of suffering (Figure 2.4), can be achieved.

In essence, the law should consider a person's long-term circumstances, not just their condition and its behavioural effects on daily life. The term 'mental disability' aims to protect a person's quality of life and the opportunities available to them. The law (or how it is interpreted) must be changed to provide greater protection for people with poor mental health, giving them greater opportunities and a better long-term quality of life, as well as protecting them when they are less able to look after themselves day-to-day.

3. A Change to the 'Hatton Propositions' to Recognise that some Occupations are Intrinsically More Dangerous to Mental Health Than Others

In passing judgement in the *Sutherland v Hatton* case at the Court of Appeal in 2002, the judge, LJ Hale, said, "no occupations should be regarded as intrinsically dangerous to mental health. The test of foreseeability is the same whatever the employment" (see chapter 5).

On the other hand, the HSE says that employers have a legal duty to protect employees from stress at work by doing a risk assessment and acting on it (HSE, online, a). In addition to this, "the law states a risk assessment must be 'suitable and sufficient'" (HSE, online, b).

The HSE seems to imply different occupations will carry different 'stress' (and presumably other different mental health) risks.

How can these two positions be reconciled? I find it unconscionable to suppose that all jobs, no matter how diverse, present the same intrinsic mental health risks to the worker.

The words "no occupation should be regarded as intrinsically dangerous to mental health" might be intended to exclude factors such as workload, management style and even bullying, as these factors are extrinsic and do not relate to the intrinsic tasks involved in performing the actual role. This nuanced argument is understood. There may be a (semantic) difference between LJ Hale's ruling and the HSE's guidance. However, the HSE's guidance isn't qualified by means of only applying to factors that are intrinsic or extrinsic to the tasks of employment. The HSE specifically requires employers to manage hazards and risks arising from an occupation, as those hazards and risks affect the worker undertaking it.

There are two points to consider here. What exactly does LJ Hale mean? And can her position be applied in actuality?

Let us check what LJ Hale means. In the case of nursing, for example, does she mean that the tasks that are intrinsic to the role (witnessing bleeding, breaks, burns, amputation, end-of-life care, dying and death) have no more an effect on the mental state of a nurse than do photocopying and filing on the mental state of a secretary, soldering on the mental state of a plumber, or traffic lights on the mental state of a taxi driver? It has been established that nurses are five times more likely to suffer with PTSD than the general population, because of the trauma they witness (chapter 1). When viewed through today's eyes, which perhaps have a different focus to those of 20 years ago, this logic seems unacceptable. On what evidence was LJ Hale's ruling based? Did she actually base her judgement on studies that set out the likely effects of an occupation upon mental health? Were such studies even available at that time? Has new evidence emerged since she passed judgement in 2002 that would lead her to change her thinking today? What do you, the reader, think? In law, we often hear about the 'reasonable person'. What do you, the reasonable person, think? Do some occupations run the risk of greater mental harm? And if so, isn't it now time for a review? If some occupations are at greater risk of mental harm than others, that greater risk must be reasonably foreseeable. The test of foreseeability seems therefore not the same whatever the employment, contrary to the 'Hatton Propositions' (see chapter 5, appendix 5.1).

Other nations already believe that some occupations run a greater risk of mental harm than others and have implemented laws accordingly (Safe Work Australia, online).

LJ Hale referred to the intrinsic nature of an occupation. But can the intrinsic nature of an occupation be separated from the person performing the occupation and any mental health consequences that accompany it? I say, no, it cannot. Sticking with the example of nursing, a nurse *will* see blood and bleeding. A nurse *will* see breaks and burns. A nurse *will* deal with dying and death. A nurse *will* see trauma, such as amputation. Witnessing such trauma is intrinsic to the nursing role and there is no escape from it. This is, among many other things, the very essence of nursing: repairing trauma. The intrinsic nature of some roles cannot be separated from the person performing it, whether for legal purposes or some other purpose.

Safe Work Australia (online) found that:

> *Over the five-year period reviewed by SWA, the occupations with the highest rate of claims for mental health conditions were:*
>
> - *defence force members, fire fighters and police (5.3 claims per million hours), specifically police (6.6)*
> - *automobile, bus and rail drivers (2.8 claims per million hours), specifically train and tram drivers (10.3)*
> - *health and welfare support workers (2.8 claims per million hours), specifically indigenous health workers (6.0)*
> - *prison and security officers (1.6 claims per million hours), specifically prison officers (4.0), and*
> - *social and welfare professionals (1.2 claims per million hours).*

Notably, verbal and physical abuse contributes towards poor mental health.

We would not apply LJ Hale's ruling to physical health. Both the intrinsic nature and extrinsic aspects of a role, as far as they affect the physical health of an employee, must be considered by employers when assessing risk and determining control measures. UK health and safety law does not limit causes of physical harm. The law expects all causes, intrinsic and extrinsic, to be controlled as far as is reasonably practicable.

Consider this. Are some occupations intrinsically more physically dangerous than others? Yes, of course. That is why a risk assessment is required and why the hierarchy of controls requires a structured approach to risk management. The approach is, by nature, to be risk-based. So, why would it be the case that all occupations carry the same level of psychological risk? They don't, as we are now seeing with the publication of study after study (chapter 1) that show certain occupations carry a higher risk of mental harm because of the intrinsic nature of the work involved.

To bring a legal claim, causation – the link between the intrinsic nature of the role and the adverse mental health effects – must still be established, of course. Here, more research will almost certainly be required. But we should not hide behind perceived difficulties arising from the legal process. The scale of the issue, and the impact it is having on people and their lives, is too great.

In my opinion, there are some acid test questions that can test this issue. Is the witnessing of traumatic events intrinsic to the nursing role? And might witnessing such events have an adverse effect on the mental health of the person performing the nursing role? A third question might relate to the frequency with which such traumatic events are witnessed, because repeated or continued exposure to trauma is known to increase adverse psychological symptoms (eg. PTSD), as Ogle et al. (2013) and Forbes et al. (2019) found. In response to these three questions, I answer 'yes' to each of them. Yes, witnessing trauma is intrinsic to the occupation of nursing. Yes, a nurse might suffer mental harm as a result of witnessing trauma. And yes, it is possible that nurses witnessing trauma on a repeated or continued basis are more likely to suffer from increased symptoms caused by that mental harm.

If, as I argue, it is the case that nursing is more intrinsically dangerous to mental health than the average occupation, then it is almost certainly the case that other occupations are too, just as Work Safe Australia (online) found.

The LJ Hale ruling was made in 2002. Now, nearly 20 years on, as we saw in chapter 1, nurses are five times more likely to suffer PTSD than the general population. Akhtar and Aydin (2019) write that the jobs in which people are particularly at risk of suicide and depression are some of the most important occupations in society, such as doctors, childcare workers and first responders. And Forbes et al. (2019) found higher than average and increasing rates of PTSD amongst soldiers. I therefore argue that LJ Hale's ruling must be reviewed.

Evidence is mounting that some professions appear more intrinsically dangerous to mental health than others. Some countries already believe this to be the case. Given this growing body of evidence, countries in which occupation is not linked with mental health face two choices:

- Let nurses, doctors, first responders, service personnel and others carry on as they are, suffering far higher (and frankly unacceptable) rates of mental ill-health, and be prepared to live with that.

- Call for an urgent review. Examine the evidence of higher levels of mental ill-health amongst certain occupations. If that evidence is flawed, continue as is. If it has merit and the evidence is robust, extend the review. Determine the laws, regulations, control measures and support that these valuable people need as they perform their often vital roles in difficult and sometimes traumatic circumstances.

We must now stop and assess whether the LJ Hale ruling of 2002 is still applicable today or whether it requires review. The evidence is mounting in favour of at least a review, and possibly change.

The UK government may not wish for this review to be undertaken. Given the nature of the professions in which people are most at risk of greater mental harm (eg. nurses, doctors, military personnel, first responders), if the law were changed as I envisage, the UK Government itself would most likely face claims under health and safety, and negligence legislation.

Mental health was barely talked of 20 years ago when LJ Hale made her ruling, and was certainly not talked about in most workplaces. Long hours and a high workload were badges of honour. They still are in some organisations. "Lunch is for wimps", right? Not anymore – today it is more likely to be a quinoa bowl with halloumi and avocado. Just as we have learned more about nutrition over the past 20 years, so we have learned far more about mental health. Increasingly, research is questioning past practice and precedents, and challenging the status quo.

To sum up, evidence is mounting that some occupations *are* more intrinsically dangerous to mental health. This would be the view of the law's 'reasonable person'. An urgent review is now required to protect those people most at risk, such as nurses. Employers of people undertaking occupations with greater psychological risk must offer their employees greater protection from mental harm. Employers failing to take reasonably practicable measures to control mental health risks must face the force of the law, which currently they do not. The 'Hatton Propositions', which currently protect employers, must be updated to recognise that some occupations are at greater risk of mental harm.

4. A Change to the 'Hatton Propositions' to Create a General Duty for Employers to Enquire About the Mental Health Of Employees

Under the Equality Act 2010, employers are currently required to do all they can be reasonably expected to do to learn of an employee's mental health condition (chapter 5). This duty aims to ensure employers make reasonable adjustments, especially for those with Protected Characteristics. However, this obligation is limited to the terms of the Equality Act 2010 and to where a 'trigger' alerts the employer that something is amiss which they should investigate (chapter 5).

If an employee does not have a Protected Characteristic or other qualifying mental disability (chapter 1), or if nothing triggers the employer to enquire about an employee's mental health, employees may well not receive any support.

Furthermore, the 'Hatton Propositions' state: 'The employer is generally entitled to take what the employee tells him or her at face value. They do not generally have to make searching enquiries of the employee or seek permission for further information from healthcare providers' (see chapter 5, appendix 5.1). In essence, this means employers have no obligation to ask the vast majority of their employees about their mental health, even though many of them may be struggling with mental health issues and even though the employer may be causing mental harm or exacerbating mental health conditions. In other words, employers can cause mental harm but need not be concerned about it and can act with impunity until they, somehow, become aware of it. This cannot be right.

Here, I call for action. I call for the obligations employers have under the Equality Act 2010 to be extended, making it a general duty that employers have to enquire about the mental health of all employees.

Simply put, employers should have a legal duty to enquire about the mental health of all employees.

This may not be as onerous as it sounds and may in some instances already be happening. A significant change may not be required. Employers already ask employees:

- questions about diversity and inclusion when they are recruited
- about workplace hazards and the effectiveness of control measures, during risk assessments and consultations
- about various aspects of employment through engagement surveys.

These existing practices can be adapted and used, alongside purpose-specific methods, to enquire about the mental health of employees.

Currently, when employers ask employees whether they have a disability or a Protected Characteristic, the questions are couched in terms defined by the Equality Act 2010 or disability-related legislation. To accommodate the change, it might be sufficient to adapt the wording of existing questions or include additional questions in existing survey forms.

If all employers ask all employees about their mental health, those employees who wish to disclose their condition, possibly with the aim of gaining support, will have a formal route through which to do so. The mechanisms that exist at the moment, which are less legal and less formal, are also proving less comprehensive, less consistent and less effective.

Before dismissing the 'general duty to enquire' proposal to change the 'Hatton Propositions', consider this. It has already been established that mental health risk assessments are a legal obligation (chapter 3). How is it possible to undertake a mental health risk assessment *without* asking employees how they are affected by mental health hazards? Again, we find the law and practice contradictory. Generally speaking, the 'Hatton Propositions' do not require employers to enquire about the mental health of employees. Yet the HSE does, through mental health risk assessments. No wonder some employers do not understand their mental health management obligations. Greater clarity is required.

Let us remind ourselves that Lord Walker stated the 'Hatton Propositions' provided useful guidance but should not be regarded as absolute (chapter 5), whereas in the UK and many other countries health and safety law is absolute. Health and safety law appears to trump the 'Hatton Propositions'.

The bottom line, in the UK at least, is that if you are not currently undertaking mental health risk assessments, including enquiring about how employees are affected by mental health hazards, you are breaking the law.

Employers not only *should* have a general duty to enquire about the mental health of employees; they already *do*. The 'Hatton Propositions' just need updating in line with this legal development.

5. A Change to the Law Relating to Employment Protection

It has been found that approximately 20% of people disclosing a mental health condition at work are demoted, disciplined, dismissed or forced to resign (chapter 1). This cannot be fair or just, and must not be allowed to continue. Given this statistic, it is evident that employers cannot always be trusted to do the right thing when employees disclose a mental health condition. Action is required.

Specifically, a change to the law is required to protect those with a 'mental disability' as it is defined and as has been discussed at 2., above.

My recommendation is that people who disclose a condition at work that meets the definition of 'mental disability' at 2. should be provided with a six-month protection period.

Disclosing their condition may afford the employee protection under the Equality Act 2010 but the Act does little to address issues such as being demoted or being forced to resign. In reality, employees in this situation often recognise that their employer no longer wants them in the organisation and, understandably, they turn their attention to finding another job. Their main worry is then about getting a favourable reference from their current position, so of course they try to leave on good terms, despite their employer's treatment of them. Of course, this is exactly what the unscrupulous employer wants; they want the employee to 'go quietly'. Employees must have greater protection than this. A more balanced and equitable arrangement is required.

During the six-month protection period I am proposing, the employer would not be able to amend in any way the employee's terms and conditions of employment. This period should be mandated in law as a time when:

- the employee's condition can be confirmed
- their symptoms can be understood
- the effects on their work-related activity can be identified

⬚   any reasonable adjustments (if required) can be determined and implemented

⬚   a periodic review can be put in place (because conditions, symptoms and effects can change).

Only by providing greater employment protection to those with mental health issues will the cycle of mental health suffering (Figure 2.4), and especially the cycle of mental health-related poverty, be slowed.

6. Health and Safety Laws to Expressly Relate to Mental Health

In the UK, many employers currently act as though health and safety laws and regulations, such as the Health and Safety at Work etc Act (HASAWA) 1974 and the Management of Health and Safety at Work Regulations (MHSWR) 1999, only apply to physical health. Perhaps this is no surprise, given that this is largely how the HSE acts; the HSE's words say one thing, their actions another.

There is a reason for this, which I have presented in chapter 5: the HSE does not believe it can meet the test required in criminal law to successfully prosecute a mental health negligence case against an employer. However, if the HSE does not try, it never will.

Codifying mental health, as has been done in Australia, New Zealand and elsewhere, would be a good start. As mental health is not expressly addressed in HASAWA and MHSWR, employers, perhaps understandably, presume they do not need to mention mental health in their own policies. This cascade effect is weakening the focus on mental health, which in turn is leading to a lack of protection for employees.

Governments around the world, including the UK government, should follow the lead of Australia, where (Safe Work Australia, online):

> The model WHS Act requires a PCBU (Person Conducting a Business or Undertaking) to ensure the health and safety of their workers, so far as is reasonably practicable. It defines health to mean both physical and psychological health.

> Under the model WHS Act, PCBUs have a duty to protect workers from psychological risks as well as physical risks.

In New Zealand, mental health is also codified. Worksafe, New Zealand (2017) states:

> Under the Health and Safety at Work Act 2015 (HSWA), Persons Conducting a Business or Undertaking (PCBUs) have a primary duty of care to provide a work environment that is without risk to health and safety, so far as is reasonably practicable. Whilst focus is typically given to reducing the risk of physical harm, HSWA importantly defines health as being both physical **and** mental.

Away from the UK and USA, other countries are seeing the need to introduce the twin track approach proposed in this book to bring mental health back to an acceptable level. These twin tracks are: 1) encouragement; and 2) legislation and regulation.

Currently, in respect of workplace mental health, the UK is failing to use legislation and regulation as a motivator of market behaviour.

I recommend the UK expressly includes mental health in health and safety law. Following such a change, the HSE must undertake a root and branch review of its policies and guidance. Currently, the HSE's current focus on psychological health is marginal, for a number of reasons:

- The majority of the HSE's guidance focuses on stress. It barely touches on other mental health issues.

- Its stress 'management standards' are far too limited. The Canadian Centre for Occupational Health and Safety (online) provides useful (if still limited) guidance. The HSE describes just six causes of stress, when there are in fact many, many more. Here, I would recommend the HSE removes detailing causes of stress. After all, it does not list the causes of physical injury; it simply expects employers to identify and manage them. The same should be the case for mental health.[3]

- The HSE's guidance relating to when it will investigate mental health incidents is far too narrow (see chapters 4 and 15). It places the onus on employees to report, as opposed to employers, and then only offers to investigate in very extreme circumstances (eg. group or mass stress). I address this specific point in action 8. below.

In the UK, I suggest that the government needs to state expressly that health and safety laws apply to mental health. A programme of communication is required to make *all* employers aware of their legal obligations. I also suggest that the HSE requires additional funding so that it can:

- lead this communication exercise

- update its position, policy and guidance

- increase the scope of inspections to include mental health

- process reportable incidents related to mental health

---

[3]   When I was researching this book, I spoke to several consultants. One of them explained that their clients felt that so long as they attempted to manage the HSE's six stress 'management standards' (HSE, online, c), they were unlikely to be found at fault. These stress 'management standards' are thus actually limiting employer mental health actions, and therefore need to be either: 1) removed, with the employer being left to assess their own risks, as happens with physical health and safety; or 2) comprehensively updated to list all causes of mental ill-health. The former approach is recommended.

■ issue notices and fines when non-compliance arises

■ prosecute employers who fail to comply with health and safety laws as they relate to mental health.

Only by bringing clarity to this otherwise ambiguous situation will we more quickly escape the trough of the mental health change curve that was set out in chapter 4.

This proposal really is not that radical. It simply follows the lead of Australia and New Zealand.

This change is coming. It is only a matter of time before the UK and other governments make mental health an intrinsic part of their health and safety laws. In the UK, I'm saying that time has come; this change is needed, *right now.*

Let me make one final point on this proposal to change health and safety law. A combination of encouragement and changes to the law led to an 84% reduction in UK workplace fatalities in the forty-five years that followed the introduction of health and safety legislation, with most of the improvement coming in the first twenty years after the changes to the law were introduced.

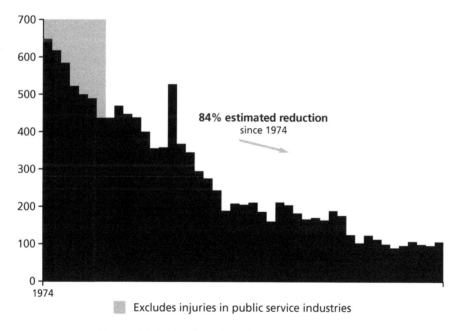

Figure 16.1 *Number of fatal injuries to employees*
Source: HSE online, c

The same twin-track approach of encouragement and changes to the law (and its enforce-ment) must now be taken if a similar seismic change is to be brought about to improve mental health.

7. A Change to the HSE's Position/Guidance on Causation

In action 6, I called for health and safety law to be changed to expressly relate to mental health. From the law, we must move to law enforcement.

The HSE's current position reflects health and safety law enforcement in the UK. On the one hand, the HSE states that employers have a legal duty to manage mental health. On the other hand, the HSE places no reporting obligations upon employers and issues no sanctions for breaches of the law as it relates to mental health. The HSE takes no action because of its flawed belief that causation – the link between cause (hazard) and effect (harm) – cannot be proven. The HSE's current position is presented in Table 16.1, which summarises the references I have made to HSE policy and practice throughout this book.

Table 16.1   *The HSE's position regarding physical and mental health*

The HSE...	Physical health	Mental health
...states employers have a legal duty to protect the health, safety and welfare of employees	Yes	Yes
...believes causation can be proven	Yes	No
...defines reportable specified injuries and illnesses	Yes	No
...requires the reporting of specified injuries	Yes	No
...inspects workplaces to ensure they are compliant with the law	Yes	No
...will investigate reports of harm	Yes	No (except where high numbers are affected)
...requires the reporting of time-based absence injuries	Yes (7-day)	No (unlimited)
...issues prohibition notices for breaches of the law	Yes	'No data available'
...issues fines for breaches of the law	Yes	'No data available'

The HSE is failing to regulate UK workplace mental health, certainly anywhere near the standard to which it regulates physical health and safety.

You should bear Table 16.1 in mind when considering actions 7, 8 and 9, which relate to the HSE's guidance on causation, the reporting of mental health incidents and sanctions for mental health breaches.

In chapter 5, I discussed a number of legal cases that established that negligence claims have and are being brought by employees against employers. These cases detailed circumstances under which employers may find themselves liable for mental health negligence. In analysing these cases, it is apparent that causation can be proven, employers can fail to foresee harm, they can have knowledge of a mental health condition upon which they fail to act, and they can act negligently.

However, the HSE's position appears to be based upon the belief they could *never* succeed in proving any of these aspects of a legal case, should they attempt to do so. In essence, the HSE is deterring employees from bringing claims against their employer for failing to provide a safe place to work, which should be at the very heart of the HSE's focus and efforts. The HSE's current position is incongruent with its own mission: 'The prevention of death, injury and ill health to those at work and those affected by work activities' (HSE, 2019).

I strongly propose that the HSE's guidance should be updated to take account of the following points:

- Employers can be found liable for mental health-related negligence, so should take steps to minimise employee distress and protect themselves from legal claims.
- Claims based upon mental health negligence may lead courts to consider wider issues than just the direct cause of poor mental health. Courts may also consider an employer's wider duties under health and safety law and whether a breach of those duties contributed to the employee suffering poor mental health. Employers must provide safe places to work, including psychological safety.

By changing its guidance, the HSE will:

- more effectively align itself with the law, as the law is being applied by courts (eg. as the law relates to the requirement to provide a safe place of work)
- encourage employers to provide more effective support for employees with mental health issues
- improve employee support at work and improve employee protection
- encourage employees to bring claims against employers, and not deter them.

In short, the HSE must change its guidance so it more effectively satisfies its mission of protecting employees from psychological injury and ill-health.

If laws related to mental health and the enforcement of these laws are to move closer to those of physical health and safety, it is recommended that enforcement is changed to more closely match the enforcement of physical health and safety laws. I am seeking two changes in particular: changes to reporting and changes to sanctions, the focus of actions 8 and 9.

8. A Change to Law Enforcement – Reporting

In physical health and safety law, an accident is reportable where a specified injury or illness occurs and where the employee is unable to perform their normal range of duties for more than seven consecutive days.

Currently, no reporting obligation exists regarding mental health injury or illness, even with a doctor's certificate stating that the cause of the mental illness is work-related, no matter how severe the injury or illness. An employee can be absent for months with mental injury, or even years, with no requirement for the organisation to report it. This is wrong.

Mental ill-health should be made reportable to the HSE where:

- there is a doctor's certificate stating that work or work-related factors have caused the mental injury or illness or have exacerbated an existing mental health condition, and

- the employee is absent or unable to perform their usual duties for more than 30 consecutive days.

This reporting requirement should be introduced as a matter of urgency; employers must have to report such incidents so the welfare of their employee can be considered by the HSE and if need be, investigated.

By creating an obligation to report '30-day' incidents, the HSE can determine the circumstances of the case and whether a more rigorous investigation is required, including looking into the extent to which the employer's actions and omissions contributed to the employee's circumstances.

At this stage I am not recommending the reporting of specified psychological injuries and illnesses. I believe this should be considered eventually, but, for now, a time-based reporting requirement of 30 days will suffice, allowing employers time to adjust to a new regime before it is further developed.

In future, the need to report specified psychological illnesses and injuries should be considered, with the following incidents being considered as being reportable:

- the dismissal of any employee with a 'mental disability'

- suicides by employees within the workplace

- employees being made the subject of a psychiatric assessment while in police custody

- employees being made the subject of an involuntary commitment or civil commitment order (eg. under the Mental Health Act).

Once the reporting of 30-day psychological injuries and illnesses has been put in place, the 30-day time frame should be reviewed to determine whether it is proving effective or a more suitable time frame (eg. 14 days) is needed. As with all aspects of health and safety, a periodical review of effectiveness is required.

It has already been established (see chapter 5) that mental health negligence claims may be brought against an employer where mental harm has arisen at work, and where negligence has caused a new injury or illness or exacerbated an existing condition.

The requirement to report such mental injuries and illnesses would strengthen the efforts of government, charities and other organisations to bring the mental health crisis under control. Employers will inevitably respond to such a reporting requirement by doing more to support employees, in order to minimise those occasions when they are required to report a mental injury or illness.

Expanding the reporting obligation will dramatically increase organisational focus on mental health, without the government having to spend significant sums of money. Costs may be incurred, say, in the recruitment of additional case handlers to administer the increased number of reports of mental ill-health but this will be a modest amount compared to the benefits that might arise from such a change.

Since 6 April 2017, employers in Britain with more than 250 staff have been required by law to publish four figures annually about gender equality:

- gender pay gap (mean and median averages)
- gender bonus gap (mean and median averages)
- proportion of men and women receiving bonuses
- proportion of men and women in each quartile of the organisation's pay structure.

This gender pay gap legal reporting requirement has led most large employers to benchmark their performance against similar organisations and develop action plans to improve it. This legal reporting requirement has pushed gender equality further up the management agenda.

Reporting must be used to push mental health up the management agenda in the same way. The reporting of mental health injuries and illnesses to the HSE provides a starting point.

Of all the recommendations in this chapter, this is by far the quickest and easiest to implement. It should be implemented with haste.

9. A Change to Law Enforcement – Sanctions

With physical health and safety management, if an employer has not complied with HSG65 (HSE, 2013b) or an equivalent method of working, they may be found negligent and face sanctions. If a mental health management system and/or standard is introduced (such as ISO45003, due to be implemented in 2021), it would help to determine whether an employer has acted appropriately or negligently in the event of a mental health incident. Such a standard judgement could then be used as the basis for determining any necessary sanction.

Mental health issues at work are up to ten times more prevalent than physical injuries and mental health accounts for 56% of all lost working days. Yet employers face no sanctions whatsoever, even where they have been negligent. This must change.

Simple changes to the law and enforcement practice would make an enormous difference to the mental health landscape, at negligible cost to the tax-payer. From the point of view of both the government and the public, the business case is a strong one that makes perfect sense.

In any operational system, demand and capacity must be balanced. Currently, the demand for public mental health services is outstripping capacity, so this needs to be brought under control. Making employers responsible for achieving some reduction in demand appears sensible. It will be a significant first step towards providing better mental health for all, especially in the workplace.

With physical health and safety, there is a cycle that drives the market (Figure 16.1). This cycle probably exists in all regulated markets. The market regulation cycle sees physical health and safety managed effectively, as assessment (eg. inspections, reportable injuries and illnesses) and enforcement (eg. notices, fines) drive market practice, learning and the process of continuous improvement.

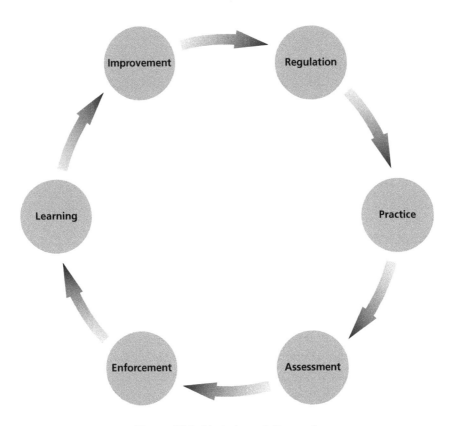

Figure 16.2 *Market regulation cycle*

With workplace mental health, the components of assessment and enforcement are currently missing from the market regulation cycle. As a result, practice in some places is poor and it is generally inconsistent. Learning is limited, with continuous improvement also limited except amongst the most progressive of employers. Perhaps it is no wonder that workplace mental health, to many employees, appears like the Wild West.

I talked at the start of this book about how the employer-employee mental health relationship is inequitable and biased towards the employer, contributing to the current mental health crisis. It is because of this that I am recommending the 10 actions in this chapter. These actions will have a dramatic effect upon mental health as they will place pressure upon employers to address mental health far more effectively.

Actions to strengthen and develop workplace mental health leadership, laws and law enforcement are required if mental health is to be significantly improved. Existing conventions must be challenged. This book provides the type of new thinking that is required.

The HSE has been very deliberate about its wording, referred to extensively in chapter 5 and in this chapter. It can be summarised as follows:

- Stress is not reportable as an occupational injury, even when it is accompanied by a medical certificate stating the stress is work-related, because it does not result from a single definable accident.

- Stress is only reportable where there is evidence that a number of staff are currently experiencing work-related stress or stress-related ill health (ie. that it is not an individual case).

- HSE is not the appropriate body to investigate concerns solely related to individual cases of bullying or harassment. The HSE fails to state the appropriate body employees should turn to.

The HSE appears to have done all it can possibly do *not* to have to regulate workplace mental health and *not* to have to take any action against employers.

How has the HSE got away with this?

10. Society's Leaders and Change Agents to Bring About Policy Changes

I haven't yet got to the most troubling of findings my research has uncovered.

Over recent years, many mental health outcomes have deteriorated or remained disappointing, as this book has demonstrated. This deterioration has been despite Stevenson and Farmer (2017), despite the efforts of leading mental health charities and despite even the intervention of members of the British royal family to raise awareness. Today we see:

- UK suicide rates have risen (ONS, online)

- nurses are suffering five times the PTSD rate of most occupations (Advisory Board, 2019)

- twice as many people are losing their job where they have a long-term mental health issue than those who do not (Stevenson and Farmer, 2017)

- the percentage of employees who feel comfortable talking to their line manager about their mental health saw no improvement between 2016 and 2019 (Business in the Community, 2019)

- managers are less confident talking about mental health than they were previously (Shaw Trust, 2018)

- too many senior managers would prefer not to work with somebody with mental health issues (Shaw Trust, 2018)

- there is a belief that people with mental health conditions are less reliable employees has almost doubled (Shaw Trust, 2018)

- the HSE is pretty much turning a blind eye to mental health failings, despite increasing civil claims being brought by employees against employers (HSE, Online, e).

More must be done to protect and support the mental health of nurses, doctors, first responders, military personnel and the others most at risk. We must unite to bring about seismic change in mental health.

Blaszczynski and Gainsbury (online) state:

> *Typically, a combination of factors leads to policy change, including political motivation, potential economic or social benefits, a strong publicly stated case by a prominent individual/group, general community support, and some evidence. The tipping point often occurs after a single or series of high profile events leading the community to demand a political/regulatory response.*

I call upon the most influential change agents among society's leaders to be the *prominent individuals/groups*, referred to by Blaszczynski and Gainsbury, to bring about policy change.

I call upon these prominent people and groups to take up this cause, to:

- consider the recommendations in this chapter

- develop these recommendations, strengthening them legally, morally and in other ways

- promote these recommendations, along with any other recommendations they wish to add

- gain Blaszczynski and Gainsbury's *general community support*

- lobby government, law-makers, academics, charities, trade associations and leading public and employer organisations, to bring about the tipping point required to achieve policy change.

The point of being a leader is to lead; to take up a significant challenge, often facing impossible odds, to bring about change to make things better. Only society's leaders can bring about the type of changes I call for; regulatory change, based upon changes in the law and law enforcement. Whatever the merits and shortcomings of my recommendations, the regulatory system must be made to apply to workplace mental health.

Of course, progressive employers could put these recommended actions into effect within their own organisation without them being codified in law. Employers could implement many of these recommendations on a self-determined basis, testing the efficacy of each recommendation and monitoring the impact they have on their organisation and its employees. So, if you are a leader of a large employer, will you step forward and consider implementing these recommendations within your organisation? Will you put in place a protection period when employees disclose a mental health issue at work? When a member of your staff has a mental health-related absence lasting more than 30 days, will you escalate it to your managing director or chief executive for review? Leaders can play a vital role in shaping mental health in their own workplace, without the need for greater regulation.

Conclusion

I do not believe I am the only person to call this out: the regulatory system is not working. The mental health of employees is being failed because of a lack of regulation.

For whatever reason, prominent workplace mental health influencers and the authors of notable workplace mental health reports have not chosen to pursue the type of legal and regulatory changes – the seismic changes – I am calling for. They are instead pursuing a 'softer' approach. However, the numerous mental health indicators presented in this book suggest their efforts to date have not proven as effective as many of us would like.

But it's not all bad news. The overall suicide rate has reduced by more than 20% since the 1980s (ONS, 2019). Additionally, twenty years ago, Mind (Read and Baker, 1996) reported that 34% of people disclosing a mental health condition at work had been dismissed or forced to resign. Today this is around 20% (Business in the Community, 2019), so some progress has been made. That said, the comparison of these results must be regarded with a degree of caution as the 1996 study had just 18% of the sample size of the 2019 study.

However, my concern relates more to the last five years and the deteriorating picture some studies present (Shaw Trust, 2018), despite far greater awareness of mental health. Surely we must all find current key mental health output indicators disappointing. Many employers are uncertain how to address mental health.

Deloitte's analysis (Hampson and Jacob, 2020) takes an encouraging tone. Its recommendations include prioritising mental health, creating an open culture and providing mental health support, and it presents a compelling commercial case for investing in mental health, which is also helpful.

But the commercial case alone will not bring about the seismic change required. The recent rise in the suicide rate and Business in the Community's statistic in Figure 2.3 (44% – *no change*) question current efforts, as do Shaw Trust's (2018) findings. No – mental health should not be about the opportunity to make money. It should be about the opportunity to improve the lives of employees by improving their mental health. That is what employers should care about, or be made to care about.

Let us remind ourselves of what the HSE (online, d), the UK's health and safety enforcer, says:

> *Whether work is causing the health issue or aggravating it, employers have a legal responsibility to help their employees. Work-related mental health issues must be assessed to measure the levels of risk to staff. Where a risk is identified, steps must be taken to remove it or reduce it as far as reasonably practicable.*

Certainly, in the UK, managing mental health is a legal obligation, just as it is in some other countries. It is not a choice based on a commercial case. Any commercial benefit should be coincidental or peripheral, not central, to the aspiration of improving employee mental health.

Despite saying that managing mental health is a legal requirement, the HSE appears to believe mental health-related cases are unlikely to succeed in court, as we have established. To some extent, I understand this point and even agree with it. However, the fact still remains that mental health is at a crisis point and employers are not doing enough to address it.

Health and safety laws and regulations should expressly include mental health. From this updated legal position, the HSE can increase inspections (as per my proposed action 6), issuing notices and sanctions, and prosecuting employers for not complying with updated laws and regulations. Here, there would be no need to prove mental harm or that negligence caused harm. All the HSE needs to do is inspect employer practice to identify whether employers, for example:

- have a health and safety policy that addresses mental health
- are undertaking mental health risk assessments that are suitable and sufficient
- are consulting their workforce on mental health.

If employers are not undertaking these activities, the HSE could issue notices and fines and/or prosecute, just as they would with physical health and safety breaches. A simplistic but effective solution is perhaps going to prove the best one, rather than getting tangled in the many complex legal issues, such as causation, identified in chapter 5.

Additionally, why not put in place a '30-day mental health absence' reporting obligation, as I suggested in action 8? This alone would buck up the ideas of many an employer, even if nothing is done with the vast majority of reported incidents. Employers *do not* like reporting to the HSE and they *will* change how they operate to avoid doing so.

Before concluding, for the sceptics amongst you, let's assume I am, indeed, wrong. What then? Mental health continues to be a problem and a growing one at that. The likelihood is that you or people you love and care for are affected by it. Do we just let nurses, doctors, first responders and our military service personnel suffer in silence? Mental health affects everyone, directly or indirectly. Do we just let the situation continue without a more significant response? I believe that poor mental health is at an unacceptable level in our society, and renewed and more significant efforts are needed to improve it. We must review every aspect of policy and practice, along with laws and regulation, to see if we can achieve greater protection of employee mental health. So, please, be part of the solution. If you don't like my ideas, that's fine, but do be open to identifying more radical solutions than have been tried to date, because these have been found wanting.

This book does not pretend to make the whole argument or even a good argument, but it does intend to start an argument. If an argument can be defined as 'a reason or set of reasons given in support of an idea, action or theory' (Lexico, online), this book proposes two sets of ideas, actions and theories:

1   A workplace mental health management system for employers
2   A 10-point plan intended to bring about a seismic change in mental health to improve the lives of employees.

It's now up to you, society's leaders and managers – the change agents amongst us – to decide if you feel the management system and 10-point plan presented in this book have merit. If you feel they do, please carry these ideas forward to the next stage, bringing about change where you can and arguing for change where you can't.

The main take-outs from this chapter focus on the 10-point plan I propose:

1   A Workplace Mental Health Tsar should be appointed to bring leadership to workplace mental health, strengthening governments' ability to bring about the changes required to make a transformational change to mental health in society.

2 A change in law (or the interpretation or definition of it) as it relates to 'mental disability' so that people with long-term conditions that affect their long-term activities (eg. getting and keeping a job) are covered by the definition.

3 A change to the 'Hatton Propositions', so that some occupations are recognised as intrinsically more harmful to mental health than other occupations.

4 A change to the 'Hatton Propositions' so the law places a general duty upon employers to periodically enquire about the mental health of all employees.

5 A change to the law as far as it offers employment protection to those with a 'mental disability' as defined by the law, to prevent employers from varying their terms and conditions of employment for six months after an employee has disclosed a mental health issue, to allow time for employers to learn of the condition and how it affects the employee, and to determine and implement any necessary reasonable adjustments.

6 Health and safety laws and regulations must expressly state that they apply to mental health, with the HSE being provided with additional funding to allow it to communicate, inspect and enforce health and safety law as it applies to mental health.

7 A change to the HSE's position, so that it recognises that causation can be established in mental health cases. The HSE should update its advice as a matter of urgency as it is misleading employees who may otherwise be considering bringing a claim against their employer.

8 A doctor's certificate has been issued which states that the cause of absence relates to a mental health issue that has been caused or exacerbated by work or work-related factors.

   a an employee is absent or unable to perform their normal duties for 30 consecutive days or longer, and

   b a doctor's certificate has been issued which states that the cause of absence relates to a mental health issue that has been caused or exacerbated by work or work-related factors.

9 A change to enforcement, whereby the HSE would issue sanctions (eg. notices, fines) against employers failing to comply with health and safety law as it relates to mental health.

10 Prominent figures are called upon to take up the challenge of bringing about these seismic, policy-level changes to workplace mental health.

References

Advisory Board (2019) *Why 1 in 4 Nurses Suffers from PTSD (and How to Help Them)*. Available at: *https://www.advisory.com/daily-briefing/2019/05/15/nurse-trauma* (accessed 3 March 2020).

Akhtar, A. and Aydin, R. (2019) Some of the jobs most at risk for suicide and depression are the most important to society. Here's a rundown of mental-health risks for doctors, childcare workers, first responders, and more. *Business Insider* 14 November. Available at: *https://www.businessinsider.com/jobs-with-mental-health-risks-like-suicide-depression-2019-10?r=US&IR=T* (accessed 8 March 2020).

Blaszczynski, A. and Gainsbury, S. (online) Tipping point: When public opinion triggers changes to policy. *Gamble Aware, UK*. Available at: *https://about.gambleaware.org/media/1520/tipping-point-brief-report.pdf* (accessed 21 March 2020).

Business in the Community (2019) Mental health at work 2019: Time to take ownership. *Business in the Community* 29 October. Available at: *https://www.bitc.org.uk/report/mental-health-at-work-2019-time-to-take-ownership/* (accessed 22 November 2019).

Canadian Centre for Occupational Health and Safety (online) *Mental health – psychosocial risk factors in the workplace*. Available at: *https://www.ccohs.ca/oshanswers/psychosocial/mentalhealth_risk.html* (accessed 25 March 2020).

Deloitte (2020) *Poor Mental Health Costs UK Employers up to £45 Billion a Year*. Press Release 22 January. Available at: *https://www2.deloitte.com/uk/en/pages/press-releases/articles/poor-mental-health-costs-uk-employers-up-to-pound-45-billion-a-year.html#* (accessed 21 March 2020).

Forbes, D., Pedlar, D., Adler, A. B., Bennett, C., Bryant, R., Busuttil, W., Cooper, J., Creamer, M.C., Fear, N.T., Greenberg, N., Heber, A., Hinton, M., Hopwood, M., Jetly, R., Lawrence-Wood, E., McFarlane, A., Metcalf, O., O'Donnell, M., Phelps, A., Richardson, J. D., Sadler, N., Schnurr, P.P., Sharp, M-L., Thompson, J.M., Ursano, R.J., Van Hooff, M., Wade D. & Wessely, S. (2019) Treatment of military-related post-traumatic stress disorder: challenges, innovations, and the way forward. *International Review of Psychiatry*, *DOI: 10.1080/09540261.2019.1595545*. Available at: https://www.kcl.ac.uk/kcmhr/publications/assetfiles/2019/forbes2019.pdf (accessed 21 March 2020).

The Guardian (2019) *The Guardian view on The Jeremy Kyle Show: TV with no moral compass*. Editorial, 15 May. Available at: *https://www.theguardian.com/commentisfree/2019/may/15/the-guardian-view-on-the-jeremy-kyle-show-tv-with-no-moral-compass* (accessed 1 April 2020).

Hampson, E. and Jacob, A. (2020) *Mental Health and Employers: Refreshing the case for investment*. London: Deloitte LLP. Available at: *https://www2.deloitte.com/content/dam/Deloitte/uk/Documents/consultancy/deloitte-uk-mental-health-and-employers.pdf* (accessed 20 March 2020).

Health and Safety Executive (2013a) Reporting injuries, diseases and dangerous occurrences in health and social care: Guidance for employers. *HSE Information Sheet No 1 (Revision 3)* (online). Available at: http://www.hse.gov.uk/pubns/hsis1.pdf (accessed 2 December 2019).

Health and Safety Executive (2013b) Managing for Health and Safety (HSG 65) (online). Available at: *https://www.hse.gov.uk/pubns/books/hsg65.htm* (accessed 2 April 2020).

Health and Safety Executive (2019) *HSE Business Plan 2019/20*. Available at: *https://www.hse. gov.uk/aboutus/strategiesandplans/businessplans/plan1920.pdf* (accessed 21 February 2020).

Health and Safety Executive (online, a) *Stress Risk Assessment*. Available at: *https://www.hse.gov. uk/stress/risk-assessment.htm* (accessed 9 March 2020).

Health and Safety Executive (online, b) *What the Law Says on Assessing Risks*. Available at: *https://www.hse.gov.uk/managing/delivering/do/profiling/the-law.htm* (accessed 9 March 2020).

Health and Safety Executive (online, c) Historical Picture Statistics in Great Britain, 2019 – Trends in work-related ill health and workplace injury. Available at: *https://www.hse.gov.uk/ statistics/history/index.htm#* (accessed 18 April 2020).

Health and Safety Executive (online, d) *Mental Health Conditions, Work and the Workplace*. Available at: *https://www.hse.gov.uk/stress/mental-health.htm* (accessed 21 February 2020).

Health and Safety Executive (online, e) *Reporting a Concern*. Available at: *https://www.hse.gov.uk/ stress/reporting-concern.htm* (accessed 20 February 2020).

Lexico (online) *Argument*. Available at: *https://www.lexico.com/definition/argument* (accessed 20 March 2020).

Office for National Statistics (online) *Suicides in the UK Statistical Bulletins*. Available at: *https:// www.ons.gov.uk/peoplepopulationandcommunity/birthsdeathsandmarriages/deaths/ bulletins/suicidesintheunitedkingdom/previousReleases* (accessed 20 February 2020).

Office for National Statistics (online). *Suicides in the UK Statistical bulletins*. Available at: *https:// www.ons.gov.uk/peoplepopulationandcommunity/birthsdeathsandmarriages/deaths/ bulletins/suicidesintheunitedkingdom/previousReleases* (accessed on 20 Feb 2020).

Ogle, C.M., Rubin, D.C. and Siegler, I.C. (2013) Cumulative exposure to traumatic events in older adults. *Aging & Mental Health* 18:3, 316–325. Available at: *https://www.ncbi.nlm.nih.gov/ pmc/articles/PMC3944195/* (accessed 5 January 2020).

Read, J. and Baker, S. (1996) *Not just Sticks & Stones. A survey of the stigma, taboos and discrimination experienced by people with mental health problems*. London: Mind. Available at: *https://disability-studies.leeds.ac.uk/wp-content/uploads/sites/40/library/MIND-MIND. pdf* (accessed 29 March 2020).

Safe Work Australia (online) *Mental Health*. Available at: *https://www.safeworkaustralia.gov.au/ topic/mental-health#mental-health-in-the-workplace* (accessed 21 March 2020).

Shaw Trust (2018) *Mental Health at Work: Still the last taboo*. Available at: *https://www.shaw-trust. org.uk/ShawTrustMediaLibraries/ShawTrust/ShawTrust/Documents/Shaw-Trust-Mental- Health-at-Work-Report-2018-full_1.pdf* (accessed 29 November 2019).

Stevenson, D. and Farmer, P. (2017) *Thriving at Work: The Stevenson/Farmer review of mental health and employers.* Available at: https://assets.publishing.service.gov.uk/government/uploads/system/uploads/attachment_data/file/658145/thriving-at-work-stevenson-farmer-review.pdf (accessed 28 October 2019).

Woodcock, A (2019). 'Government Announces £70m for Community Mental Health Services', *Independent,* 29 September 2019. (Online). Available at: *https://www.independent.co.uk/news/uk/politics/conservative-tory-conference-mental-health-services-johnson-a9124821.html* (accessed 20 April 2020).

Worksafe, New Zealand (2017) Health isn't just physical. *Safeguard* April. Available at: *https://worksafe.govt.nz/topic-and-industry/work-related-health/work-related-health-updates/health-isnt-just-physical/* (accessed 25 March 2020).

17

SUMMARY

In the course of this book I have endeavoured to give you a comprehensive understanding of workplace mental health management, including an appreciation of the workplace mental health backstory, related laws, management methods and policy issues. It is my hope that you now feel better placed to become a mental health leader within your workplace.

In this final chapter, I give a short summary of the main points from each chapter and offer a few words to bring the book to a close.

In Part I, I explored the scale of the mental health issue with the aim of building readers' empathy with employees who have mental health issues. I presented some of the methods through which physical health and safety is managed, and considered the differences between the management of physical health and safety and mental health. I explored aspects of the law that employers should take into account when developing a mental health programme. I then considered the positive case for employing people with mental ill-health, and explored some of the challenges employers may face when managing employees with mental health issues.

In Part II, I presented the case for using a management systems approach to manage mental health. I presented my '7 Principles' model for managing workplace mental health, which comprises: the mental health management system itself; commitment; policy; risk assessments; the hierarchy of controls; consultation; and reporting. I concluded Part II by proposing a 10-point plan of action that recommends the appointment of a Workplace Mental Health Tsar, changes to the law and to law enforcement, and which called upon prominent figures in society to bring about seismic, policy-level change to workplace mental health management.

In chapter 1, I identified that between one in four and one in five people suffers with a mental health issue each year. Many of them are in work. The World Health Organization estimates that depression and anxiety lead to $1 trillion dollars a year in lost productivity worldwide. However, studies have shown that organisations can improve productivity by as much as 25% when they invest in a mental health and wellbeing programme. Such programmes should seek to address the causes of poor mental health, which can be rooted in the person themselves, their circumstances and/or their relationships. At any given time, everyone, including employees, is in one of four mental health states: distress, coping, managing or contentment. Studies suggest that up to 70% of employees have experienced a condition related to mental health, and work-related circumstances can cause or contribute towards poor mental health. There is a correlation between the number of traumatic events a person has experienced and PTSD symptoms. The more trauma people suffer, the worse their symptoms appear to get. Distress arising from poor mental health can be caused by factors at work or outside of work. A compound effect can occur, with the last in a long succession of stressors being the *one small thing* that may cause an employee to become distressed. Employers should be proactive in avoiding the *one small thing* occurring at work, by reducing known workplace mental health risk factors. People in some occupations were found to be more at risk of mental harm than others. Current employer responses – which include speaking out, resilience training and mental health first aid – are mostly tactical and not strategic. The reasons employers do not take more strategic action to address mental health is linked to a lack of understanding and uncertainty. Employers should take a strategic, structured and systematic approach to managing mental health, such as that set out in this book.

In chapter 2, I presented the five-stage discovery process experienced by people who have mental health issues. This journey has five stages: no known condition; ignorance; awareness; diagnosis; and treatment. Some people may only complete part of the journey of discovery. The process can be short or lengthy, simple or complex, with few or numerous people involved. Some people may self-diagnose, and employers should be cautious about this. Others may seek a professional opinion. Having established they have a condition, employees with mental health issues will weigh up whether to tell their employer about it. Many of them will feel this is a major decision, with the fear of reprisals and stigma being uppermost amongst their concerns. Approximately 20% of employees who disclose a mental health condition at work are demoted, disciplined, dismissed or forced to resign. Many employers see employees with mental health issues as a 'significant risk' to their organisation, so it is no wonder employees may be reticent to disclose their condition. It was noted that stigma only arises where there is a failure of leadership. Anti-bullying policies must be enforced if a pro-mental-health culture is to develop. Employees with mental health issues are likely to suffer from knock-on effects, such as worries about their children having the same condition and low income levels, arising from repeatedly being sacked, that can lead to financial problems and poor living conditions. A cycle of suffering can emerge. Employers can help break this cycle by being more supportive of employees with mental health issues. I also identified that employers might believe an employee has a mental health condition without the employee being aware of it themselves. Employers must act with caution before raising this with the employee, and should take care not to risk making the situation worse.

I presented an introduction to health and safety (H&S) management in chapter 3. I established that H&S is managed in a similar way in many parts of the developed world, and that it is most effectively managed using a strategic, systematic and structured approach. Most H&S management systems possess seven core elements: the management system itself; leadership and commitment; policy; risk assessments; the hierarchy of controls; consultation; and reporting. The whole organisation should demonstrate *commitment* to managing H&S effectively, with leaders establishing the culture and framework for doing so. The *policy* for managing H&S should set out the statement of intent, the organisation and management structure through which H&S will be managed and controlled, and the arrangements through which H&S will be implemented and integrated into the processes of the organisation. *Risk assessments* should be undertaken using a five-step approach, so that every part of the population that might be affected by the organisation's activities is protected as far as is reasonably practicable. The five steps are: identify what can cause harm; determine who can be harmed and how; assess the risks and determine control measures; write up the risk assessment and implement it; and review the risk assessment. I introduced the *hierarchy of controls*, which provides a structured approach to the planning and implementing of measures that control risks, with elimination and substitution being considered the most effective and preferred methods, and with administrative controls and personal protective equipment (PPE) being the least effective and least preferred. I presented workforce *consultation*, at whole organisation and local levels, as part of the H&S management system. Consultations provide an effective method for sharing information, discussing and agreeing improvements, and deciding upon the best solutions to problems. Consultations were revealed to be a way of bringing together strategic aspiration and practical insight based upon employee input. Finally, *reporting* provides the means of monitoring practice and performance. I discussed legal reporting requirements, and identified specified and 7-day injury reporting requirements. Reporting can be used to determine the adequacy and effectiveness of control measures, provide a method for investigating incidents, and provide strategic insight into organisational performance over time through statistical and trend analysis. I also identified that benchmarking reports can be considered to determine organisational H&S performance within a given industrial sector.

There are significant differences between physical H&S management and mental health management. These differences were the subject of chapter 4. The length of time each management practice has been established has a major bearing on how it is managed today. Physical H&S has been managed systematically for 50 years, whereas mental health management is a recently emerging discipline. The intangible nature of mental health can make it more difficult to understand and manage. Neither mental health hazards nor the controls required to reduce harm may be visible. Technical ambiguity can occur too, with confusion occurring at macro (national) and micro (organisational) levels. At the macro level, laws and regulation, psychology and management methods are not being considered as a whole. At the micro level, the expertise relevant to mental health across health and safety (H&S), human resources and occupational health may fail to become unified, leading to ambiguity within the organisation. If mental health is to be effectively managed, the organisation needs to consider aspects from all three functions, probably as well as introducing new thinking. In terms of law enforcement, between £20m and £50m of fines are issued for breaches of physical H&S in the UK each year. By comparison, few (if any) fines are issued by the HSE, the UK's H&S enforcer, for breaches of the law as they relate to workplace mental health. I argue that, under current conditions, those employers that cause mental harm do so with impunity, unless employees bring civil claims against them. Mental health is a subset of wellbeing; the two are different. Mental wellbeing, physical wellbeing and interactive wellbeing feed each other. One can provide a kick-start to the others, or drive improvement in them. Employers should develop a feeling-doing-treating (FDT) approach, to ensure that work-related factors that could cause or contribute to poor mental health are properly managed, including how employees treat one another. Mental health programmes should be risk-based, with a focus on the elimination of hazards, and should not simply focus on managing symptoms (through initiatives such as resilience building and mindfulness, which may not provide an actual solution to the cause of poor mental health). Actions to improve mental health must be tailored to the individual to maximise their effectiveness, as individuals may have a unique reaction to common circumstances.

The law as it relates to workplace mental health was the subject of chapter 5. 'Mental disability' was defined, as set out within the Equality Act 2010. A mental disability is said to exist where a condition has a substantial effect on a person's life, lasting in the long-term (12 months or more) and affecting their day-to-day activities. The law protects people with long-term conditions that affect short-term activities. The law fails to protect people with long-term conditions that affect long-term activities, like getting and keeping a job. The Health and Safety at Work etc Act 1974 (HASAWA) already provides employers with mental health management obligations, especially in Sections 2 and 7. As I established in chapter 4, enforcement of HASAWA as it relates to mental health is incredibly limited. The Data Protection Act 2018 gives employees with mental health issues the right to keep their mental health information (referred to as special category data) confidential. Under the Equality Act 2010, where an employer has knowledge of a mental health condition or ought reasonably to know of it, the employer has a duty to act on that knowledge. The 'Hatton Propositions' state that all occupations carry the same risk of mental harm, contradicting the research presented in chapter 1. The 'Hatton Propositions' also state that employers have no general duty to enquire about the mental health of employees. Any case brought by employees against employers has to pass the four tests of negligence: the employer owed the employee a duty of care; the duty of care was breached; the employee suffered harm and that harm was foreseeable; and the employer's negligence led to the harm suffered. Excluding those circumstances, and where internal procedures (eg. grievance) fail, should employees be unable or unwilling to bring civil claims against employers, my argument is that there is nothing to stop unscrupulous employers causing unlimited mental harm with impunity. Current laws and law enforcement are biased in favour of employers, and are failing many people with mental health issues.

In chapter 6, I presented the positive case for employing people with mental health issues, based upon legal, moral, technical and commercial arguments. The legal case argued that people with certain mental health conditions are protected from discrimination in law. The moral case suggested that organisations with strong social values may wish to increase their social wellbeing 'reach' and might be more generous when considering employing people with mental ill-health. Instead of simply supporting mental health charities, organisations can show their commitment to mental health by employing people with mental ill-health. The technical case considered the 'superpowers' some people with mental health issues possess; they might prove to be highly creative, be able to apply an ability to hyper-focus or be talented at problem-solving. The commercial case showed how investing in wellbeing and mental health can increase productivity by up to 25%, as well as increasing employee retention and reducing sickness absence. When making recruitment decisions, employers might wish to guide their hiring managers by using an 'expertise-need' matrix. Although pigeon-holing feels clumsy, this framework may help encourage and guide managers when they are making recruitment decisions about people with mental health issues, partly by giving hiring managers permission to make such decisions and partly to minimise any prejudice in the recruitment process.

In chapter 7, I considered some of the challenges employers face when trying to establish a positive mental health culture, which should include making arrangements for people to be able to talk openly about their mental health. Currently, too many employees are not willing to be open about their mental health and many lie to their employer to keep it a secret. For employees to feel able to disclose their condition, they must believe their employer's culture is positive towards mental health. Employees will judge elements of the culture (eg. policies, procedures and training), the examples set by leaders in speaking out about their own experience, and the precedents leaders have set in how they have treated other employees who have disclosed their condition. Speaking about their own lived experience is one of the most powerful things the leaders (especially the directors) of an organisation can do. Leaders must also ensure, through their own actions and through the actions of other leaders and managers, that all employees who disclose a mental health issue are treated fairly. Leaders are encouraged to look at the facts, not the perception, when contemplating employing people with mental health issues. Of course, there are risks involved in employing people with mental health issues, just as there are with all recruitment decisions, but these are balanced by the legal, moral, technical and commercial benefits. The main risk to workplace productivity appears to be in failing to manage mental health, not in employees' actual mental health issues. On balance, there is strong justification for employing people with mental health issues, and most of the risks appear manageable.

In chapter 8, I recommended using a management system for workplace mental health, as this provides a strategic structured and systematic approach. Mental health may not at first glance seem the type of issue that can or should be managed using an impersonal, bureaucratic management system. However, other aspects of society where high levels of care and compassion are required (eg. maternity units, primary schools) use a strategic, structured management system approach to managing the people they care for. A management system approach is used wherever high levels of control and certainty are required. Policies and procedures prescribe the best course of action for the people being cared for and minimise the chance of employees making mistakes. Given that mental health can be regarded as a complex and potentially problematic aspect of management, a management system approach seems appropriate and, some might argue, necessary. I propose a workplace mental health management system that comprises a '7 Principles' approach: the management system itself; commitment; policy; risk assessments; the hierarchy of controls; consultation; and reporting. Leaders and managers may have fears about mental health and how best to manage it, as well as concerns relating to how to ensure they do the right thing and how to avoid getting it wrong with employees and creating potential liabilities. These fears can be allayed by effectively planning and controlling how workplace mental health is managed – through a management system approach.

In chapter 9, I presented the first of the '7 Principles', the *management system* itself. I summarised the other principles of the management systems and revisited the Plan-Do-Check-Act (PDCA) approach to management, offering examples of workplace mental health programme actions set out within a PDCA framework. I went on to establish the role that leaders should play in the management of mental health as it relates to managing business/ organisational risks. As with all risk management practices, I stressed that leaders should develop a mental health risk register, consider governance and oversight, given the legal compliance requirement, and consider using external advisors and auditors where internal expertise is lacking and to avoid complacency. Leaders must also create belief and purpose, garner the support of other leaders within the organisation, allocate resources and set the strategic direction. They must lead by example, delegate authority and review progress. This book only intends to provide leaders and managers with a 'straw man' of a management system, so I stressed that organisations should develop the management system for their own purposes, improving, expanding and adapting it to better meet their own requirements and those of their employees.

The second principle, *commitment*, was the subject of chapter 10. I discussed guidance from the HSE that commitment can be gained, in part, through leaders being involved, allocating resources and delegating authority. I explored the reasons for gaining commitment, which included the need to address mental health at work in terms of the law, and the opportunity it offers to improve productivity. I explained that commitment starts with the executive leadership team (ELT), and stressed the need for every member of the ELT to be committed to mental health. As with trust, a single erroneous act can cause lasting damage. Leaders must establish the cycle of commitment, which has six steps: 1) leadership; 2) practice; 3) perception; 4) trust; 5) commitment; and 6) recognition. Leaders must not only be committed to mental health, they must also be seen to be supportive of it. Leaders can show their commitment to mental health by monitoring, enforcing and reviewing the mental health policy and related practices. Leaders must not break the cycle of commitment or allow it to be broken. They must address threats to the cycle and any wrongful behaviours (eg. bullying); if wrongful behaviours are allowed to occur and be perpetuated, it will undermine any pro-mental-health culture. Leaders must combat four complacencies: poor leadership commitment; poor leadership involvement; poor enforcement; and poor treatment. By implementing the commitment cycle effectively, leaders will demonstrate that *all* employees are included, respected and valued, which in turn will have a positive effect, driving organisational productivity and performance.

In chapter 11, I presented the third principle, the mental health *policy*. I described how leaders should decide whether to have a specific mental health policy, or whether to combine the mental health policy with their health and safety policy, or with their diversity and inclusion policy. Given the strategic nature and scale of the mental health issue, a separate policy may seem appropriate. The policy should comprise at least three aspects: statement of intent; organisation and management structure; and arrangements. The statement of intent sets out the organisation's commitment to mental health, along with the goals of the mental health programme. The organisation and management structure establishes who will implement and control the mental health programme. A director will usually head up this management structure. A competent person should be appointed and their position in the management structure made clear. The arrangements section should include details of all the procedures the organisation implements through which workplace mental health is to be managed. The policy should be widely communicated throughout the organisation. A means of checking policy compliance must be adopted, such as internal audits and inspections. The policy should be reviewed annually or when any significant change occurs that necessitates a policy review.

I explored the fourth principle, mental health *risk assessments*, in chapter 12. These should be undertaken using the same risk assessment process that is applied to physical health and safety. The five steps of the risk assessment process are: 1) identify what can cause harm; 2) identify who can be harmed and how; 3) determine the risk and what control measures are required; 4) write up the risk assessment and implement it; and 5) review the risk assessment. I identified the 12 general mental health risk factors (many of which are not related to work) and the 12 workplace mental health risk factors. These provide the basis of my 12 x 12 workplace risk assessment approach, which answers the question: 'What risks should I assess?' When assessing risks, employers might gather information from a number of sources, including employees, analysis and observation. Employers must foresee mental health risks, using all the information in their possession. A 9-point or 25-point scoring system should be applied to each risk, based on the likelihood of the risk arising and the severity of its impact. Risks with high scores should be managed as a priority. Risk assessments should be audited to ensure they have been properly undertaken, properly implemented and are proving effective.

The approach to controlling risk should be structured. In chapter 13, I explored a structured approach to risk control in the form of the fifth principle, the *hierarchy of controls*. This well-known approach to hazard and risk control will almost certainly be included in any external assessment of adequacy an employer faces when their health and safety management practices are scrutinised (eg. to assess their compliance with the OHSAS 18001 standard). The hierarchy of controls requires employers to take a preventative approach and to be proactive; employers cannot simply expect employees to be wholly responsible for their own mental health. The hierarchy requires employers to consider five (or six) stages of risk control: 1) elimination; 2) substitution; 3) isolation (in some instances); 4) engineering controls; 5) administrative controls; and 6) personal protective equipment (PPE). Each control method has a varying degree of effectiveness. Elimination of mental harm is considered the most effective control, with PPE being the least effective. Employers should prioritise the most effective methods (elimination and substitution). The hierarchy of controls can be applied once risk assessments have been completed to identify workplace mental health hazards, which can be managed by applying a systematic approach of 'cause, effect and control'. Employers should focus on reducing causes of mental harm as far as is reasonably practicable. New thinking may also be required. I gave the example of increasing notice periods to reduce stress, at very low cost. Organisations must develop new levels of expertise and bring innovative thinking to bear, if they are to address causes of mental harm.

The sixth principle, *consultation*, was the subject of chapter 14. Employers in the UK have a legal obligation to consult their workforce on matters relating to health and safety. Elsewhere in the world, doing so is at least recommended. Consulting with employees about mental health is necessary: because of the scale of the mental health issue; to gain buy-in to any mental health programme and related initiatives; to help reveal the otherwise intangible nature of mental health issues; and to align the perceptions of leaders and employees. Where mental health consultations are a legal requirement, consideration must be given to the governance and compliance of consultations. A form of independent audit of the consultation group and its processes is advisable. Group and individual consultations should be held, with representatives from all employee groups and with individuals who have no known mental health issues. All employees must be consulted, especially in light of the fact that about half of employees with mental health issues keep their condition to themselves so their employer will not know about it. Group consultations can be held through meetings, engagement events and engagement surveys. Engagement survey questions need not refer directly to mental health. Questions can be based on the known risk factors, established from the 12 x 12 workplace risk assessment approach, and mental health effects can be inferred from employees' answers. Critics of this approach may not like its reliance on causality, but there is a danger of more bias arising from other approaches. When consulting with employees, confidentiality and anonymity must be respected, and individual consultations should obviously be held in a confidential setting, especially to identify issues such as bullying.

I explored *reporting*, the seventh and final principle of the mental health management system, in chapter 15. Reporting should be used to monitor mental health practice and mental health performance. In the UK, there is no legal requirement for employers to report mental health incidents to the health and safety regulator, the Health and Safety Executive (HSE). Mental health reports should include inspection/audit reports, incident reports, statistical and trend reports, and benchmarking reports. A wide variety of mental health performance measures are available. Many of these will be similar to those used when managing other aspects of organisational performance, especially aspects related to other protected characteristics, such as gender, race and religion. Organisations should monitor mental health performance for a variety of reasons, including to identify the current state of mental health in the organisation, to ensure mental health initiatives are proving effective and to ensure compliance with the law. A degree of caution should be applied when reviewing report results, as errors and bias may well affect the results, given employees may be reluctant to disclose mental health issues or lie about them. When applying the Plan-Do-Check-Act model, reporting forms part of the 'check' phase. If the results are not in accordance with expectations, corrective action will be required. Urgent action may occasionally be required, especially when vulnerable groups are involved. The organisation's efforts to manage mental health, and the effects of those efforts, should be monitored through reporting. The inputs and outputs of the mental health programme should be measured, along with direct and indirect measures. Strategic measures of the mental health programme will include attendance, engagement, productivity and retention. Leaders should develop mental health measures that best suit their organisation. Having assessed the results of the mental health programme and related initiatives, a process of continual improvement should be adopted.

In chapter 16, I presented a 10-point plan of action aimed at bringing about a seismic change in mental health in the workplace and throughout society. I started by calling for the UK Government to appointment of a Workplace Mental Health Tsar, to strengthen leadership. I proposed a change in the law and the legal definition of 'mental disability', to cover people with long-term conditions that affect their *long-term activities* (eg. getting and keeping a job). I recommended a change to the 'Hatton Propositions' so that some occupations, such as nursing, are recognised as being intrinsically more dangerous to mental health; and so that employers have a general duty to enquire about the mental health of all employees (necessary, in any case, when conducting mental health risk assessments). I also proposed that the law be changed to prevent employers changing employment terms and conditions for six months following an employee disclosing a mental health condition. I went on to recommend that health and safety law should be expressly applied to mental health and that HSE funding must be increased to allow the HSE to undertake related communications, inspections and enforcement. I called for changes to the HSE's approach, including to its guidance, which I believe should state that the cause of mental ill-health can be proven. I also recommended that the HSE should require employers to report any mental health injuries and illnesses that lead to an employee being absent or unable to perform their usual duties for 30 consecutive days or longer. The HSE should also issue sanctions against those employers committing the most serious of breaches to health and safety law as it relates to mental health. Finally, I called upon prominent figures in society to take forward these recommendations and help to bring about the seismic change they attempt to achieve. In summary, I believe the regulatory system fails to protect employee mental health and call for it to be changed.

This book has attempted to achieve two things:

- Provide employers with a management system, along with easy-to-understand, easy-to-implement initiatives and ideas, to help them manage the mental health of their employees more effectively.

■ Present a 10-point plan aimed at bringing about a seismic change not only to workplace mental health but also to the mental health of society as a whole.

Employers provide a ready-made network through which to manage mental health. If mental health management can be improved in every country's top 500 employers, the effect will directly benefit millions of people. It will also have an indirect effect on the families and friends of these millions of employees. The management system and recommendations presented in this book have the potential to create a tidal wave of mental positivity throughout workforces around the world.

Like climate change, mental health provides a global challenge. Like climate change, a combination of encouragement and regulation is required to bring about change. This book gives encouragement to employers that are progressive and calls for regulatory changes to tackle those that are not.

At this book's heart is *hope*. The hope that every employer takes good care of the mental wellbeing of each and every one of their employees, so making a positive contribution, not just to their organisation, but to society as a whole.

AFTERWORD
A Thought for People on the Front Line

In this book, I have presented some worrying statistics not only about the mental health of nurses and doctors, but also relating to PTSD rates amongst soldiers. Even the most elite special operations soldiers are not immune and may suffer nearly twice the rate of PTSD as conventional army units (Hing et al, 2012; Rayment, 2018).

In light of the growing weight of evidence about PTSD rates amongst public servants, some of whom witness trauma all too regularly, perhaps we should do as they have done in Australia, where they recognise that some occupations are more dangerous to mental health and compensate workers accordingly. Nurses, military personnel and others on the front line loyally serve their country, seeing trauma after trauma, day in, day out, for no more than the average annual wage. Soldiers put their life on the line, time and time again, in Iraq, in Afghanistan, in Syria and elsewhere, with little respite between tours, coming close to death and seeing their mates injured and dying. Surely, we can look after these and other heroes and heroines better than we do currently.

Now is the time to consider a 'traumatic exposure compensation scheme' for all frontline workers whose occupations are intrinsically more dangerous to mental health because they repeatedly experience and witness trauma. In Australia, a scheme like this is already in operation across civil service occupations, not just the military. While I welcome the UK Government's review of the Armed Forces Compensation Scheme (House of Commons, 2019), more needs to be done. Not just for military personnel but for other occupations too, such as nursing, where rates of PTSD are at an unacceptably high level.

Setting aside compensation, new thinking is required to prevent mental harm occurring in the first instance. Perhaps a predisposition to PTSD should be assessed, through psychological testing, during the recruitment process for roles which expose employees to trauma. Perhaps greater efforts should be made to control exposure to trauma, say, through more regular role rotation. Perhaps workers should be assessed more frequently, through health screening of mental health, to determine how close to their resilience threshold workers are, so timely action can be taken to prevent distress. More effective preventative action must be taken to minimise mental harm, which will minimise the number of people experiencing mental health issues and, in turn, reduce the demand for mental health care and support services.

One thing is certain. Front line workers who experience and witness trauma deserve better support than they receive today.

REFERENCES

Hing, M., Cabrera, J., Barstow, C. and Forsten, R. (2012) Special operations forces and incidence of post-traumatic stress disorder symptoms. *Journal of Special Operations Medicine* 12:3, 23–35. Abstract available at: *https://www.ncbi.nlm.nih.gov/pubmed/23032317* (accessed 1 April 2020).

House of Commons (2019) Mental Health and the Armed Forces, Part Two: The Provision of Care: Government Response to the Committee's Fourteenth Report of Session 2017–19. Eighteenth Special Report of Session 2017–19. HC 2213. Available at: *https://publications.parliament.uk/pa/cm201719/cmselect/cmdfence/2213/2213.pdf* (accessed 2 April 2020).

Rayment. S. (2018) SAS soldiers suffer PTSD thanks to 'Wheel of Death' lifestyle that 'could drive elite troops to suicide'. *Mirror* 29 September. Available at: *https://www.mirror.co.uk/news/uk-news/sas-soldiers-suffer-ptsd-thanks-13332578* (accessed 1 April 2020).

Safe Work Australia (2014) *Workers' Compensation Legislation and Psychological Injury. Fact sheet.* Available at:

INDEX

Lightning Source UK Ltd.
Milton Keynes UK
UKHW031001260720
367198UK00004B/124

How To Become A
MENTAL HEALTH LEADER
Within The Workplace